Microsoft

Microsoft® Office Word 2007
Plain & Simple

Jerry Joyce
Marianne Moon

PUBLISHED BY
Microsoft Press
A Division of Microsoft Corporation
One Microsoft Way
Redmond, Washington 98052-6399

Library of Congress Control Number: 2006937712

Printed and bound in the United States of America.

2 3 4 5 6 7 8 9   QWT   2 1 0 9 8 7

Distributed in Canada by H.B. Fenn and Company Ltd.

A CIP catalogue record for this book is available from the British Library.

Microsoft Press books are available through booksellers and distributors worldwide. For further information about international editions, contact your local Microsoft Corporation office or contact Microsoft Press International directly at fax (425) 936-7329. Visit our Web site at www.microsoft.com/mspress. Send comments to mspinput@microsoft.com.

Acquisitions Editor: Juliana Aldous Atkinson
Developmental Editor: Sandra Haynes
Project Editor: Kathleen Atkins
Technical Editor: Jerry Joyce
Manuscript Editor: Marianne Moon

Typographer: Kari Fera
Proofreader/Copyeditor: Alice Copp Smith
Indexer: Jan Wright, Wright Information

Body Part No. X12-48762

Contents

Acknowledgments . . . . *xii*

About This Book   1

No Computerspeak! 1
A Quick Overview 2
What's New in Word 2007? 4
A Few Assumptions 5
A Final Word (or Two) 6

Reading and Writing   7

What's Where in Word? 8
Creating a New Document. 10
Working with an Existing Document 12
Editing Text. 13
Working with Old Documents. 14
Reading a Document. 16
Using Only the Keyboard 18
So Many Ways to View It 20
Changing Your View 22
Researching a Subject 23
Translating Foreign-Language Text. 24

What do you think of this book? We want to hear from you!

Microsoft is interested in hearing your feedback so we can continually improve our books and learning resources for you. To participate in a brief online survey, please visit:

www.microsoft.com/learning/booksurvey/

Finding Text 26

Replacing Text 28

Adding Page Numbers 29

Inserting Frequently Used Content. 30

Correcting Your Spelling and Grammar 32

Correcting Text Automatically 34

Moving and Copying Text 36

So Many Ways to Do It 38

Printing a Document. 40

Getting Help. 42

Designing Your Documents   43

Formatting Text 44

Controlling the Look: Themes, Styles, and Fonts 46

Using Any Style 48

Switching Quick Styles. 49

Changing Character Fonts 50

Adjusting Paragraph Line Spacing 52

Setting Paragraph Alignment 54

Indenting a Paragraph 55

Formatting with Tabs. 56

Adding Emphasis and Special Formatting. 58

Creating an Inline Heading 59

Adjusting the Spacing Between Characters. 60

Copying Your Formatting. 61

Setting the Overall Look. 62

Placing a Line Border Around a Page. 64

Placing an Art Border Around a Page. 65

Adding a Decorative Horizontal Line 66

Adding a Border or Shading to a Paragraph. 67
Creating a Bulleted or Numbered List 68
Creating a Multilevel List 70
Formatting a List 71
Formatting a Table. 72

Creating a Layout   73

Laying Out the Page 74
Changing Page Orientation Within a Document 76
Changing Margins Within a Document 77
Improving the Layout with Hyphenation. 78
Fine-Tuning Your Layout. 80
Flowing Text into Columns. 82
Creating Chapters 83
Creating a Table from Scratch 84
Using a Predesigned Table 85
Creating a Table from Text 86
The Anatomy of a Table 87
Adding or Deleting Rows and Columns. 88
Positioning Elements in a Table 89
Customizing a Table Layout 90
Aligning a Table 92
Moving a Table. 93
Creating a Side-by-Side Layout. 94

Creating Specialized Documents   95

Composing Different Types of Documents 96
Word's File Formats 98
Creating an Online Document. 99

Writing and Publishing a Blog. 100
Printing an Envelope. 102
Printing a Mailing Label 103
Mail Merge: The Power and the Pain 104
Creating a Form Letter 106
Personalizing a Form Letter 108
Addressing Envelopes from a Mailing List. 110
Switching Templates 111
Creating Running Heads. 112
Creating Variable Running Heads 114
Organizing Your Information 116
Reorganizing a Document 118
Creating a Master Document. 120

Adding Graphics to Your Documents 121

Inserting a Picture 122
Changing the Size of a Picture. 123
Adding Clip Art 124
Adding Shapes. 125
Editing a Picture. 126
Wrapping Text Around a Graphic 128
Formatting a Shape. 130
Arranging Multiple Graphics 131
Positioning Graphics on the Page 132
Combining Graphics 133
Creating Stylized Text 134
Inserting a Relational Diagram 136
Creating a Chart. 138
Inserting an Excel Chart 140

7 Adding Specialized Content

Inserting a Cover Page 142
Numbering Headings 143
Adding Line Numbers 144
Inserting an Equation 145
Creating an Equation 146
Inserting Microsoft Excel Data 148
Using Hyperlinks 150
Inserting Special Characters 152
Adding a Sidebar or a Pull Quote 153
Creating Custom Text Boxes 154
Creating a Dropped Capital Letter 156
Creating Footnotes and Endnotes 157
Creating Cross-References 158
Inserting a Bookmark 159
Inserting Information with Smart Tags 160
Inserting a Watermark 161
Adding Document Properties 162
Having Word Insert Information for You 164
Adding Captions to Tables and Figures 165
Creating a Table of Figures, Equations, or Tables 166
Creating a Table of Contents 167
Inserting a Citation 168
Inserting a Bibliography 170
Creating a Table of Authorities 171
Creating an Index 172

8 Reviewing and Finalizing

Marking Changes in a Document 176
Comparing Changes in a Document 178

Combining Reviews. 180
Comparing Documents Side by Side 181
Comparing Different Parts of a Single Document .182
Standardizing the Formatting 183
Proofreading in Another Language 184
Checking the Word Count 186
Checking the Compatibility 187
Finalizing Your Document 188

9 Customizing Your Content 189

Creating Your Own Styles. 190
Creating a Table Style 192
Creating a Quick Style Set 193
Creating a Custom Cover Page 194
Creating a Custom Table of Contents. 196
Creating a Custom Table of Tables or Figures 198
Saving Your Custom Table Design. 199
Customizing a Template 200
Designing a Template 202
Customizing a List 204
Customizing a Multilevel List. 206
Customizing the Page Numbers 207
Organizing with Styles. 208

10 Customizing and Securing Word 209

Customizing the Quick Access Toolbar. 210
Customizing the Window. 212
Creating Keyboard Shortcuts. 214
Specifying What You Want Word to Display. 215

Changing Your User Information. 216
Changing the Way Word Saves Files. 217
Customizing the Way Word Checks Spelling and Grammar. 218
Customizing Your Spelling Dictionaries 219
Creating Your Own Commands. 220
Transferring Styles and Macros 221
Safeguarding a Document 222
Restricting Access to a Document. 223
Restricting Changes to a Document 224
Signing a Document with a Certificate. 225
Signing a Document with a Visible Signature. 226
Protecting a Document with a Password 228
Controlling Macros, Add-Ins, and ActiveX Controls. 230
Fixing Word 231
Adding or Removing Word Components. 232

Index 233

What do you think of this book? We want to hear from you!

Microsoft is interested in hearing your feedback so we can continually improve our books and learning resources for you. To participate in a brief online survey, please visit:

www.microsoft.com/learning/booksurvey/

Acknowledgments

This book is the result of the combined efforts of a team of skilled professionals whose work we trust and admire and whose friendship we value highly. Kari Fera, our wonderful longtime typographer who's worked on almost all our books, did the work of two people and did it graciously. She not only refined and produced the graphics but also laid out the complex design, wrestling with problems ranging from limited space to logical arrangement of numbered steps. We appreciate her excellent work. Our dear friend Alice Copp Smith has helped us improve every one of the books we've written. Alice does so much more than proofread and copyedit: Her gentle and witty chiding on countless yellow sticky notes makes us groan (and laugh) but teaches us to write better and, always, to get rid of those danglers! And we are fortunate indeed to be able to work with indexer *par excellence* Jan Wright, whose index reveals in microcosm the soul of the book. We thank this dedicated and hardworking trio for their exceptional work and their unwavering good humor in the face of grueling deadlines.

At Microsoft Press we thank Lucinda Rowley and Juliana Aldous Atkinson for asking us to write this book, and we thank Kathleen Atkins for her valuable insight and helpful suggestions. Thanks also to Jim Kramer, Sandra Haynes, Victoria Thulman, Bill Teel, and Sally Stickney.

We also thank, in spirit, Oscar Tschirky, longtime *maître d'hôtel* at The Waldorf (now The Waldorf-Astoria) in New York City, whose book *The Cook Book by "Oscar" of The Waldorf,* first published in 1896, is a family heirloom and the source of the sample text in many of our screen shots.

On the home front, we thank our beautiful grandchild, Zuzu, for love, laughter, and many hours of Monopoly, at which she routinely beats both of us and winds up with more money than the bank.

Last but not least, we thank each other—for everything.

1

About This Book

In this section:

- No Computerspeak!
- A Quick Overview
- What's New in Word 2007?
- A Few Assumptions
- A Final Word (or Two)

If you want to get the most from your computer and your software with the least amount of time and effort—and who doesn't?—this book is for you. You'll find *Microsoft Office Word 2007 Plain & Simple* to be a straightforward, easy-to-read reference tool. With the premise that your computer should work for you, not you for it, this book's purpose is to help you get your work done quickly and efficiently so that you can get away from the computer and live your life.

No Computerspeak!

Let's face it—when there's a task you don't know how to do but you need to get it done in a hurry, or when you're stuck in the middle of a task and can't figure out what to do next, there's nothing more frustrating than having to read page after page of technical background material. You want the information you need—nothing more, nothing less—and you want it now! *And* it should be easy to find and understand.

That's what this book is about. It's written in plain English— no technical jargon and no computerspeak. No single task in the book takes more than two pages. Just look up the task in the index or the table of contents, turn to the page, and there's the information you need, laid out in an illustrated step-by-step format. You don't get bogged down by the whys and wherefores: Just follow the steps and get your work done with a minimum of hassle. Occasionally you might have to turn to another page if the procedure you're working on is accompanied by a *See Also*. That's because there's a lot of overlap among tasks, and we didn't want to keep repeating ourselves. We've scattered some useful *Tips* here and there, pointed out some features that are new in this version of Word, and thrown in a *Try This* or a *Caution* once in a while. By and large, however, we've tried to remain true to the heart and soul of the book, which is that the information you need should be available to you at a glance and it should be *plain and simple!*

Useful Tasks...

Whether you use Microsoft Word 2007 for work, school, personal correspondence, or some of each, we've tried to pack this book with procedures for everything we could think of that you might want to do, from the simplest tasks to some of the more esoteric ones.

...And the Easiest Way to Do Them

Another thing we've tried to do in this book is to find and document the easiest way to accomplish a task. Word often provides a multitude of methods for achieving a single end result—and that can be daunting or delightful, depending on the way you like to work. If you tend to stick with one favorite and familiar approach, we think the methods described in this book are the way to go. If you like trying out alternative techniques, go ahead! The intuitiveness of Microsoft Word invites exploration, and you're likely to discover ways of doing things that you think are easier or that you like better than ours. If you do, that's great! It's exactly what the developers of Word had in mind when they provided so many alternatives.

A Quick Overview

First, we're assuming that Word is already installed on your computer as a part of The 2007 Microsoft Office System. If it isn't, Windows makes installation so simple that you won't need our help anyway. So, unlike many computer books, this one doesn't start with installation instructions and a list of system requirements. If Word is installed on its own without the other 2007 Office System programs, you can still use everything in this book except the instructions for those tasks that incorporate material from other Office components.

Next, you don't have to read this book in any particular order. It's designed so that you can jump in, get the information you need, and then close the book and keep it near your computer until the next time you need it. But that doesn't mean we scattered the information about with wild abandon. The tasks you want to accomplish are arranged in two levels. The overall type of task you're looking for is under a main heading such as "Creating a New Document" or "Laying Out the Page." Then, in each section of the book, the smaller tasks within each main task are arranged in a loose progression from the simplest to the more complex. OK, so what's where in this book?

Section 2 covers the basic tasks—and a few slightly more complex ones—that you can use to produce professional-looking documents: starting, saving, reopening, and closing a Word document; entering, editing, formatting, copying, and moving text; working with documents that were created in an earlier version of Word; using Word's research tools; translating foreign-language text; learning how to use the spelling- and grammar-checking tools; printing your documents; and getting some help if you need it.

Section 3 takes you well beyond the basics and focuses on designing and formatting your documents, using themes, styles, and fonts to create letters, memos, and other types of frequently used documents. You'll see how simple it is to use

Word's Quick Styles feature to create your own styles: custom-formatting text, paragraphs, or an entire document; choosing a theme or creating your own theme to produce documents with consistent design elements; adding decorative touches such as borders and shading; and creating and formatting lists and tables. We'll also cover some of the refinements you can apply to your text, such as *kerning*—that is, adjusting the spacing between characters—and adjusting line spacing in and between paragraphs.

Section 4 is about laying out the page, whether you're creating a simple one-page report or a long document or book whose pages will be printed on both sides and eventually bound. We'll walk you through the steps that are entailed in creating a layout: setting up the margins, flowing text into columns, creating chapters, and fine-tuning the finished document before you print it, including *breaking lines* and eliminating those sad-sounding and unsightly *widows* and *orphans*. We'll also spend some time in this section discussing tables—creating and customizing them—and we'll clue you in on how useful a table can be in certain layouts.

Section 5 is about composing different types of specialized documents. If you have your own online *blog* (Web log), for example, you'll find all the information you need in this section to create and publish your blog entries directly in Word. You'll also find information here about using templates, creating *running heads,* using Outline view to organize or reorganize your information, and creating a single *master document* when writings by several people need to be incorporated into a cohesive whole. And let's not forget that much-maligned phrase "mail merge"! Yes, we know—mail merge has a bad reputation, but if you need to send a bunch of letters to a large group of people, Word's mail merge feature is the way to go. It's not as daunting as you might think, and we'll help you sail smoothly through the process, from setting up your master document and *data source* to printing your envelopes or mailing labels.

Section 6 focuses on using your own creativity to spice up your documents with pictures, clip art, drawings, and so on. You'll learn how to insert a picture into a document; edit, recolor, or resize the picture; add a border or special effects to it—soft edges, glow, 3-D formats, and so on—or wrap text around it; and turn ordinary text into eye-popping art with WordArt. We'll also show you how to create and format diagrams and charts that can enliven dry statistics and make them not only more friendly to the eye but more understandable than plain old worksheets and endless columns and rows of numbers.

Section 7 examines specialized design and other elements that are common to such seemingly dissimilar documents as company reports, short stories, scientific papers, or your Great American Novel. Just a few of the topics we cover here are choosing and inserting an appropriate cover page; numbering headings and lines, and creating footnotes, endnotes, figure captions, citations, cross-references, and a bibliography—all of which are often required in scientific and scholarly documents; building and inserting mathematical equations; adding hyperlinks; creating design elements such as *drop caps, pull quotes, sidebars,* and *watermarks;* creating a table of contents and other types of tables, including the tables of authorities that are used in the world of legal language; and compiling and creating a comprehensive index.

Section 8 is where you'll find information about reviewing and finalizing your documents, and you'll find this section especially useful if you send your writing out to be reviewed, edited, or commented on by your peers or coworkers. Word's Track Changes feature keeps track of each reviewer's changes, which you can then accept or reject. If your reviewers didn't use the Track Changes feature, you can use Word's Compare feature to compare the original document with the edited version, and you can specify which elements you want marked to show what was changed. When you've decided which edits you want to use, you can then merge all of them into one final document. There's also the Window Split bar, which you can use when you want to compare different sections of the same document on your screen. When you need to stay within a certain word count or page count, Word can keep track of either or both for you. And if you sometimes use other languages in your work, Word can proofread those foreign-language documents for you.

Section 9 is about customizing the content of your documents. You'll learn how to modify existing styles or create your own styles for templates, tables, cover pages, and other design elements if you don't want to use Word's predesigned templates and styles. We'll also walk you through the customizations you can make to templates, tables of contents, bulleted or numbered lists, page numbers, and so on. It's a great way to create highly individual-looking documents and, at the same time, to educate yourself as to what does and doesn't work in a design and why.

While section 9 was about customizing your content, section 10 is about customizing Word itself. You can take control of just about every aspect of Word—adding items to the Quick Access toolbar; customizing the status bar and the color scheme; showing or minimizing the Ribbon; creating your own macros; customizing the way Word checks for spelling and grammar errors; adding or removing Word components; changing the way Word saves your files; and much more. This section also shows you how you can protect your documents, make your system more secure, and—if you encounter problems—run some diagnostic tests to find out what's wrong and how to fix it.

What's New in Word 2007?

Microsoft Word 2007 has been built on an entirely new structure, and you'll find that its features look different from those of earlier versions and work quite a bit differently as well. The first conspicuously new feature you'll encounter when you start Word will undoubtedly be the *Ribbon*. And where are the menus and toolbars? That's the beauty of the Ribbon. No longer do you have to wander through the maze of menus, submenus, and toolbars searching for what you want—they're all right there, in plain sight, at a glance. On the Ribbon are all the commands, styles, and resources, arranged on task-oriented tabs. Click the Page Layout tab to see all the tools and resources you need to lay out your document's pages. Click the Insert tab to insert something into your document—how simple, and how sensible! The one and only menu remaining from earlier versions of Word is the Office menu—hidden until you click the big, round Office button—which gives you access to most of your file-management commands. The one remaining toolbar is the Quick Access toolbar, where you can place your most frequently used commands and resources for easy access, regardless of which tab of the Ribbon is active.

Another aspect of replacing Word's menus was the development of the *galleries*. These are the graphical equivalents of drop-down menus, except that they show you samples of all the choices that are available for you to "try on." There are many different galleries—for styles, for themes, for page numbers, and so on. The galleries provide you with the ability to look before you leap. With *Live Preview,* you can see how the formatting you choose will change your text, pictures, or other content, or how the overall look of your document will change when you switch the theme simply by pointing to the different items in the galleries.

So what else is new in Word besides the entire interface? Plenty! Some of the biggest changes that you'll encounter are the new file types. Word uses a whole new file structure that, unfortunately, isn't directly compatible with earlier versions of Word. Of course, you can open and use files from earlier versions, but people who are using any earlier version of Word will need to download and install a converter so that they can open the documents you create using the Word 2007 file format. However, the good news is that the new file format is what enables many of the improvements in Word 2007.

Word 2007 also includes an entirely new graphics tool, *SmartArt,* which is designed to help you create diagrams and lists that graphically present your information—and, by the way, will surely impress those who see your work. If you work with technical or legal documents into which you need to insert citations, a full bibliography, a list of works cited, or a legal table of authorities, you'll find that Word's bibliography and citations features are great new ways to take care of these often tedious and time-consuming chores.

And it's not only all the new stuff that's great. Some of Word's existing features have been greatly enhanced too. Checking your grammar and spelling has become much more accurate. Now you can check the contextual use of words: for example, should it be "to" or "too," "there" or "their," "road" or "rowed"? You get the picture. If you're involved in mathematics, science, or engineering, you'll appreciate the enhanced Equations feature, which not only supplies some predesigned equations that you can edit but also makes it easy to create your own equations and save them for future use. Whether you need legal blacklining to indicate changes in a document or you need to track the changes reviewers make to your documents, you'll find the enhancements to the Track Changes feature—including the ability to distinguish between what has been added or deleted and what has been moved— really invaluable.

Word 2007 has also greatly improved document safety and security. You'll be better able to control access to your documents—for example, you can indicate when a document is completed and that no further changes may be made to it. You can easily check for and remove any sensitive or personal information in your documents that you don't want other people to have access to. You can digitally sign a document to provide verification in the electronic file that it really *was*

you who signed it, and you can even attach a scanned image of your signature right there in the document. With Word's improved document-recovery system, your files are now more secure from loss, and the new file system also assists you in being able to recover files if they've become corrupted. And if you end up with system problems involving Word and your computer, you can easily run a series of diagnostics that can determine the problem and either fix it or get you the help you need to get it fixed.

A Few Assumptions

We had to make a few educated guesses about you, our audience, when we started writing this book. Perhaps your computer is solely for personal use—e-mail, the Internet, and so on. Or you might run a small business or work for a giant corporation. After taking these quite varied possibilities into account, we assumed that you're familiar with computer basics—the keyboard and your little friend the mouse, for example—and that you're connected to the Internet and/or a company intranet. We also assumed, if you're working on a corporate network, that you're familiar with the specialized and customized tools, such as a SharePoint site or a file-management system, that are used on the network. We also assumed that you're using and familiar with the basics of Windows Vista, and that you have the Aero glass appearance enabled. However, if you're running Microsoft Windows XP, you'll still be able to use this book, although you might find that the look and function of the windows and dialog boxes on your screen are a bit different from those shown in this book. Whichever version of Windows you're using, we'd like to recommend two other books we've written that you'll find helpful: *Windows Vista Plain & Simple* and *Microsoft Windows XP Plain & Simple—2nd Edition.* If you need information about using other Office programs, we also recommend our book *The 2007 Microsoft Office System Plain & Simple.*

The appearance of Word 2007 is very dynamic, so the look of the Ribbon will change depending on the screen resolution you're using. That is, with a high resolution, you'll see many more individual items on the Ribbon than you will if you're using a low resolution. With a low resolution, you'll find that items are contained under a button, and only when you click the button are the items then displayed. To see this effect, resize the width of your Word window, and note that items are hidden when you make the window smaller and that they appear when you make the window larger. Word 2007 was designed using a screen resolution of 1024 by 768 pixels, so this is the resolution we used as we wrote this book.

A Final Word (or Two)

We had three goals in writing this book:

- Whatever you want to do, we want the book to help you get it done.
- We want the book to help you discover how to do things you *didn't* know you wanted to do.
- And, finally, if we've achieved the first two goals, we'll be well on the way to the third, which is for our book to help you *enjoy* using Word. We think that's the best gift we could give you to thank you for buying our book.

We hope you'll have as much fun using *Microsoft Office Word 2007 Plain & Simple* as we've had writing it. The best way to learn is by *doing,* and that's how we hope you'll use this book.

2 Reading and Writing

In this section:

- What's Where in Word?
- Working with New and Existing Documents
- Using Only the Keyboard
- Changing Your View
- Researching a Subject
- Translating Foreign-Language Text
- Finding and Replacing Text
- Adding Page Numbers
- Inserting Frequently Used Content
- Correcting Your Spelling and Grammar
- Correcting Text Automatically
- Moving and Copying Text
- Getting Help

The radical new design of Microsoft Office Word 2007 makes creating professional-looking documents faster and easier than ever. If you're new to Word, the logical layout of its tools and the ease of finding just what you need for the job at hand will quickly make you feel like an expert. If you're a longtime user, you'll probably say, as we did, *"Why didn't they think of this before?"*

In this section, we'll introduce that new interface and cover the basic skills you'll use every day: creating documents, editing and formatting text, printing documents, and getting help if you need it. If you're not familiar with Word, step through the first few tasks and see just how easily you can produce great-looking documents. You'll find it easy and rewarding to explore and try things out—in other words, you'll learn by doing. If you're already a Word aficionado, you'll quickly see how the new design will eliminate that all-too-familiar "Now *which* menu was that command on?" Hallelujah! No more digging through menu after menu looking for that elusive command!

Turn the page for a short visual tour of Word's new interface. Then jump right in! If you get stuck in some way, you'll find the answers to most of your questions in other sections of this book, or in Word's Help system.

What's Where in Word?

Microsoft Word 2007 has many faces and can be customized in countless ways. The pictures on these two pages show many of the common features you'll see when you're working in Word, and they also introduce just a few of the customizations you can use. We've identified many of the screen elements for you, but it's a good idea to explore Word's interface while you're looking at these two pages. For example, click each of the command tabs and familiarize yourself with what's on the different parts of the Ribbon. If you're not sure what the buttons are used for, point to one of them. In a moment or two, you'll see a *ScreenTip* that tells you the button's name and gives you a pretty good idea of that particular tool's function.

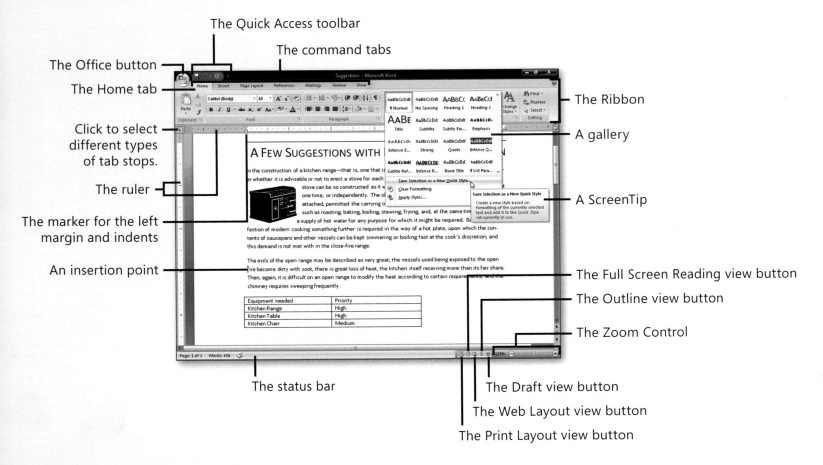

The Quick Access toolbar

The command tabs

The Office button

The Home tab

Click to select different types of tab stops.

The ruler

The marker for the left margin and indents

An insertion point

The status bar

The Ribbon

A gallery

A ScreenTip

The Full Screen Reading view button

The Outline view button

The Zoom Control

The Draft view button

The Web Layout view button

The Print Layout view button

The picture below shows more of Word's interface. As you experiment with it, you'll find that Word has many looks: different tabs on the Ribbon for different tasks, a toolbar that you can customize, items that appear exactly when you need them for the job you're doing right that minute, and much more.

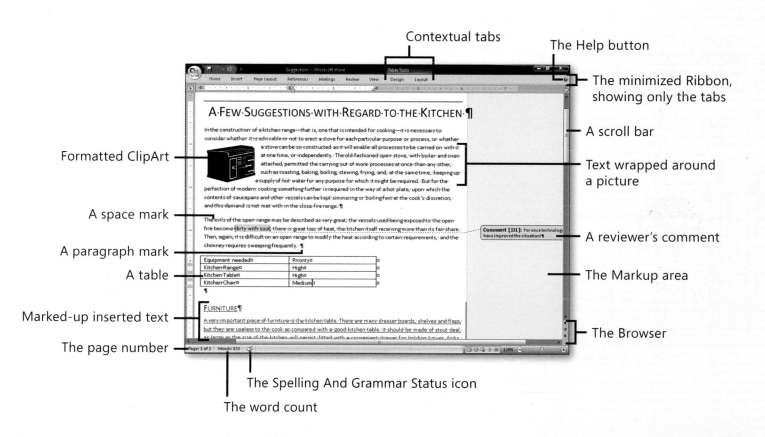

Contextual tabs

The Help button

The minimized Ribbon, showing only the tabs

A scroll bar

Formatted ClipArt

Text wrapped around a picture

A space mark

A reviewer's comment

A paragraph mark

A table

The Markup area

Marked-up inserted text

The Browser

The page number

The Spelling And Grammar Status icon

The word count

Creating a New Document

You can start Word in several different ways, depending on how it was installed, but the tried-and-true method is to choose Microsoft Word from the Windows Start menu. When Word starts, it automatically opens a new blank document for you. If you've been experimenting and Word is already running, you can open a new blank document with a few mouse clicks.

Start Word and Enter Some Text

1. If Word is already running and you've entered some text, choose New from the Office menu to display the New Document dialog box, and double-click Blank Document to create a new blank document. If Word isn't running, start it from the Windows Start menu.

2. To show paragraph marks and other formatting marks such as spaces and tabs, on the Home tab, click the Show/Hide ¶ button. Click the button again if you want to hide the marks.

3. Type your text. When you reach the end of a line, continue typing. Word automatically moves, or *wraps*, your words onto the next line.

4. Press Enter to start a new paragraph.

Tip

To better see the formatting marks, as well as your text, use the Zoom Control at the bottom of the window to increase the magnification, as shown here.

See Also

"Correcting Your Spelling and Grammar" on pages 32–33 for information about working with the spelling and grammar checkers.

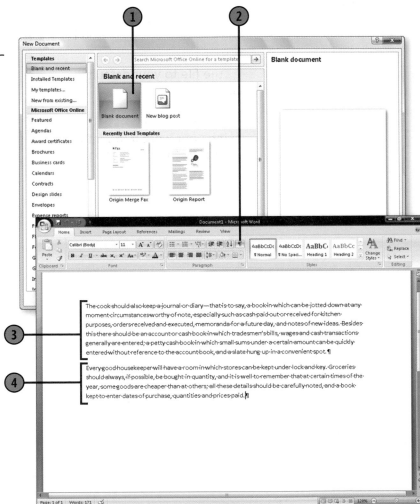

Save the Document

1 Click the Save button on the Quick Access toolbar.

2 Type a name for the document in the File Name box if you don't want the name that Word proposes. File names can be as long as 250 characters and can include spaces, but you can't use the \ / * ? < > and | characters.

3 If you'll always want to save the file to your default location, click Hide Folders.

4 Click Save.

5 Work on the document, saving your work frequently by clicking the Save button or pressing the keyboard shortcut Ctrl+S.

Tip

If you're running Windows XP instead of Windows Vista, the Save As dialog box looks different but functions in a similar way.

Tip

After you've saved your document for the first time, the Save As dialog box won't appear for subsequent saves. To save the document using a different location, name, or file format, choose Save As from the Office menu.

See Also

"Word's File Formats" on page 98 for information about using a different file format to save your document.

Working with an Existing Document

Unless you always create short documents—letters, memos, and so on—you'll often need to continue working on a document that you started but didn't complete in an earlier session. Simply open the saved document, add more text, and then save and close the document again.

Open a Document

1 Start Word if it isn't already running, and click the Office button to open the Office menu.

2 If the document you want to use is listed, click it to open it, and then skip to step 6.

3 If the document isn't listed, click Open.

4 Use the Favorite Links section to locate the document you want, or click the Folders button to navigate through your folders to locate the document.

5 Double-click the document to open it.

6 Add new text or edit the existing text.

7 Click the Save button periodically to save the document, and click the button again when you've finished working on the document.

8 Close the document.

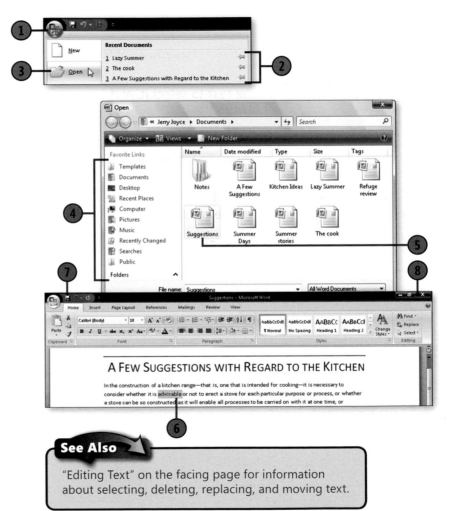

Tip

To open a document as a copy or as a read-only file, choose Open from the Office menu, and click the file you want in the list. Click the down arrow at the right of the Open button, and choose the option you want from the menu. Read-only lets you open the document but doesn't allow you to save it to the same folder using the same file name.

See Also

"Editing Text" on the facing page for information about selecting, deleting, replacing, and moving text.

Editing Text

Whether you're creating a business letter, a financial report, or the Great American Novel, it's a sure bet that you're going to need to go back into your document and do some editing.

Word provides a great variety of ways to edit. To edit existing content, you simply select it and make your changes or, if you prefer, type over some existing text.

Select and Modify Text

1. Click at the beginning of the text that you want to delete.

2. Drag the mouse over all the text to select it, and then release the mouse button.

3. Press the Delete key. The selected text is deleted.

4. Select some text that you want to replace with new typing.

5. Type the new text. The selected text is automatically deleted and replaced by the new typing.

6. Click Save.

Tip

If you accidentally delete some text, immediately click the Undo button on the Quick Access toolbar to restore the deleted text.

Tip

If you prefer to type over text without selecting it, use Overtype mode. To turn it on, choose Word Options from the Office menu, click the Advanced category, and select the Use The Insert Key To Control Overtype Mode check box. Click OK, and then press the Insert key to turn on Overtype mode; press Insert again to turn off overtyping.

A very important piece of furniture is the kitchen table. There are many dresser boards, shelves and flaps, but they are useless to the cook as compared with a good kitchen table. It should be made of stout deal, as large as the size of the kitchen will permit, fitted with a convenient drawer for holding knives, forks, spoons, clean kitchen cloths, and other necessaries.

A very important piece of furniture is the kitchen table. It should be made of stout deal, as large as the size of the kitchen will permit, fitted with a convenient drawer for holding knives, forks, spoons, clean kitchen cloths, and other necessaries.

A very important piece of furniture is the kitchen table. It should be made of stout deal, as large as the size of the kitchen will permit, fitted with a convenient drawer for holding knives, forks, spoons, clean kitchen cloths, and other necessaries.

A very important piece of furniture is the kitchen table. It should be made of pine planks, as large as the size of the kitchen will permit, fitted with a convenient drawer for holding knives, forks, spoons, clean kitchen cloths, and other necessaries.

See Also

"So Many Ways to Do It" on page 38 for more information about different ways to select text.

Working with Old Documents

When you open a document that was created in an earlier version of Word, you're working in Compatibility mode, which means that some of the new features of Word aren't available.

However, you'll maintain full compatibility with anyone who's using an earlier version. You can also convert your document so that you can use all the features in Word 2007.

Work in Compatibility Mode

(1) Choose Open from the Office menu to display the Open dialog box, and double-click the file to open it.

(2) Work on the document as you normally would.

(3) If you encounter a grayed (unavailable) feature, such as Themes, simply ignore that feature because you can't use it.

(4) Click the Save button to save the file in its original format.

The label indicates that you're working in Compatibility mode.

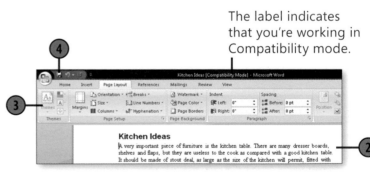

Tip ✓

Some features work differently in Compatibility mode. For example, equations are inserted as pictures, and SmartArt graphics are limited to the diagrams used in earlier versions of Word. These modifications are necessary so that you can open the file in your earlier version of Word.

Convert the Document

(1) With your Word 97–2003 format document open, choose Convert from the Office menu.

(2) If you see a dialog box asking you whether you want to convert, click OK. The original file won't be overwritten because its file extension is different from that of the updated file.

(3) Work on your document, using all the features in Word.

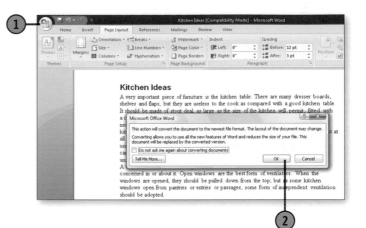

Caution

If you upgrade the file format of the document, the file won't be usable by people who have earlier versions of Word unless they've installed the Office Compatibility pack, which enables them to read and save this type of file.

Tip

If you need to send an upgraded file to someone who has an earlier version of Word but doesn't have the Office Compatibility pack, point to the arrow at the right of the Save As command on the Office menu, and choose Word 97–2003 Document from the gallery that appears. You might lose some advanced features in your document, but at least other people will be able to read it.

Reading a Document

To help you cut down on the amount of paper piled up in the so-called "paperless office," Word's Full Screen Reading view is designed to make it simple and pleasant to read documents without printing them. If you like it, that's great—you'll save some trees, as well as some clutter.

Read

1. If you're not already in Full Screen Reading view, click the Full Screen Reading button on the status bar to display your document for easy reading.

2. Move the mouse to the left or right edge of the screen until the cursor turns into a hand. Click to move to the previous page or pair of pages (left edge) or to the next page or pair of pages (right edge).

3. Open the View Options menu, and choose

   - Increase Text Size or Decrease Text Size to change the size of the screen text.

   - Show One Page or Show Two Pages to view a single page or a pair of pages.

   - Show Printed Page to view the page as it will look when printed, and Margin Settings to specify whether the margins should be shown correctly or shrunk so that the text can be shown in a larger size.

   - Allow Typing to edit the text as you read it, and Track Changes to mark all changes.

   - Show Comments And Changes to display all comments and marked changes, and to indicate which types of changes came from which reviewers.

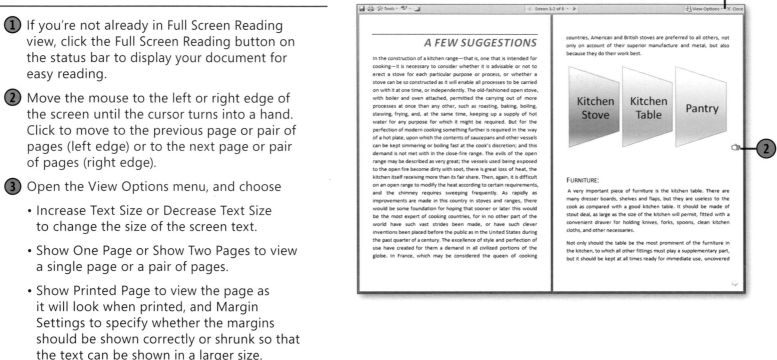

Tip

Word is set to display any Word attachments in your e-mail in Full Screen Reading view. If you prefer not to use this view, you can turn it off on the View Options menu.

Navigate

① Click the Page button to go to a specific page, location, or heading, or to display the Document Map or Thumbnails pane.

② If the Thumbnails pane is displayed, click a thumbnail to jump to that page.

③ If the Document Map pane is displayed, click a heading to jump to that heading.

④ When you've finished, press the Esc key or click the Close button to exit Full Screen Reading view.

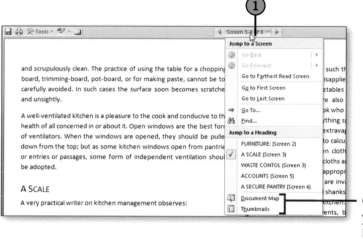

Choose whether you want to view Document Map or Thumbnails.

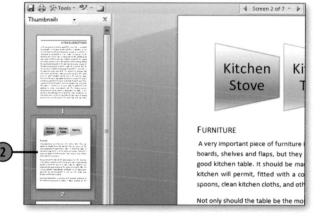

Tip

The Thumbnails and Document Map panes are available in all views by selecting the one you want from the View command tab on the Ribbon.

See Also

"Marking Changes in a Document" on pages 176–177 for information about adding comments or tracking changes.

Using Only the Keyboard

If you prefer to keep your hands on the keyboard instead of using the mouse, you can do almost everything using Word's keyboard shortcuts. By activating the command tabs and the Ribbon, you can use the displayed keys to navigate and to execute commands and activities. There are also many keyboard shortcuts you can use to execute some of the most common commands and activities.

Browse with Your Keyboard

1. Press and release the Alt key to display the KeyTips for access to the tabs and the Ribbon.

2. Type the letter for the tab you want. You can also type the letter for any item on the Quick Access toolbar or to open the Office menu.

3. Type the key or key combination to access the item you want on the Ribbon. If a gallery or a drop-down menu appears, use the arrow keys to select the item you want, and then press Enter.

4. If you want to access items on the status bar, press the F6 key until an item on the status bar is selected. Use the arrow keys to select items on the status bar, and press Enter to execute your choice.

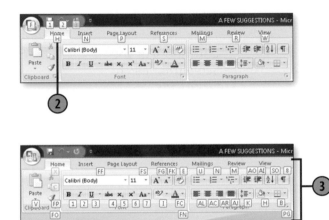

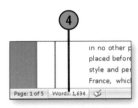

Tip

If you decide you don't want to execute an action after you've pressed the Alt key, press the Esc key to return to your work.

See Also

"Creating Keyboard Shortcuts" on page 214 for information about assigning your own keyboard shortcuts to commands.

Use Keyboard Shortcuts

① Use any of the keyboard shortcuts shown in the table to execute the action you want.

② If you want to switch from mouse methods to keyboard methods, point to the button or other item you want to work with, and note the keyboard shortcut in the ScreenTip. Then use that keyboard shortcut.

③ If you don't see the keyboard shortcut you want in the table or in a ScreenTip, search Word Help for "keyboard shortcuts."

See Also

"Getting Help" on page 42 for information about using Word Help.

Common Keyboard Shortcuts

Action	Keyboard shortcut
Copy and delete (cut) selected content	Ctrl+X
Copy selected content	Ctrl+C
Paste content	Ctrl+V
Hide or minimize Ribbon	Ctrl+F1
Apply/remove bold formatting	Ctrl+B
Apply/remove italic formatting	Ctrl+I
Apply/remove underline formatting	Ctrl+U
Align paragraph left	Ctrl+L
Align paragraph center	Ctrl+E
Align paragraph right	Ctrl+R
Add/remove space before paragraph	Ctrl+0 (zero)
Apply double line-spacing	Ctrl+2
Apply single line-spacing	Ctrl+1
Apply Normal style	Ctrl+Shift+N
Apply Heading 1 style	Alt+Shift+1
Apply Heading 2 style	Alt+Shift+2
Apply Heading 3 style	Alt+Shift+3
Change case	Shift+F3
Undo last action	Ctrl+Z
Redo last action	Ctrl+Y
Open shortcut menu	Shift+F10
Check spelling	F7
Save document	Ctrl+S
Save As	F12
Print (show Print dialog box)	Ctrl+P
Open Help	F1

So Many Ways to View It

Word gives you several ways to view your document as you work on it, and you'll find that your efficiency increases and your work becomes easier when you use the optimal view for the task at hand. You can use either the View tab on the Ribbon or any of the five view buttons at the bottom-right of the window to change your view.

Print Layout View

The standard working view for print documents, Print Layout view shows you how your document will look when it's printed—the placement of pictures, the arrangement of columns, the distance of the text from the edge of the page, and so on.

Full Screen Reading View

Full Screen Reading view makes it easy to read documents on your screen. The text is laid out in long vertical pages (or screens), just like those you see in most books. If you increase the size of the text for better readability, the content simply flows from one screen to the next. To maximize the area of the screen that's available for the document's content, the elements you normally see in the other views—the tabs, the Ribbon, and the status bar, for example—are no longer visible.

Web Layout View

Web Layout view is exclusively for working with online documents as if they were Web pages. That is, all the elements are displayed, but font size, line length, and page length all adjust to fit the window, just as they do on many Web pages.

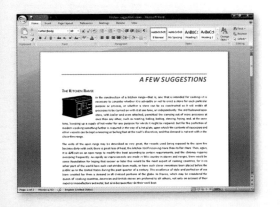

Although the six views shown on these two pages are the ones you'll probably use most often, there are other views and options that are useful in various circumstances: Thumbnails, Document Map, draft font, picture placeholders, and more.

You'll find information about many of these items elsewhere in this book in the discussions of the tasks and procedures where their use is the most relevant.

Outline View

Outline view displays your document as an outline, with the paragraph formatting defining the levels of the outline. By default, Word's standard heading styles have corresponding outline levels—Heading 1 is level one, Heading 2 is level two, and so on—and other paragraph styles, such as Normal, are treated as regular text. You can use Outline view to organize your topics before you start writing, or you can use it to reorganize an existing document.

Draft View

Draft view is designed for speed of entry and editing. It's based on the commercial publishing technique of creating *galleys*. You place the text and other elements in one long, continuous column that flows from one page to the next, and you deal with the placement of elements after you've ironed out any content problems. Draft view was called Normal view in earlier versions of Word.

Print Preview

Print Preview is designed to show you just how your document will look when you print it. You can see a close-up view, one page at a time, or two or more pages at once. Use Print Preview to make sure your document's layout is exactly the way you want before you go ahead and print it.

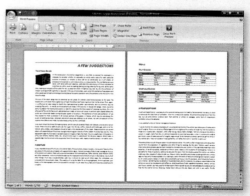

Changing Your View

A new perspective can often spark creativity and new ideas, so why not adjust your view of Word to the way you like it? Not only can you zoom in or out, but you can hide Word elements to maximize the area for your document.

Set the View

1 In any view other than Full Screen Reading view, click the view you want on the View tab.

2 To set a specific level, click the Zoom button.

3 Select the magnification or the display you want. (Not all options are available in all views.)

4 Click OK.

5 Clear the check boxes to maximize your work area or to hide any elements you don't want or need.

6 If the Quick Access toolbar takes up a line of its own, click the Customize Quick Access Toolbar button, and choose Show Above The Ribbon from the drop-down menu.

7 Double-click the active tab (or press Ctrl+F1) to minimize the Ribbon. Click any tab to temporarily display the entire Ribbon, or double-click the tab to keep the entire Ribbon visible.

Tip ✓

You can also change the magnification by dragging the Zoom Control slider at the bottom-right of the window or by clicking the plus or minus signs next to the Zoom Control slider. You can also change the magnification by holding down the Ctrl key and turning the wheel on your mouse.

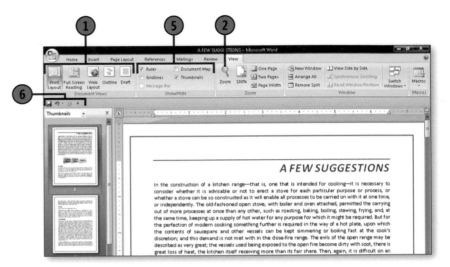

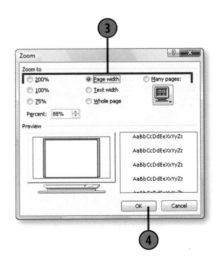

Researching a Subject

Wouldn't it be great to look up the definition of a word? Or to get information about something simply by clicking a word or a name? Well, you can do this in Word using the built-in research feature and access to the Internet.

Do Some Research

(1) Click in a word (or select a group of words) that you want information about.

(2) On the Review tab, click the Research button.

(3) Select the resource or the types of resources you want to use.

(4) Review the results.

(5) If you want to look up something more, type the word or words, and press Enter.

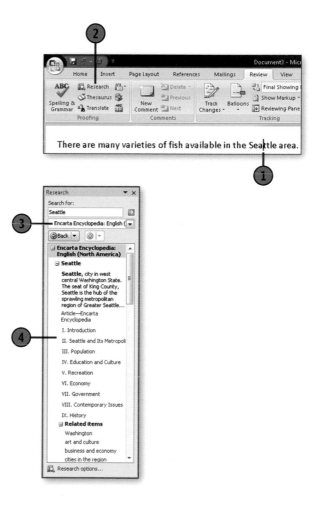

Tip

To quickly open the Research pane, hold down the Alt key and click the word to be looked up.

Caution

Some research services charge to view the full content of their results. If there's a charge, you'll see an icon indicating the amount next to the search result.

Translating Foreign-Language Text

You can translate a word, a common phrase, or an entire document into or from another language by using one of the language dictionaries installed on your computer. When you work in the Translate task pane, you can translate several words, or you can obtain additional resources either to translate in languages for which you don't have dictionaries or to translate large sections of text, including entire documents.

See a Translation

1. On the Review tab, click the Translation ScreenTip button, and choose the language into which you want to translate a word.

2. Move the mouse pointer over a word you want translated and wait until the ScreenTip with the translation appears.

3. If you no longer want to see the ScreenTip, click the Translation ScreenTip button again, and click Turn Off Translation ScreenTip.

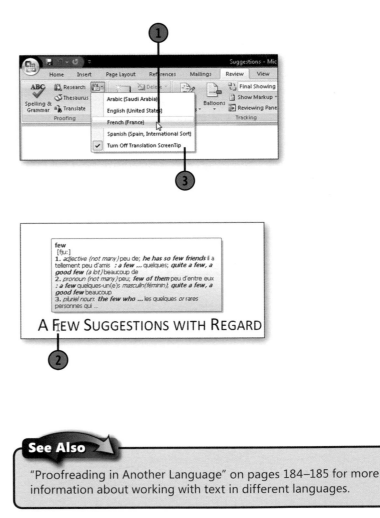

See Also

"Proofreading in Another Language" on pages 184–185 for more information about working with text in different languages.

Tip ✓

Word provides three translation resources. The Translation ScreenTip's translation is based on the dictionaries installed on your computer. In the Research pane, if the required dictionary isn't installed, Word will try to use an online dictionary. To translate large amounts of text, Word can link you directly to a translation service on the Internet through the Office Marketplace. Because these Web services aren't part of Office and aren't provided by Microsoft, there might be differences in the way each one works.

Do More Translating

1 Click in a word or select a short phrase you want translated.

2 On the Review tab, click the Translate button.

3 In the Research pane that appears, specify the language of the selected text, and then select the language into which you want the word or phrase translated.

4 If you want to insert the translation into your document, double-click the translated word or phrase to select it, or select only the words you want to use. Then right-click the selected word or words, choose Copy from the shortcut menu, and paste the translation into your document.

Tip

To quickly open the Research pane and translate a word, hold down the Alt key and click the word.

Finding Text

If you're not sure where to find some text in your document, Word can locate it for you. You can broaden the search so that Word finds similar words, or you can narrow the search to a designated part of the document or to text that uses specific formatting.

Find Text One Instance at a Time

1 On the Home tab, click the Find button (or press Ctrl+F) to display the Find And Replace dialog box.

2 Type the text you want to find.

3 Click Find Next. Continue to click Find Next as you move through the document, finding each instance of the text.

Tip

To limit the search to a specific part of a document, select that part of the document before you open the Find And Replace dialog box. To search text boxes or headers and footers, click the Find In button, and choose the location.

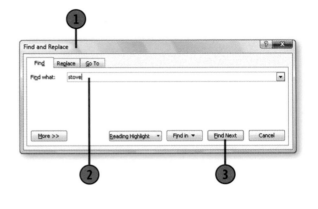

Find All Instances of Text

1 Click Reading Highlight, and then choose Highlight All to highlight all the words that match the search.

2 To remove highlighting from the text, click the Reading Highlight button, and choose Clear Highlighting from the menu.

3 Click Close when you've finished (the Cancel button changes to Close after you've conducted a search).

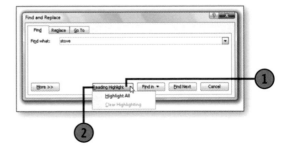

Modify the Search

 Click the More button, if it's displayed, to show the full Find And Replace dialog box.

 Click Up, Down, or All to search all or part of the document.

3 To customize the search, select

- Match Case to find only text that exactly matches the capitalization of the text in the Find What box.

- Find Whole Words Only to find text only if the matching text consists of whole words, not parts of words.

- Use Wildcards to use certain characters as wildcard characters.

- Sounds Like to find words that sound the same but are spelled differently (*their* and *there,* for example).

- Find All Word Forms to find all words that are forms of the word (its plural or its past tense, for example).

- Match Prefix to find words that begin with the search text, or Match Suffix to find words that end with the search text.

- Ignore Punctuation Characters to find text whether or not all the punctuation is the same, or Ignore White-Space Characters to find text whether or not it contains the same white-space characters (spaces or paragraph marks, for example).

4 Click Format to specify the formatting of the search text.

5 Click Special to search for any special element that's associated with the text or to choose wildcard characters.

6 Use the Reading Highlight or the Find Next button to search for the text.

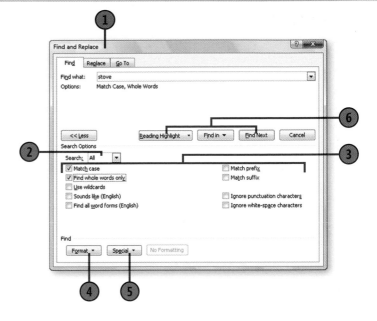

Tip

"Wildcard" characters are used to represent other characters. The most commonly used wildcards are ? and *. The ? wildcard represents any single character, and the * wildcard represents any number of characters. For a complete list of wildcards, select the Use Wildcards check box, and click the Special button.

Replacing Text

When you need to replace a word or phrase with a different word or phrase in several places in your document, let Word do it for you. It's a great way to use Word's speed and power to make quick work of those tedious document-wide changes.

Replace Text

① On the Home tab, click the Replace button (or press Ctrl+H) to display the Find And Replace dialog box with the Replace tab selected. Click the More button, if it's displayed, to show the full dialog box.

② Type the text you want to find.

③ To narrow the search, click Format, and specify the formatting of the text you're searching for.

④ To replace non-text items, click Special, and specify any element that's associated with the text.

⑤ Type the replacement text. Click the Format button to specify any formatting the replacement text should have. Use the Special button to specify a non-text element.

⑥ Click one of the following:

- Replace to replace the found text and find the next instance of the search text

- Replace All to replace all instances of the search text with the replacement text

- Find Next to find the next instance of the search text without replacing it

⑦ Click Close when you've finished (the Cancel button changes to Close after you've conducted a search).

Tip

If you used the Replace All button and the results aren't what you expected, click the Undo button on the Quick Access toolbar. You can then try the replacement again, this time with more specific search parameters.

See Also

"Finding Text" on pages 26–27 for information about broadening or narrowing a search.

"Standardizing the Formatting" on page 183 for information about replacing formatting only.

Adding Page Numbers

It's a wise practice to add page numbers to any document that's more than a few pages in length. We all know what a time-consuming hassle it is to try to put the unnumbered pages of a long document back in the right order after they've gone flying all over the place. Don't let this happen to you!

Insert Page Numbers

1 On the Insert tab, click the Page Number button. On the drop-down menu that appears, point to the location where you want the page number to appear.

2 Click the page-numbering design you want in the gallery that appears.

3 If you want to change the numbering format or the way the pages are numbered in a multi-section document, click Page Number again, and choose Format Page Numbers from the menu that appears.

4 Select the numbering format you want.

5 If you have more than one section in your document, specify whether you want the page numbering to be continuous or to restart at the beginning of each section.

6 Click OK.

7 If you don't like the way the page number looks or where it's positioned, click the Page Number button, choose Remove Page Numbers, and then choose a different numbering format.

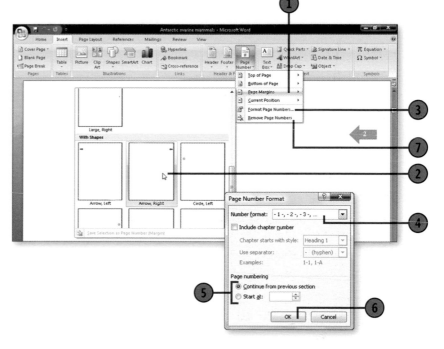

See Also

"Creating Running Heads" on pages 112–113 for information about incorporating page numbers with other information.

"Customizing the Page Numbers" on page 207 for information about changing the appearance of the page numbers.

Inserting Frequently Used Content

If you type the same word or phrase repeatedly, you can save yourself a lot of time (especially if you use long technical terms or difficult names) by saving that word or phrase as a Quick Parts entry. You assign the Quick Part a short name—a nickname of sorts, with at least four letters—and when you type the nickname, you can insert the Quick Part into your document. And the Quick Parts feature isn't limited to text; the information can be anything you can put into a document: pictures, tables, whole new pages, even fields. Word comes already equipped with numerous Quick Parts entries for some of the most common types of information.

Store the Information

1. In your document, select all the information you want to include in the Quick Parts entry.

2. On the Insert tab, click the Quick Parts button, and choose Save Selection To Quick Part Gallery (or press Alt+F3) to display the Create New Building Block dialog box.

3. Accept the suggested name, or type a new name for the entry.

4. Select Quick Parts if it isn't already displayed in the Gallery list.

5. Select a category for the entry, or choose Create New Category to create and select an additional category.

6. Specify where you want to save the entry—in the current template, the global Normal template, or the global Building Blocks collection.

7. Specify the way you want the material to be inserted.

8. Click OK.

Insert the Information

1 Place the insertion point where you want the content to be inserted, type the Quick Parts name, and press the F3 key to insert the content.

2 Check your document to verify that Word inserted the correct information.

Find and Insert an AutoText Entry

1 On the Insert tab, click the Quick Parts button.

2 In the gallery that appears, scroll through the list to find the item you want to insert, and do either of the following:

- Click the Quick Parts entry you want to insert at the insertion point in the document.

- Right-click the entry, and choose the way you want it to be inserted.

Tip

If you frequently use the Quick Parts gallery to insert content, open the gallery, right-click it, and choose to add the gallery to the Quick Access toolbar. That way, you'll be able to access the gallery while you're working on any command tab in Word.

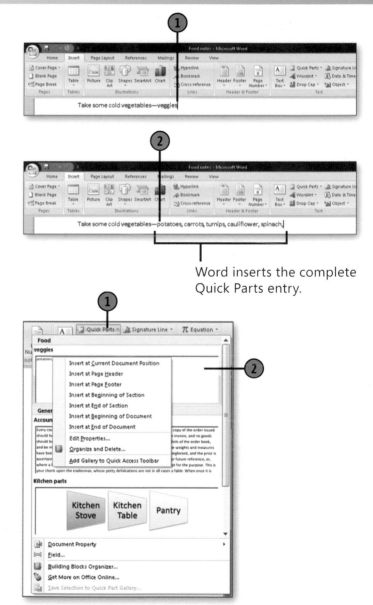

Word inserts the complete Quick Parts entry.

Correcting Your Spelling and Grammar

You can avoid the embarrassment of distributing a document full of misspellings, incorrectly used words, or poor grammar even if you don't have a proofreader or an editor at your disposal. Word comes to the rescue by discreetly pointing out your spelling errors, word usage problems, and grammatical no-no's. When you see one of those helpful little squiggles under a word or phrase, you can choose what you want to do to correct the mistake—if it really is a mistake.

Correct a Spelling Error

1 Right-click a red squiggle to see one or more suggestions for correcting the error.

2 Click the suggestion you want to use.

3 If you believe that what you have isn't an error but is something that isn't recognized by Word, click Ignore or Ignore All to tell Word to ignore the word throughout this document, or click Add To Dictionary to have Word ignore the word throughout all your documents.

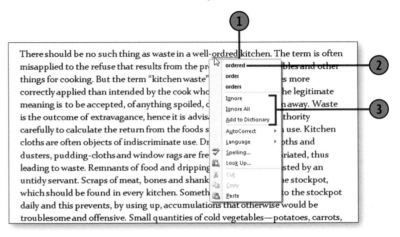

There should be no such thing as waste in a well-ordered kitchen. The term is often misapplied to the refuse that results from the pr[...] things for cooking. But the term "kitchen waste" [...] s more correctly applied than intended by the cook who [...] he legitimate meaning is to be accepted, of anything spoiled, [...] n away. Waste is the outcome of extravagance, hence it is advis[...] thority carefully to calculate the return from the foods s[...] use. Kitchen cloths are often objects of indiscriminate use. Dr[...] oths and dusters, pudding-cloths and window rags are fre[...] riated, thus leading to waste. Remnants of food and dripping [...] sted by an untidy servant. Scraps of meat, bones and shank[...] e stockpot, which should be found in every kitchen. Someth[...] to the stockpot daily and this prevents, by using up, accumulations that otherwise would be troublesome and offensive. Small quantities of cold vegetables—potatoes, carrots,

ordered
order
orders
Ignore
Ignore All
Add to Dictionary
AutoCorrect ▸
Language ▸
Spelling...
Look Up...
Cut
Copy
Paste

Tip

If Word didn't offer any suggestions when you right-clicked a squiggle, return to your document and try to correct the error yourself. If the squiggle remains, right-click it, and see whether there are any suggestions now.

Tip

To get correction suggestions and to correct errors using the keyboard, move the insertion point into the misspelled word, press the F7 key, and use the Spelling And Grammar dialog box to make your changes.

See Also

"Correcting Text Automatically" on pages 34–35 for information about having Word automatically correct the spelling of words you frequently misspell.

"Customizing the Way Word Checks Spelling and Grammar" on page 218 for information about enabling or disabling spelling and grammar checking.

"Customizing Your Spelling Dictionaries" on page 219 for information about adding and modifying the dictionaries that are used in the spelling check.

"Adding or Removing Word Components" on page 232 for information about installing Office components, including multiple-language proofreading tools, if they aren't already installed.

Correct a Contextual Spelling Error

① Right-click a blue squiggle to see one or more suggestions for fixing improper word usage.

② Click the suggestion you want, or choose to ignore this error or this word throughout the document.

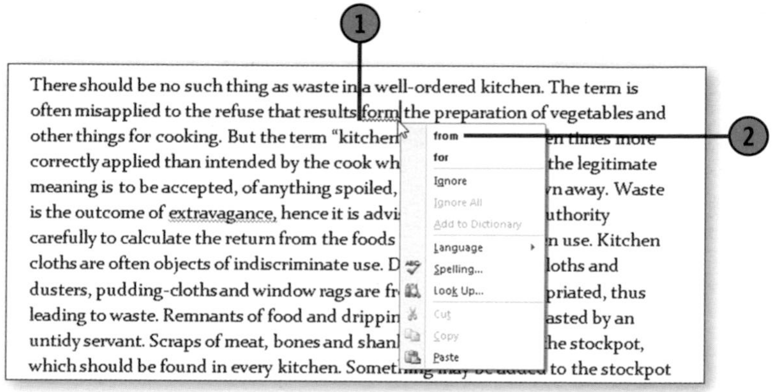

There should be no such thing as waste in a well-ordered kitchen. The term is often misapplied to the refuse that results form the preparation of vegetables and other things for cooking. But the term "kitchen" ... en times more correctly applied than intended by the cook wh ... the legitimate meaning is to be accepted, of anything spoiled, ... n away. Waste is the outcome of extravagance, hence it is advi ... uthority carefully to calculate the return from the foods ... n use. Kitchen cloths are often objects of indiscriminate use. D ... loths and dusters, pudding-cloths and window rags are fr ... priated, thus leading to waste. Remnants of food and drippin ... asted by an untidy servant. Scraps of meat, bones and shan ... he stockpot, which should be found in every kitchen. Somet ... to the stockpot

Shortcut menu: from / for / Ignore / Ignore All / Add to Dictionary / Language ▶ / Spelling... / Look Up... / Cut / Copy / Paste

---

Tip

If you chose to ignore misspelled words or improper grammar but you're now having second thoughts, choose Word Options from the Office menu, and, with the Proofing category selected, click the Recheck Document button to remove all your Ignore choices.

Try This!

In a document that has spelling and/or grammar errors, click the Proofing Errors icon on the status bar. Correct the error, and then click the icon again to find the next error. Continue finding and correcting your spelling and grammar errors until your document is error-free.

Correct the Grammar

① Right-click a green squiggle.

② If the shortcut menu suggests alternative phrasing, click to use the alternative. If only a description of the problem is shown, click in the document and edit the text as suggested.

③ If you're sure your grammar is correct, click Ignore Once.

④ If you want to know why the text was marked, click About This Sentence for an explanation of the grammar rules involved.

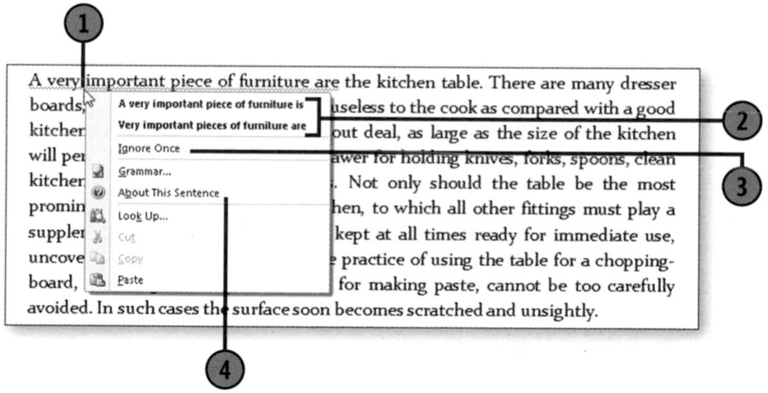

A very important piece of furniture are the kitchen table. There are many dresser boards, ... useless to the cook as compared with a good kitchen ... out deal, as large as the size of the kitchen will per ... awer for holding knives, forks, spoons, clean kitchen ... . Not only should the table be the most promin ... hen, to which all other fittings must play a suppler ... kept at all times ready for immediate use, uncove ... e practice of using the table for a chopping-board, ... for making paste, cannot be too carefully avoided. In such cases the surface soon becomes scratched and unsightly.

Shortcut menu: A very important piece of furniture is / Very important pieces of furniture are / Ignore Once / Grammar... / About This Sentence / Look Up... / Cut / Copy / Paste

Correcting Text Automatically

Word provides an exceptionally useful feature called Auto-Correct that you can use to correct common misspellings of certain words. You can also customize the AutoCorrect feature to include your own common repetitive typing errors and misspellings, and you can make AutoCorrect work even harder for you by defining special AutoCorrect entries.

Add Your Own Misspellings

1. Right-click one of your own common misspellings, point to AutoCorrect on the shortcut menu, and choose the correct spelling from the list of suggestions that appears.

2. Check your document, and observe that the correct spelling has replaced your misspelling. Continue composing your document. Note that if the same misspelling occurs again, Word corrects it for you.

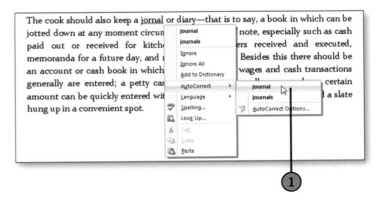

Add Other Entries

1. Choose Word Options from the Office menu, click the Proofing category, and click the AutoCorrect Options button to display the AutoCorrect dialog box.

2. On the AutoCorrect tab, with the Replace Text As You Type check box selected, enter the abbreviated or incorrect text that you'll type.

3. Type the text that you want to replace the text you typed.

4. Click Add.

5. Add other entries if desired. Click OK when you've finished.

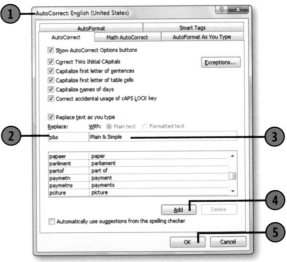

Control the Corrections

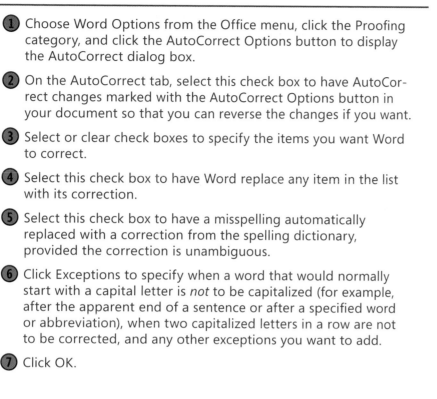

1 Choose Word Options from the Office menu, click the Proofing category, and click the AutoCorrect Options button to display the AutoCorrect dialog box.

2 On the AutoCorrect tab, select this check box to have AutoCorrect changes marked with the AutoCorrect Options button in your document so that you can reverse the changes if you want.

3 Select or clear check boxes to specify the items you want Word to correct.

4 Select this check box to have Word replace any item in the list with its correction.

5 Select this check box to have a misspelling automatically replaced with a correction from the spelling dictionary, provided the correction is unambiguous.

6 Click Exceptions to specify when a word that would normally start with a capital letter is *not* to be capitalized (for example, after the apparent end of a sentence or after a specified word or abbreviation), when two capitalized letters in a row are not to be corrected, and any other exceptions you want to add.

7 Click OK.

Tip

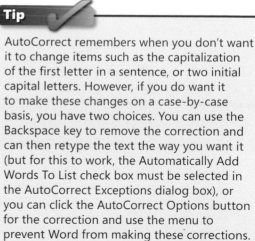

AutoCorrect remembers when you don't want it to change items such as the capitalization of the first letter in a sentence, or two initial capital letters. However, if you do want it to make these changes on a case-by-case basis, you have two choices. You can use the Backspace key to remove the correction and can then retype the text the way you want it (but for this to work, the Automatically Add Words To List check box must be selected in the AutoCorrect Exceptions dialog box), or you can click the AutoCorrect Options button for the correction and use the menu to prevent Word from making these corrections.

Moving and Copying Text

Word uses a tool called the *Clipboard* as a temporary holding area for text and other content that you want to move or copy to another part of your document, to another document in the same program, or to a document in another program. You simply park your content on the Clipboard and then, when you're ready, you retrieve it and "paste" it into its new location. Word uses two different Clipboards: the Windows Clipboard, which stores the item most recently cut or copied; and the Office Clipboard, which can store as many as 24 different items, including the most recently cut or copied item, but which works only with Office programs. You'll probably use the Paste button when you're pasting the last item you cut or copied, and the Windows Clipboard when you want to move several different pieces of text from one place to another.

Cut or Copy Text

 Select the text you want to cut or copy.

Do either of the following:

- Click the Cut button (or press Ctrl+X) to delete the selected text and store it on the Clipboard.

- Click the Copy button (or press Ctrl+C) to keep the selected text where it is and place a copy on the Clipboard.

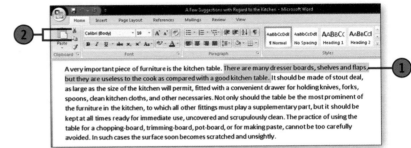

Paste the Cut or Copied Text

Click in your document where you want to insert the text.

Click the Paste button (or press Ctrl+V).

If the inserted text looks strange because it doesn't match the look (that is, the formatting) of the surrounding text, click the Paste Options button that appears, and choose Match Destination Formatting from the menu.

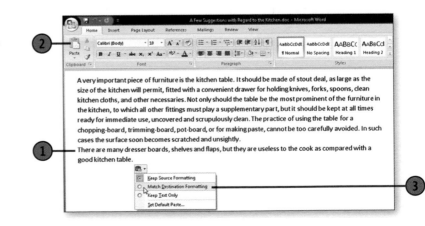

Copy and Paste Multiple Items

① On the Home tab, click the Clipboard button to display the Clipboard, and select and cut or copy the items you want in this document, or in any other Word or Office document.

② If necessary, switch to the document into which you want to paste some or all of the items you cut or copied. Click where you want to insert one of the items.

③ Click the item to be inserted. Continue inserting, cutting, and copying text as necessary.

④ To paste all the items you copied into one location, click Paste All.

⑤ Click Clear All when you no longer need any of the copied items and want to empty the Clipboard to collect and store new items.

The Office Clipboard

Tip

To change the default way Word pastes content in different circumstances, click the Paste Options button, and choose Set Default Paste from the menu to display the Word Options dialog box. If the Paste Options button doesn't appear, choose Word Options from the Office menu, and, in the Cut, Copy, And Paste section of the Advanced category, select the Show Paste Options Buttons check box. Click OK.

See Also

"So Many Ways to Do It" on pages 38–39 for information about the many different ways to copy and move text.

So Many Ways to Do It

Word offers you a variety of ways to do most things. You might, for example, be able to use a button, a menu item, a keyboard shortcut, a gallery, or a mouse-click to accomplish the same result. Why are there so many choices? Well, one reason is that we all work differently. Given several choices, we usually do some experimenting, find the way that works best for us and that we're most comfortable with, and then stick with it. Another reason is that certain methods work best in certain situations.

You can accomplish two frequently used procedures—selecting text and moving or copying it—using quite a few different methods, some of which might cause you a bit of difficulty if you use them in the wrong situation. The tips we offer here will help you choose which method to use in which circumstances.

Try these common methods of selecting text to see which work best for you. Of course, there are other ways to select text, and, depending on whether and how you've customized Word, some selection methods might work a bit differently from those described here. For information about customizing Word, see section 10, "Customizing and Securing Word," starting on page 209.

Text-Selection Methods

To select	Use this method
Characters in a word	Drag the mouse over the characters.
A word	Double-click the word.
Several words	Drag the mouse over the words.
A sentence	Hold down the Ctrl key and click anywhere in the sentence.
A line of text	Move the pointer to the far left of the window, and click when you see a right-pointing arrow.
A paragraph	Move the pointer to the far left of the window, and double-click when you see a right-pointing arrow.
A long passage	Click at the beginning of the passage, and then hold down the Shift key and click at the end of the passage.
Noncontiguous blocks of text	Drag the mouse to select the first block. Hold down the Ctrl key and drag the mouse to select the second block.
A vertical block of text	Click at the top-left corner of the text block. Hold down the Alt key and drag the mouse over the text block.
The entire document	Press Ctrl+A.

After you've selected the text, your next step might be to move it or copy it. Again, some methods are better than others, depending on the situation.

The process of moving or copying contents uses different tools, depending on what you want to do. When you use the F2 key or the Shift+F2 key combination, the selected material is stored in Word's short-term memory, where it's remembered only until you paste it into another location or execute any other Word activity.

The Cut and Copy buttons on the Clipboard store the selected material on the Office Clipboard, from where you can retrieve the information once or numerous times. The Office Clipboard stores up to 24 items, which you can retrieve one at a time or all at once. For more information about the Office Clipboard, see "Moving and Copying Text" on pages 36–37.

If these seem like an overwhelming number of ways to accomplish the same tasks, get ready for a surprise—there are even more ways. If you really want to explore the full range of different ways to do these tasks, take a stroll through Word's Help and try out some of the other methods.

Copying and Moving Methods

To do this	Use this method after you've selected the text
Move a short distance	Drag the selection to the new location.
Copy a short distance	Hold down the Ctrl key, drag the selection to the new location, and release the Ctrl key.
Move a long distance or to a different document or program	Click the Cut button, click at the new location, and click the Paste button. OR press Ctrl+X, click at the new location, and press Ctrl+V.
Copy a long distance or to a different document or program	Click the Copy button, click at the new location, and click the Paste button. OR press Ctrl+C, click at the new location, and press Ctrl+V.
Copy several items and insert all at one place	Click the Copy button, select the next item, click the Copy button again, and repeat to copy up to 24 items. OR hold down the Ctrl key, select multiple items, and then click the Copy button. Click at the new location, and then click the Paste All button on the Clipboard.
Move a long or short distance	Press the F2 key, click at the new location, and press Enter.
Copy a long or short distance	Press Shift+F2, click at the new location, and press Enter.

Printing a Document

E-mail and Web documents are bringing the paperless office closer to reality, but the most common way to distribute a finished document is still to print it. Printing is mostly a job for Windows—Word prepares your document, and then hands it off to Windows.

Check Your Layout

1. On the Office menu, point to the arrow next to the Print command, and click Print Preview in the gallery that appears.

2. Scroll through the document, using the scroll bars or the Page Up and Page Down keys to examine the layout of your pages.

3. Use the Zoom buttons to change your view of the document. To take a closer look, with the Magnifier check box selected, move the mouse over the document, and click to enlarge the page. Click the mouse again to restore the original view.

4. Scroll to the last page of the document. If it contains only a few words and you don't want to print a mostly blank page, click the Shrink One Page button to see whether Word can make minor formatting changes to move the remaining text onto the previous page.

5. If you're not happy with the way the document looks, use the tools in the Page Setup group to make the changes you want in the layout.

6. Click Print to display the Print dialog box and print your perfect document.

7. Click Close Print Preview to return to your normal view.

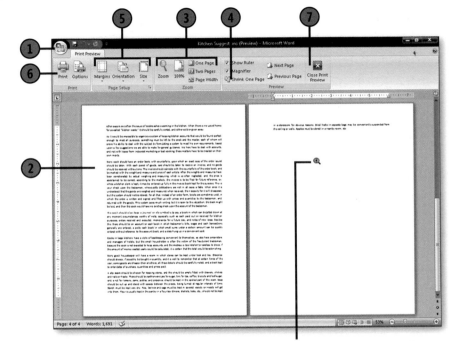

The mouse cursor shows when the Magnifier is available.

> **Tip**
>
> If you're using a mouse with a scroll wheel, turn the wheel to move through the pages of Print Preview.

Print the Document

1 Look over your document to make sure it's complete and free of errors. Then choose Print from the File menu to display the Print dialog box.

2 Specify whether you want to print the entire document, a single page, some selected text, or a range of pages.

3 Specify the printer to be used.

4 Specify the number of copies you want.

5 If you're printing multiple copies, specify whether the pages are to be printed in order (collated) or whether all copies of the same page are to be printed at one time.

6 Specify a scaling size if you want to print on paper that's a different size from the paper the document was originally set up for.

7 Click OK to print the document.

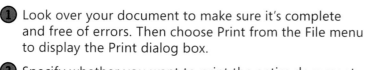

Tip

If you don't need to change any settings in the Print dialog box, you can quickly print a document to your default printer by pointing to the arrow next to the Print command on the Office menu and then clicking Quick Print in the gallery.

Tip

Although you should close Print Preview before you make any substantial changes to the document, you can make small edits in Print Preview by clearing the Magnifier check box and then clicking in your document.

Tip

To print special material—for example, a list of markups in the document, document properties, styles, or shortcut-key assignments—specify the item to be printed in the Print What list box. To print only odd pages or only even pages, specify what you want to print in the Print list box.

Getting Help

Nothing can replace this book, of course, but Word does provide you with other resources to help solve problems you might encounter. Word's Help system has several different ways to render assistance.

Browse for Help

 Press the F1 key to display the Word Help window.

 Click a category to expand the list.

 Click an appropriate topic, and then click an article that seems most relevant to your question.

④ If the font size is too small or too large, click the Change Font Size button, and choose a font size from the menu.

⑤ To print the topic, click the Print button.

⑥ To return to either the list or the articles, click the Back button. To return to the list of categories, click the Back button again.

Search for Help

① Type your Search text.

② If you want to specify which Help resource you want, click the Search down arrow, and then click the resource.

③ Click Search.

④ Click a search result that seems relevant. If there's more than one page of results, click the Next button at the top of the search results to see any additional pages.

⑤ Close the window when you've finished.

Go back and forth between topics you've already opened.

Click to keep window on top.

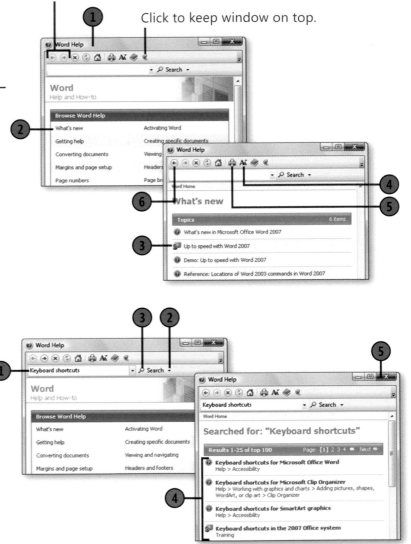

3

Designing Your Documents

In this section:

- **Formatting Text with Themes, Styles, and Fonts**
- **Adding Emphasis and Special Formatting**
- **Creating an Inline Heading**
- **Adjusting the Spacing Between Characters**
- **Copying Your Formatting**
- **Setting the Overall Look**
- **Placing a Line Border or an Art Border Around a Page**
- **Adding a Decorative Horizontal Line**
- **Adding a Border or Shading to a Paragraph**
- **Creating and Formatting Lists and Tables**

Even if you don't have the time, inclination, or experience to design the documents you use every day, you can still produce professional-looking, well-designed letters, reports, memos, faxes, and even the Great American Novel. You do this by using the themes, styles, fonts, colors, borders, shading, decorative lines, and other design elements that Microsoft Office Word 2007 provides to help you create, design, and maintain consistency throughout the documents you produce at work, at school, or at play. Depending on your desired end result and how little or how much involvement you want in the design, you can use the predesigned themes and style sets just as they come, without changing a thing; you can modify the existing ones a little or a lot; or, with a bit of time and experimentation, you can create your own highly individual designs.

In this section, we'll walk you through some of the procedures that will get you comfortable with the tools on Word's Ribbon and in the galleries—what they do and how you use them to achieve the look you want for your documents. Because Word's new interface is so visual and intuitive, you'll find that experimenting with the tools is a lot of fun, and that "trying on" a bunch of different designs just to see how they look can build your confidence and unleash your creativity.

Formatting Text

Rarely, except possibly in a short note or e-mail, is a document composed of just plain old text, with all the paragraphs in the same font and font size and with the same indents and line spacing. In Microsoft Word, you can quickly add formatting to selected text or set all the formatting for a paragraph to give your documents a professional look. You can apply formatting whenever you want—before you type, while you're typing, or after you've typed all your text.

Apply Character Formatting

① Click the Home tab if it isn't already selected.

② Select the text you want to format.

③ Point to any style that isn't a paragraph style—that is, any one that doesn't have a small paragraph mark (¶) at the left of its name—to see how the formatting of your selected text has changed. If you like the formatting, click the style to apply it to the selected text. If you don't like what you see, use the scroll arrows to scroll through the list of styles until you find a style you want to use.

Tip

Paragraph styles define both the character formatting and the paragraph layout.

Tip

Quick Styles are sets of styles that are designed to coordinate with the theme used to control the overall look of the document. There are multiple sets of Quick Styles for each theme and different sets for different themes.

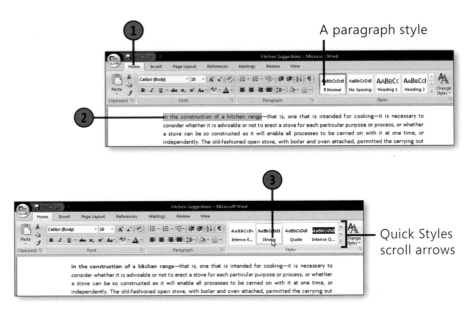

A paragraph style

Quick Styles scroll arrows

See Also

"Switching Quick Styles" on page 49 for information about changing the set of Quick Styles used in a theme, and "Setting the Overall Look" on pages 62–63 for information about changing the overall theme for the document.

Apply a Quick Style to a Paragraph

1. Click in the paragraph that you want to format, or select multiple paragraphs to which you want to apply the same formatting.

2. Point to a style you might want to use.

3. Inspect the paragraph or paragraphs to see whether you like the way the paragraph or paragraphs will look with this style.

4. If you like the look, click the style.

5. If you don't like the look, point to different styles to see alternative appearances, and click the style you want to use.

Tip

If you don't see any changes to the formatting of your paragraphs, you might not have the Live Preview feature enabled. To enable it, choose Word Options from the Office menu, and, with the Popular category selected in the Word Options dialog box, select the Enable Live Preview check box, and click OK.

See Also

"Creating Your Own Styles" on pages 190–191 for information about adding your custom styles to the Quick Styles gallery.

Tip

Styles provide a quick way to maintain consistency in formatting throughout a document. You can, however, apply direct formatting within text or paragraph formatting to modify the appearance whether or not you've applied a Quick Style.

Controlling the Look: Themes, Styles, and Fonts

Microsoft Office Word 2007 provides powerful tools that make it possible for you to easily create professional-looking documents. To simplify the design process—and thereby avoid the chaos that's often a problem in heavily formatted documents—Word's tools help you build consistent layouts with a minimum of hassle.

Themes: The master controllers of the design, themes set many elements, including the default fonts; the color schemes for text, horizontal and vertical lines, and backgrounds; and the shading and shadow effects in graphics. When you change a theme, you change the entire appearance of your document. You can change the whole theme or only individual elements—the default fonts, for example, or the color scheme or shading effects. Word comes with many built-in themes, but you can also design and save your own themes.

Paragraph Styles: These styles define the layout of your paragraphs—line spacing, indents, tab spacing, borders, and so on.

Character Styles: These styles define the look of individual text characters—for example, boldfaced, italicized, or underlined emphasis; strikethrough, superscript, color, and shadow effects; and spacing between characters. If you specify the font as something other than the theme's default font, the character style can also define the font and font size. Otherwise, the font is determined by the chosen theme.

Linked Styles: These styles define both paragraph and character formatting—for example, in a single style you can define the paragraph layout, including the alignment and line spacing, as well as the appearance of the characters for the entire paragraph, including font, font size, emphasis, and effects.

Table Styles: These styles define the appearance of your tables—for example, the shading of rows or columns and the thickness of the gridlines.

List Styles: These styles determine the appearance of your bulleted and numbered lists—for example, the kind of bullet used and how far the paragraph is indented.

Direct Formatting: You can use direct formatting to create customized words, paragraphs, or blocks of text. For example, you can apply bold formatting to a couple of words for emphasis, or select a quotation and add italics to it. Although you'll want to use styles most of the time to maintain a consistent look, direct formatting is a useful tool in certain instances. If you use direct formatting and later want to use the same formatting again, you can either use that formatting to create a new style or copy the formatting and apply it elsewhere with the Format Painter tool.

Direct formatting

A paragraph style

A linked style

A character style

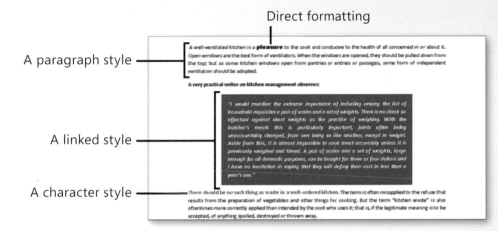

A font that has been specified
isn't changed by the theme.

Changing the theme changes
the default font and the entire
appearance of the text.

Using Any Style

Sometimes there are styles you want that aren't part of the Quick Styles set. You can access these styles and use them wherever you want.

Access Your Styles

1. On the Home tab, click the Show The Styles Window button at the bottom-right of the Styles group.

2. Select the Show Preview check box if it isn't already selected.

3. Click in a paragraph, or select the text or paragraphs to which you want to apply the same formatting.

4. Click the style you want to apply.

5. If the style you want isn't listed, click Options, and, in the Styles Pane Options dialog box, under Select Styles To Show, click All Styles, click OK, and then click the style you want.

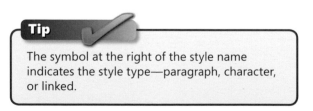

Tip

The symbol at the right of the style name indicates the style type—paragraph, character, or linked.

Try This!

Open the Quick Styles gallery and click Apply Styles to display the Apply Styles window. Click in a paragraph, or select the text you want to format. Click the Apply Styles window and start typing the name of the style you want. Press Enter when the name of the style you want is displayed.

Switching Quick Styles

Quick Styles exist in sets, and each set is designed to have a certain look, or mood, which is coordinated with the overall theme of the document. Some sets have a formal look; others are casual or emphatic. You can choose among these sets of styles to apply the look and feel you want to your document.

Select a Style Set

1. On the Home tab, with your document open, click the Change Styles button, point to Style Set, and, on the submenu, point to the Quick Style set you want.

2. If you like the way your document looks, click the style set to apply it. If you want to try out some different style sets, point to other style sets until you find the one you like, and then click that style set.

3. If you want this to be the style set you'll use in other documents based on this template, click Change Styles again, and then choose Set As Default from the menu that appears.

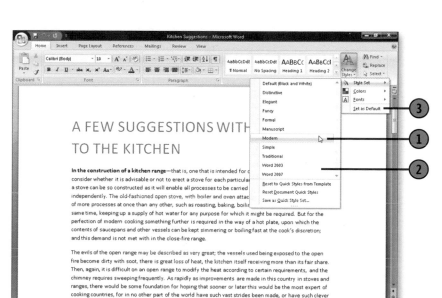

See Also

"Creating Your Own Styles" on pages 190–191 for information about defining your own Quick Styles.

Caution

In most business settings, it's best (unless you've been given permission) not to modify the style set that's been designed for a specific template, because most companies want all their documents to have the same coordinated look. If you modify the style set and later find out—ooops!—that you shouldn't have done so, click the Change Styles button, point to Style Set, and click Reset To Quick Styles From Template.

Changing Character Fonts

The combination of font and font size greatly determines the look of your content. You can easily set both of these elements for all or part of your content with just a few clicks on the Ribbon. Font and font size affect the selected character or characters.

Change the Font

1 Select the text whose font you want to change.

2 On the Home tab, click the Font list down arrow.

3 Click the font you want to use.

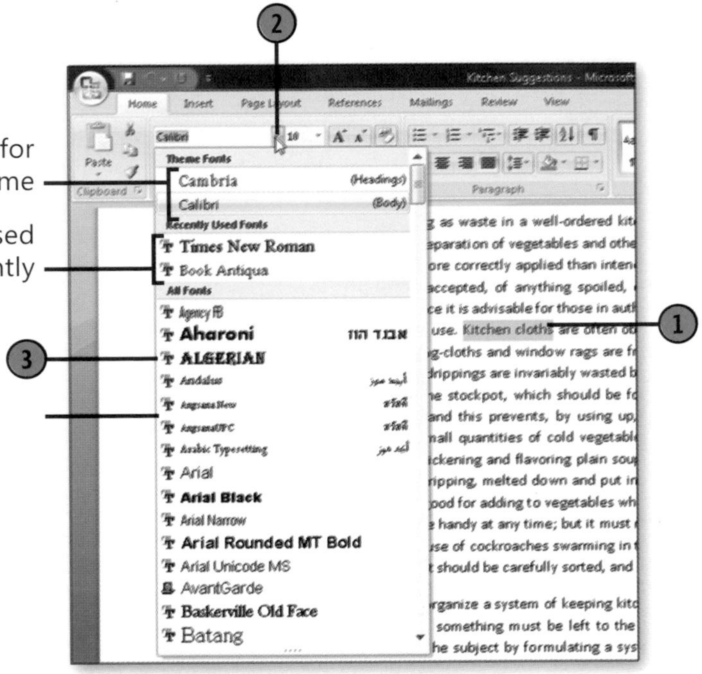

Fonts recommended for the current theme

Fonts that you've used recently

List of all fonts

Tip

Use Quick Styles or custom styles to apply consistent font formatting for similar content throughout your document. Use direct formatting for special formatting or to design and create new styles.

Tip

You can also change the font and font size using the Mini toolbar that appears when you select some text and keep the mouse pointer pointing to the selected text.

Try This!

Create and select some text in your document. On the Home tab, click the Font list down arrow, point to a font, and drag your mouse slowly down the list. Note that the font of the selected text changes to the font you're pointing to. When you see the font you like, click it to use that font.

Change the Font Size

1. Select the text whose font size you want to change.

2. On the Home tab, do any of the following:

   - Click the Font Size down arrow, and select a font size from the drop-down list that appears.

   - Click the Font Size list, and type the font size you want.

   - Click the Grow Font button or the Shrink Font button to increase or decrease the font size.

The Grow Font button — The Shrink Font button

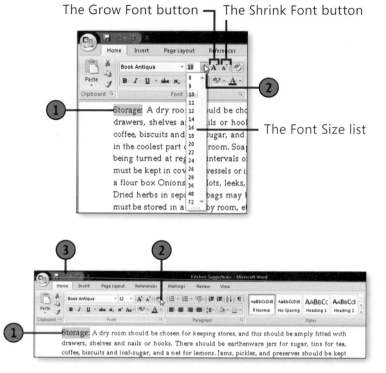

The Font Size list

Restore the Default Font and Font Size

1. Select the text to which you want to restore the default settings for that style.

2. On the Home tab, click the Clear Formatting button.

3. If you don't like the results, click the Undo button on the Quick Access toolbar, and use the formatting buttons to modify the formatting of the selected text.

See Also

"So Many Ways to Do It" on pages 38–39 for information about different methods of selecting text, including selecting noncontiguous blocks of text.

"Modify a Theme" on page 63 for information about setting the default heading and body text fonts for your theme.

"Creating Your Own Styles" on pages 190–191 for information about using existing formatting to create or modify a style.

Caution

The Clear Formatting button changes not only the font and font size, but also any emphasis—bold, italic, or underline—that you've applied.

Adjusting Paragraph Line Spacing

You can improve the readability of your text by adjusting the spacing, or *leading* (pronounced "ledding"), between the lines. Too little space makes the lines of text looked squashed together and difficult to read; too much space also makes the text difficult to read because the reader's eye has to search for the beginning of the next line.

Set the Line Spacing Within a Paragraph

(1) Click in a paragraph, or select all the paragraphs whose line spacing you want to set.

(2) On the Home tab, click the Line Spacing button.

(3) Select the line spacing you want.

(4) If you don't see the spacing you want, click Line Spacing Options.

(5) In the Paragraph dialog box that appears, select the type of line spacing you want:

- Exactly to create a specific space between lines regardless of the font size used

- At Least to create a minimum space between lines, which can increase if large font sizes are used

- Multiple to specify how many lines of space you want between the lines of text

(6) Use the arrows or type a value. For Exactly and At Least settings, this is a distance measurement, usually in points; for Multiple, this is the number of lines of space. Click OK.

Tip

The default measure for spacing is the *point*, abbreviated as "pt." A point is a typographic measure: 72 points equal one inch (or about 28.57 points equal one centimeter).

Tip

Some commonly used keyboard shortcuts are for line spacing and "space-before" spacing. Press Ctrl+1 for single spacing, Ctrl+5 for 1.5 line spacing, Ctrl+2 for double spacing, and Ctrl+0 (zero) for 1 line before the paragraph. Ctrl+0 is a toggle, so you can use it to change a paragraph from 1 line before to no lines before.

Set the Line Spacing Between Paragraphs

1 Click in a paragraph, or select all the paragraphs for which you want to set the spacing.

2 On the Home tab, click the Line Spacing button.

3 Click the command for adding space before or after the paragraph or paragraphs.

4 If you want to customize the spacing, click Line Spacing Options to display the Paragraph dialog box.

5 In the Before and After boxes, use the arrows or type a value for the space before (above) the first line of the paragraph and for the space after (below) the last line of the paragraph.

6 Select this check box if you don't want space between paragraphs of the same style.

7 Click OK.

8 If you want to remove the space before or after the selected paragraph or paragraphs, click the Line Spacing button again, and choose Remove Space Before Paragraph or Remove Space After Paragraph from the menu.

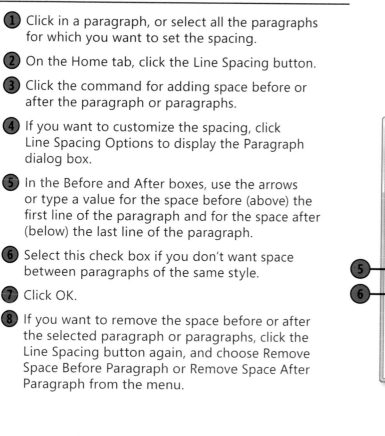

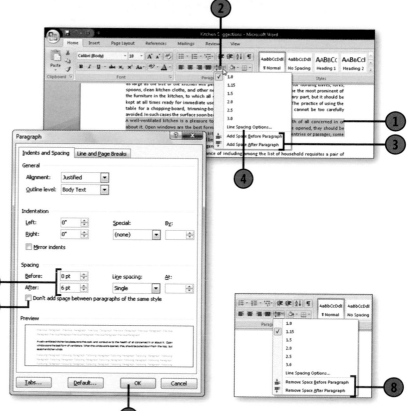

Caution

Note that the distance between two paragraphs is the sum of the space below the first paragraph and the space above the second paragraph. Keep this in mind so that you don't end up with a bigger space between paragraphs than you intended.

Setting Paragraph Alignment

The alignment you choose for a paragraph creates a distinctive appearance, and you can experiment with the various alignments to achieve just the right look for the way you'll be using that particular paragraph. With Word, you can adjust the alignment of one paragraph, several paragraphs, or even all your paragraphs.

Set the Alignment

1. Click in a paragraph, or select all the paragraphs whose alignment you want to set.

2. On the Home tab, click

   - The Align Left button to align the paragraph with the left margin or left indent, creating a ragged right edge.

   - The Center button to equalize the distance between the left margin or left indent and the left side of the paragraph with the distance between the right side of the paragraph and the right margin or right indent.

   - The Align Right button to align the paragraph with the right margin or right indent, creating a ragged left edge.

   - The Justify button to align the paragraph with both the left margin or left indent and the right margin or right indent by adding any necessary space between words.

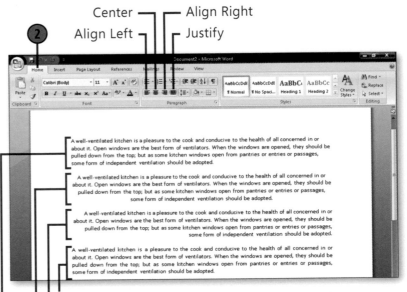

Justified alignment is often used in presentations and multicolumn pages.

Right alignment is often used when text wraps around objects or for special effects.

Center alignment is often used in titles, pull quotes, and special layout designs.

Left alignment is often used in standard paragraphs for ease of reading.

Tip

Consider using a style instead direct formatting to ensure consistency in your document if you're going to use this formatting more than once.

Indenting a Paragraph

An indent is the distance a paragraph or a first line is moved in from the left and/or right margin. Indenting a paragraph sets it off from other paragraphs. The indent can be as simple as slightly indenting the first line to indicate the start of a new paragraph, or as complex as indenting both the left and right sides of the paragraph to create a separate block of text.

Indent a Paragraph

(1) Click in a paragraph, or select all the paragraphs for which you want to set an indent.

(2) On the Home tab, click the Paragraph button to display the Paragraph dialog box.

(3) Click in the Left box, and use the arrows or type a value for the distance you want the indent from the left margin.

(4) Click in the Right box, and set the distance for the right indent from the right margin.

(5) Select this check box if you want the left and right indents to switch depending on whether they're on odd or even pages. This option is designed for two-sided documents, so you'll notice that the Left label changes to Inside and the Right label changes to Outside.

(6) Click in the Special box, and select

• First Line to indent the first line.

• Hanging to indent all the lines in the paragraph except the first line.

(7) Click in the By box, and use the arrows or type a value for the size you want the indent to be.

(8) Click OK.

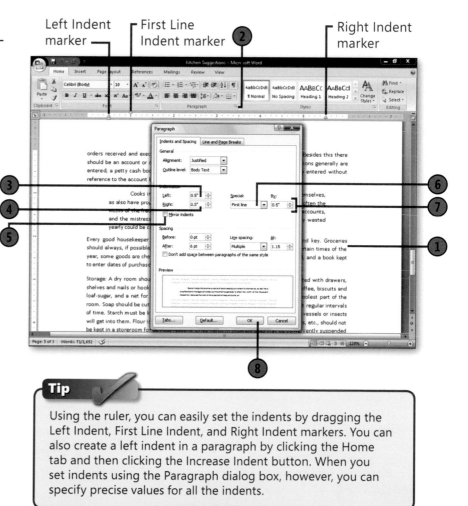

Left Indent marker

First Line Indent marker

Right Indent marker

Tip

Using the ruler, you can easily set the indents by dragging the Left Indent, First Line Indent, and Right Indent markers. You can also create a left indent in a paragraph by clicking the Home tab and then clicking the Increase Indent button. When you set indents using the Paragraph dialog box, however, you can specify precise values for all the indents.

Formatting with Tabs

You can use tabs to position text horizontally on a line simply by pressing the Tab key. All you need to do is specify the location of each tab and the alignment for the tab stop.

You can also set different types of leaders—dotted, dashed, or plain lines—that appear before the tab stop.

Set Your Tabs

1 If the ruler isn't already displayed, click the View Ruler button to display the ruler.

2 Click in a paragraph, or select all the paragraphs in which you want to set the tabs.

3 Click to select the type of tab you want. Each click selects a different type of tab or other ruler marker.

4 Click in the ruler where you want the tabs. If necessary, drag a tab stop to a new location to adjust it.

5 Repeat steps 3 and 4 to set additional tab stops.

6 Drag a tab stop off the ruler to delete that tab stop.

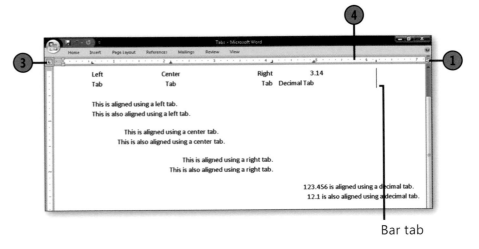

Bar tab

Tip ✓

If you don't set any tab stops, Word provides default tab stops that are usually set at 0.5 inch all the way across the line of text. You can change this default value in the Tabs dialog box, which you can open by double-clicking any tab stop on the ruler.

Tip ✓

Consider using a table instead of tab stops when you want to align several lines of text into columns.

See Also ➤

"Creating a Table from Scratch" on page 84 for information about setting tabs in table cells.

Modify the Tabs

① Double-click any tab stop on the ruler to display the Tabs dialog box.

② Select the tab stop you want to modify.

③ Select an alignment for the tab stop.

④ Select a leader for the tab stop.

⑤ Click Set.

⑥ Do any of the following:

- Specify a position for a new tab stop, set its alignment and leader, and click Set.

- Select an existing tab stop, and click Clear to delete it.

- Set a new value for the default tab stops.

⑦ Click OK.

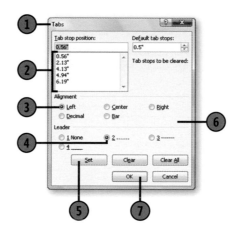

Tip ✔

You can also display the Tabs dialog box by clicking the Home tab, clicking the Paragraph button, and then clicking the Tabs button in the Paragraph dialog box.

Tip ✔

If the Page Setup dialog box appears instead of the Tabs dialog box, you clicked an inactive part of the ruler instead of a tab stop. Try again!

Dotted leader

No leader   Dashed leader   Underline leader

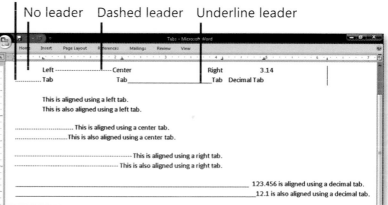

Adding Emphasis and Special Formatting

You'll often want to add special formatting to some text: for example, italics to use in a reference, bold to draw attention to something specific, strikethrough to show what has been deleted, and so on. Word gives you a large array of special formatting options.

Format the Text

 Select the text you want to format.

2 On the Home tab, use any combination of the formatting buttons on the Ribbon to add the formatting you want. Click a button a second time to remove that formatting.

3 If there isn't a button for the formatting you want, click the Font button to display the Font dialog box.

4 Do any of the following:

- Select a font color.

- Select the type of underline and the underline color you want.

- Select any effect or combination of effects. Note that there are some effects that can't be combined with others.

5 Click OK.

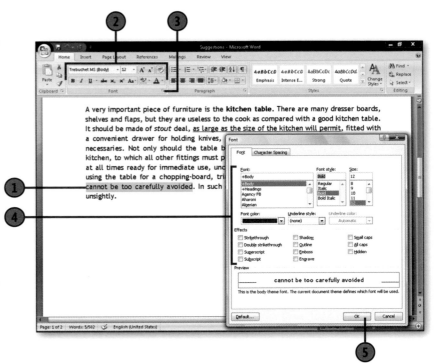

> **Tip**
>
> If you're not sure what a formatting button does, point to it, and wait for the ScreenTip to appear. In addition to describing the button's function, the ScreenTip also shows you which keyboard shortcut you can use instead of clicking the button with the mouse.

> **See Also**
>
> "Switching Quick Styles" on page 49 for information about using Quick Styles to add emphasis.

Creating an Inline Heading

Many document designs use *inline* headings—that is, the first sentence (or part of the first sentence) of a paragraph is formatted as a bold or an italic subheading. An inline heading is also called a *run-in* heading because, unlike more prominent headings, it doesn't have its own separate paragraph but is run in with the paragraph text. Although you can use direct formatting to create this type of heading, using a style will provide consistency for all the headings of this type throughout your document.

Create an Inline Heading

① Type your paragraph, including the text for the inline heading. Use the appropriate paragraph style, but don't worry about the formatting of the heading.

② Select the text that you want for the inline heading.

③ On the Home tab, point to a Quick Style. Look at the selected text and see whether you like the way its appearance has changed.

④ Point to other Quick Styles, and watch the selected text as it changes. Note that paragraph Quick Styles (those with a paragraph mark next to the name) affect the entire paragraph, while the character and linked styles affect the appearance of the selected text only.

⑤ Click the Quick Style when you see the result you want.

See Also

"Creating Your Own Styles" on pages 190–191 for information about creating a custom inline-heading character style that can specify different fonts, font sizes, colors, and other formatting.

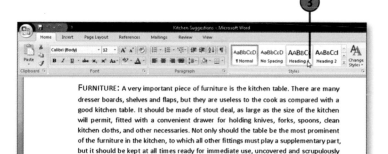

Adjusting the Spacing Between Characters

Sometimes you'll need to squeeze a little more text onto a line; at other times you'll want to spread the text out to fill up a line. Perhaps you want to create a special look in a heading by condensing or expanding the text. You can achieve all of these effects by adjusting the widths of characters and the spaces between characters and between words.

Adjust the Spacing

1 Select the text whose spacing you want to adjust.

2 On the Home tab, click the Font button to display the Font dialog box, and click the Character Spacing tab.

3 Change the settings to adjust the spacing:

- In the Scale box, click a percentage in the list, or type the percentage by which you want to expand or condense the width of each character.

- In the Spacing box, click Expanded or Condensed in the list, and, in the By text box, enter a value to expand or condense the spacing between characters.

4 To *kern*—that is, to decrease the spacing between—certain pairs of letters, select this check box, and specify a minimum font size to be kerned. (Word uses its own list to determine which letter pairs, in which fonts, can be kerned.)

5 Click OK.

The Font button 2

See Also

"Creating Stylized Text" on pages 134–135 for information about adjusting the character spacing in WordArt.

Caution

As a side effect of your increasing or decreasing the character spacing, Word also adjusts the spacing between words.

Copying Your Formatting

If you've created some formatting that you like, you can copy it and apply it to any text or paragraph that you want to have the same look. On the other hand, if you've created some formatting that you don't like or that looks really weird, you can replace it with a copy of any of your good formatting.

Copy a Character Format

① If paragraph marks aren't displayed in your text, click the Home tab, and then click the Show/Hide ¶ button.

② Select the text whose formatting you want to copy. If you want to copy paragraph formatting, make sure your selection includes the paragraph mark at the end of the paragraph.

③ On the Home tab, click the Format Painter button.

④ Drag the Format Painter over the selected text to apply the formatting, and then release the button.

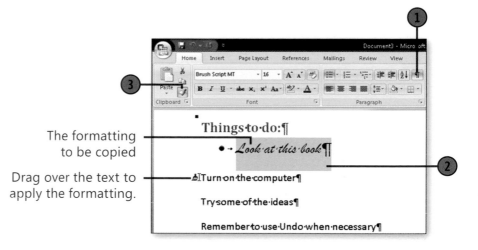

The formatting to be copied

Drag over the text to apply the formatting.

Tip ✓

To copy formatting to several locations, double-click the Format Painter button after you've selected your text. You can now copy the formatting to as many places as you want. When you've finished, press the Esc key or click the Format Painter button again.

Tip ✓

To copy only paragraph formatting, select only the paragraph mark before you click the Format Painter button.

Caution !

You can't copy multiple types of formatting at one time. For example, in a selection where the first word is formatted in bold and the next word is in italics, only the bold formatting will be applied when you use the Format Painter.

Setting the Overall Look

Themes define the look of your entire document—the color scheme, the pairing of the default fonts used for body and heading text, and even the shading effects on graphics.

Once you've selected a theme, you can use the font pairing and the color palette in your formatting to apply a unified look to your document design.

Choose a Theme

① On the Page Layout tab, click the Themes button to display the Themes gallery.

② Do any of the following:

- Point to a theme to see how your document will look if you use that theme.

- Click the theme you want to use.

- Click More Themes On Microsoft Office Online to find more themes on line, and select the theme you want.

- Click Browse For Themes to display the Choose Theme Or Themed Document dialog box. Select a theme or a document that contains the theme you want, and click Open.

- Click Reset To Theme From Template to revert to the original theme for the document.

③ Use the tools on the Home and Insert tabs as you normally would, selecting from the theme fonts and colors shown or selecting non-theme fonts and colors for special effects.

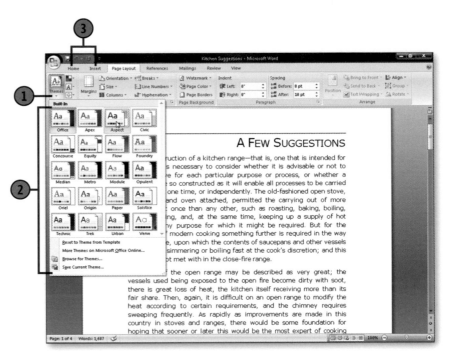

Tip

You're not limited to the fonts or colors of your theme. The theme fonts and colors are suggested and usually appear at the top of your formatting choices, but you can choose any fonts and colors you want.

Modify a Theme

1 On the Page Layout tab, click the Theme Colors button to display the gallery of color groupings, and click the color grouping you want.

2 Click the Theme Fonts button, and select the font pairing from the gallery that appears.

3 Click the Theme Effects button, and select the shadow and shading effects you want for SmartArt graphics and graphs from the gallery that appears.

4 Use the theme fonts, colors, and effects in your document.

5 If you like your customized theme, on the Page Layout tab, click the Themes button, and choose Save Theme. In the Save Current Theme dialog box, type a name for the theme, and click Save.

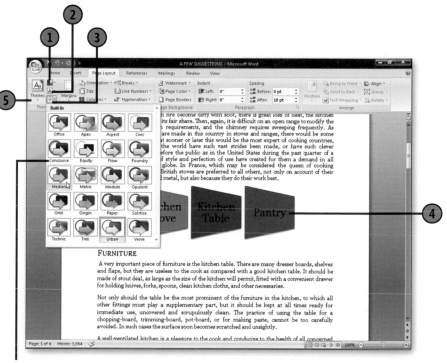

The Theme Effects gallery

See Also

"Switching Quick Styles" on page 49 for information about using different Quick Style sets for a theme.

Placing a Line Border Around a Page

You can add a very nice finishing touch to a page by placing a border around it. Word provides a wide variety of easily applied customizable line styles.

Create a Page Border

① On the View tab, click the One Page button to display one entire page of your document.

② On the Page Layout tab, click the Page Borders button, and, in the Borders And Shading dialog box that appears, click the Page Border tab.

③ Click the type of border you want.

④ Specify a line style, color, and width.

⑤ To remove an existing border from one side of the page, click the border button that represents the side of the page whose border you want to remove. To add a border, click a border button that represents a side of the page that doesn't have a border.

⑥ Specify the part of the document that you want to have this border.

⑦ Click Options to change the distance of the border from the edge of the page or the text, and to specify whether you want the running heads to be surrounded by this border.

⑧ Click OK.

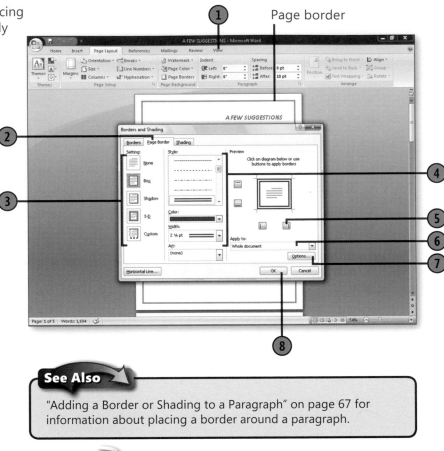

Page border

See Also

"Adding a Border or Shading to a Paragraph" on page 67 for information about placing a border around a paragraph.

Try This!

Insert a page border. Click a button to remove the border from one side. Specify a different line style, width, or color, and click the same border button. Repeat to modify the other sides to create a custom border.

Placing an Art Border Around a Page

You can go beyond line borders and add one of Word's attractive and fanciful art borders around a page. How about a border of cupcakes or ice-cream cones for a party invitation, palm trees for a travel brochure, or ladybugs for an environmental newsletter? Playing with the different looks you can create with this huge collection of art borders is almost irresistible, and it's so easy and satisfying to do!

Create an Art Border

1. On the View tab, click the One Page button to display one entire page of your document.

2. On the Page Layout tab, click the Page Borders button, and click the Page Border tab of the Borders And Shading dialog box.

3. Click the Box setting.

4. Specify the art you want to use for your border.

5. Specify the width you want for the border art and, if the Color list is available, the color you want.

6. Click a border button if you want to remove the border from the side of the page the button represents. To replace the border, click the button again.

7. Specify the part of the document that you want to have the selected border.

8. Click Options if you want to change the distance of the border from the page edge or from the text.

9. Click OK.

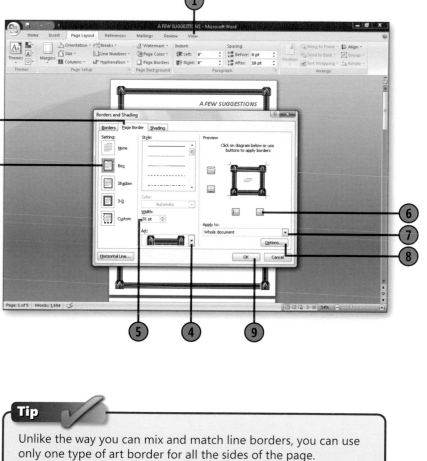

Tip ✔

Unlike the way you can mix and match line borders, you can use only one type of art border for all the sides of the page.

Adding a Decorative Horizontal Line

A horizontal line can be more than just a line. In Word it can be a curvy, colorful line or picture, or it can be as simple as a series of dots and dashes. Whichever style of horizontal line you choose, you can customize it to be the perfect divider between parts of your document.

Add a Line

(1) Click in your document where you want the horizontal line to appear.

(2) On the Page Layout tab, click the Page Borders button, and click the Horizontal Line button in the Borders And Shading dialog box to display the Horizontal Line dialog box.

(3) Browse through the horizontal lines, and double-click the one you want to use.

(4) To modify the line, double-click it to display the Format Horizontal Line dialog box.

(5) On the Horizontal Line tab, make any modifications you want to the line.

(6) On the Picture tab, make any further adjustments.

(7) Click OK.

Type a keyword if you want to search for a specific type of line.

Select this check box if you want to search Office Online for additional lines that match your keyword search.

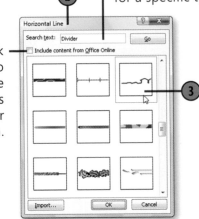

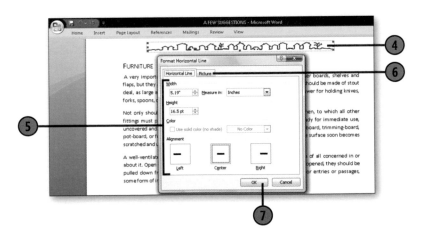

Adding a Border or Shading to a Paragraph

A great way to separate a paragraph from the rest of the text in the document, or to highlight specific information, is to surround the paragraph with a border and/or add shading to the paragraph.

Add a Border

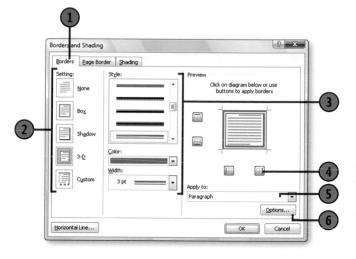

① On the Page Layout tab, with the insertion point in the paragraph that is to have the border, click the Page Borders button, and click the Borders tab of the Borders And Shading dialog box if it isn't already displayed.

② Click the type of border you want.

③ Specify a line style, color, and width.

④ Click a border button if you want to remove the border from the side of the paragraph the button represents. To replace the border, click the button again.

⑤ Specify Paragraph.

⑥ Click Options if you want to change the distance of the border from the text. Click OK.

Add Shading

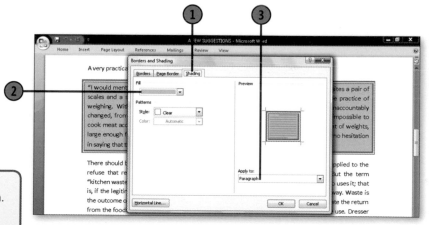

① On the Layout tab, click the Page Borders button, and, in the Borders and Shading dialog box, click the Shading tab.

② Click the color you want.

③ Specify Paragraph, and then click OK.

Try This!

Select a word or a sentence, but don't select a whole paragraph. Open the Borders And Shading dialog box, add a border and some shading, and, in the Apply To box, specify Text. Click OK.

Creating a Bulleted or Numbered List

An excellent way to clearly provide information is to present it in a numbered or bulleted list. Not only does Word add numbers or bullets to your list, with consistent spacing between the number or bullet and the text, but it keeps track of your list so that if you move an item within a numbered list, Word will renumber the list to keep the items in the correct order. You can also have the numbering skip paragraphs and can even split lists by restarting a series at 1.

Create a List

1. Start typing the first line of your list. Make sure you're using the paragraph style you want for the list.

2. On the Home tab, click the Numbering button for a numbered list or the Bullets button for a bulleted list.

3. After completing the first line, press Enter to start the second list item.

4. When you've completed the list, press Enter twice to create an empty paragraph and to turn off the list formatting.

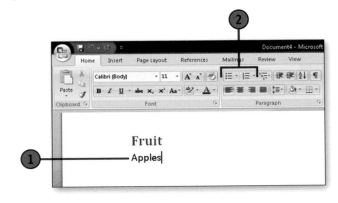

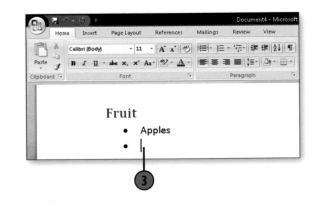

See Also

"Creating a Multilevel List" on page 70 for information about placing a list inside another list.

"Adding Captions to Tables and Figures" on page 165 for information about numbering tables, figures, and more.

"Customizing a List" on pages 204–205 for information about changing the look of a list.

Create a Discontinuous Numbered List

 Create the first part of the numbered list.

 Click the Numbering button to turn off the numbers.

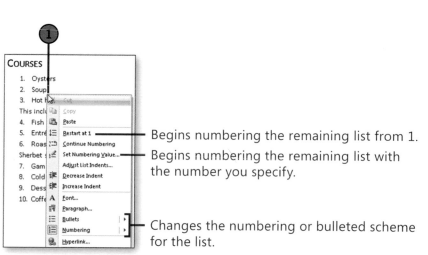 Type at least one non-list paragraph.

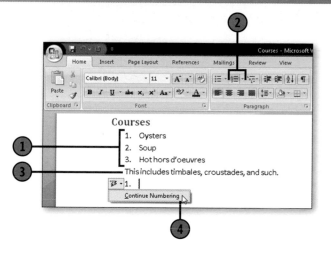 In a blank paragraph, click the Numbering button to turn the numbers on again, click the AutoCorrect Options button that appears, and choose Continue Numbering from the drop-down menu.

Modify the List

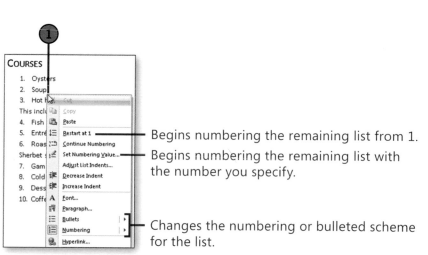

 Right-click in the paragraph you want to change.

 From the shortcut menu, choose the action you want for that item in the list.

Begins numbering the remaining list from 1.

Begins numbering the remaining list with the number you specify.

Changes the numbering or bulleted scheme for the list.

Creating a Multilevel List

Sometimes a regular list just doesn't do the job for you. If you want a list within a list (called a *nested* list), or if you need to classify the relationship of items by listing them under specific categories, you can quickly and easily create a multilevel list.

Create a Multilevel List

(1) Start typing the first line of your list.

(2) On the Home tab, click either the Numbering or the Bullets button to format the type of list you want.

(3) Continue creating the list of items that are all at the same level.

(4) At the beginning of the paragraph with which you want to start the second level of the list, press the Tab key. Type the item, and press Enter. Continue entering the items that belong in this level of the list.

(5) At the beginning of the paragraph with which you want to start the third level of the list, press the Tab key again.

(6) To return to the second level of the list, press Shift+Tab. Press Shift+Tab a second time to move from the third level to the first level of the list.

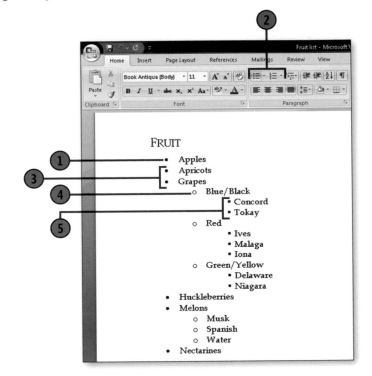

Tip ✓

You can create a list with as many as nine levels. If you need more than nine levels, you might want to reconsider your organizational structure!

Tip ✓

If you don't like a sublevel's indent, point to the number or the bullet, and drag it to where you want the indent. All the items in the list at that level will move to the new indent.

Formatting a List

The standard bulleted or numbering system is fine for a simple document, but if you want to give your document some extra pizzazz, or if you need to create a document with a specific outline-numbering scheme, you can adjust the look of the list.

Change the Format

① Select your entire list.

② On the Home tab, click the down arrow at the right of either the Bullets, the Numbering, or the Outline Numbering button to display the gallery for that button.

③ Move the mouse pointer over the different bulleted or numbering schemes, and preview the way the list will look with each selection.

④ Click the bulleted or numbering scheme you want.

When you point to an item in the gallery...

...you see a live preview of that numbering scheme in your text.

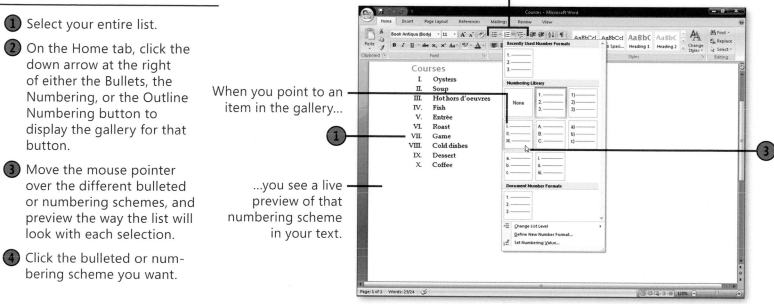

Formatting a Table

A table is a superb way to organize almost any kind of information, and you can add interest and clarity to any table with the styles and formatting options Word provides. For example, you can use shading to delineate certain cell groupings, add borders to draw attention to particular cells, or use the formatting tools to vary the dimensions and alignment of the text.

Format a Table

1. Click anywhere inside the table.

2. On the Design tab that appears, select a style for the table.

3. Select or clear the check boxes to turn the various formatting options on or off, as desired.

4. Select the cell or cells to which you want to add or from which you want to remove shading, click the Shading button, and select a color to add shading, or select No Color to remove shading.

5. Select the cell or cells to which you want to add or from which you want to remove borders, click the Borders button, and select the borders you want, or select No Borders to remove the borders.

6. Click the Layout tab, and use the tools to add or delete rows or columns, to set the dimensions of the rows and columns, and to set the text alignment, direction—that is, horizontal or vertical—and margins.

See Also

"Using a Predesigned Table" on page 85 for information about using a template to create a preformatted table.

4

Creating a Layout

In this section:

- Laying Out the Page
- Changing Page Orientation Within a Document
- Changing Margins Within a Document
- Improving the Layout with Hyphenation
- Fine-Tuning Your Layout
- Flowing Text into Columns
- Creating Chapters
- Creating a Table from Scratch
- Using a Predesigned Table
- Creating a Table from Text
- Customizing a Table Layout
- Moving a Table

Your layout is a lot like the "bones" of your document—the beneath-the-surface underpinning that gives the finished work its strength and beauty. As you work through this section of the book, whether you're actually putting your layout together now or just getting ideas for an upcoming project, you'll see that Microsoft Office Word 2007 gives you a multitude of ways to create the foundation on which to build your document.

If you've done this before, you'll appreciate the way Word's extremely visual and intuitive interface puts the tools you need right at your fingertips. If laying out a document is new to you, you'll learn the meaning of some probably unfamiliar terms: *widows, orphans, running feet, page breaks, line breaks, optional hyphens*. We'll help you decide whether to use portrait or land-scape orientation, and we'll show you how to flow your text into columns, use left-aligned or justified text, shape your paragraphs with hyphenation, organize your information using tables, create chapters or sections, and so on.

Keep in mind, if all this sounds a bit daunting, that there's no harm done if you don't like the end result you see on your screen. You can simply click an Undo button and start the process all over again!

Laying Out the Page

When you create a document that will be printed, you need to tell Word how you want the page to be set up—what size paper you're using, whether the page will be printed in landscape or portrait orientation, the size of the margins, and so on. If the document will be printed on both sides of the paper or is going to be bound, you can tell Word to accommodate those design elements. A good template will usually set up the specifics for you, but you might need to readjust the settings a bit to get everything exactly right.

Set Up a Standard Page

① On the Page Layout tab, click the Size button, and, in the gallery that appears, select the size of the paper you want. If that size isn't listed, click More Paper Sizes, and specify your paper size on the Paper tab of the Page Setup dialog box.

② Click the Margins button, and select the margins you want. If that size isn't listed, click Custom Margins, and specify your margins on the Margins tab of the Page Setup dialog box.

③ Click the Orientation button, and select the orientation: Portrait (longer than wide) or Landscape (wider than long).

See Also

"Creating Variable Running Heads" on pages 114–115 for information about using different headers and footers in a two-sided document.

Tip

The gutter is the extra space you add to the margin where the document is to be bound so that the text won't be hidden by the binding.

Set Up a Two-Sided Document

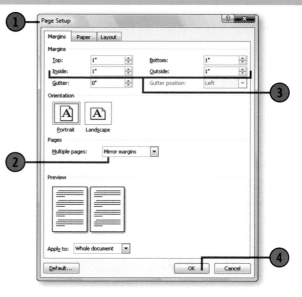

1 On the Page Layout tab, click the Margins button, and choose Custom Margins from the gallery to display the Page Setup dialog box.

2 On the Margins tab, click Mirror Margins in the Multiple Pages list.

3 Set the document's side margins using the Inside and Outside boxes. The Inside margin will be on the left side of odd-numbered (right-hand, or *recto*) pages and on the right side of even-numbered (left-hand, or *verso*) pages.

4 Click OK.

Tip

You can apply a gutter to any document layout. For a document that's set up for one-sided printing, you can specify the gutter location as the left side of the paper or the top of the paper. For a multiple-page layout, Word uses the default location of the gutter for the type of layout you choose. Use the preview to see the placement of the gutter.

Set Up a Bound Document

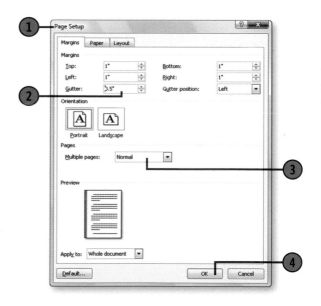

1 Click the Margins button, and choose Custom Margins from the gallery to display the Page Setup dialog box.

2 On the Margins tab, specify a value for the gutter.

3 If the Multiple Pages list is set to Normal, specify whether the gutter (and therefore the binding) should be on the left side or at the top of the page. For other Multiple Pages settings, the gutter position is set automatically.

4 Click OK.

Changing Page Orientation Within a Document

Different parts of a long document sometimes require different layouts. For example, although most of the document's text is in portrait orientation, there might be one or two pages that contain tables, figures, or other special elements that need to be set up in landscape orientation because of their width. By dividing the document into sections, you can set up each section with its own orientation.

Change the Page Orientation

1. Select the part of the document whose page orientation you want to change.

2. On the Page Layout tab, click the Margins button, and choose Custom Margins from the gallery to display the Page Setup dialog box.

3. Click the orientation you want.

4. Specify Selected Text.

5. Click OK.

6. Use the Zoom Control on the status bar to see your pages in detail, and verify that the layout is what you want.

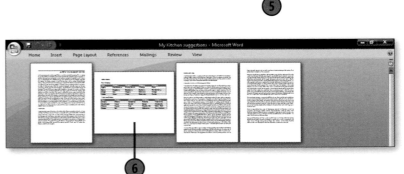

Tip

When you change the orientation of selected text, you're actually creating two new sections: one for the selected text and another for the text that follows the selection.

Changing Margins Within a Document

Usually, a document has one set of margins, and you use paragraph indents to control the layout of individual paragraphs. Sometimes, though, a long document might have several large sections that need different margins. Setting different margins for different sections would be extremely time-consuming and tedious to do using paragraph indents. Instead, you can set each section to start on a new page, or even to start on the same page as a section that has different margins.

Change the Margins

(1) Select the part of the document whose margins you want to change.

(2) On the Page Layout tab, click the Margins button, and click Custom Margins in the gallery to display the Page Setup dialog box.

(3) Set the new margins.

(4) Specify Selected Text.

(5) Click the Layout tab, and specify the point at which the section with the changed margins will start. Specify Continuous if you want the changed section to begin on the same page as the previous section. Click OK.

(6) Click in the following section, click the Margins button, click Custom Margins in the gallery again, and, on the Layout tab, specify where you want this section to start. Click OK when you've finished. (Word creates section breaks between the areas that have different margins. If you don't see the section-break markers, click the Show/Hide ¶ button. Don't delete the markers, or you'll lose your margin settings.)

See Also

"Flowing Text into Columns" on page 82 for information about using a multiple-column layout.

Improving the Layout with Hyphenation

Sometimes the right edges of left-aligned paragraphs look way too ragged and uneven. Justified paragraphs can contain big white spaces between words, especially in columnar text. You can easily repair these common problems with automatic hyphenation, or, if you want more control, you can have Word suggest where you should hyphenate. You can then decide whether or not to insert the hyphen and where in the word you should insert it.

Set Automatic Hyphenation

① On the Page Layout tab, click the Hyphenation button, and choose Automatic from the drop-down menu.

② If you don't like the way Word hyphenates, click the Hyphenation button again, and choose Hyphenation Options from the menu to display the Hyphenation dialog box.

③ Specify whether or not you want to hyphenate capitalized words.

④ Specify the maximum distance between the end of the last word and the edge of the column.

⑤ Specify whether you want to limit the number of consecutive end-of-line hyphens. (In many books, including this one, a limit of two consecutive end-of-line hyphens is customary.)

⑥ Click OK.

See Also

"Fine-Tuning Your Layout" on pages 80–81 for information about manually inserting optional hyphens, as well as information about other ways to change line breaks (or word, column, or page breaks).

Tip

If you want to use automatic hyphenation in a document but don't want a few specific paragraphs hyphenated, create and use a separate paragraph style (or use direct paragraph formatting) for those paragraphs, making sure that, on the Line And Page Breaks tab of the Paragraph dialog box, you've selected the Don't Hyphenate check box.

Hyphenate Manually

 On the Page Layout tab, click the Hyphenation button, and choose Manual from the drop-down menu to display the Manual Hyphenation dialog box.

② When Word proposes hyphenating a word, do any of the following:

- Click Yes to accept the proposed hyphenation.

- Click No to skip the current word and locate the next candidate for hyphenation.

- Click at another proposed break, and then click Yes to hyphenate at that point.

Tip ✓

To see any optional hyphens in your text that aren't at the end of a line, turn on the Show/ Hide ¶ button on the Home tab. Optional hyphens look like regular hyphens with a little downward "tail" on the right side.

Tip ✓

Use the Hyphenation feature instead of inserting hyphens with the hyphen key. When you use either Automatic or Manual hyphenation, Word inserts an *optional hyphen.* An optional hyphen shows up only when a whole word won't fit on a line, so if a hyphenated word moves from the end of a line because of changes in your text, the optional hyphen will magically disappear. Be aware that if you use the hyphen key to hyphenate manually, the hyphen will stay where it is even if the hyphenated word moves to the middle of a line.

Fine-Tuning Your Layout

After you've composed your document, you can adjust the text flow—especially when a paragraph *breaks* across pages—to improve the look of the document. Word does much of this automatically, but you can make a few adjustments yourself.

Control Widows and Orphans

1. Select the paragraph or paragraphs in which you want to make changes.

2. On the Home tab, click the Paragraph button to display the Paragraph dialog box.

3. Click the Line And Page Breaks tab.

4. Select or clear this check box to control the way paragraphs break across consecutive pages.

5. Select this check box if the paragraph is a heading that must always be on the same page as the beginning of the following paragraph.

6. Select this check box if you never want to allow a paragraph to break across pages.

7. Click OK.

The Paragraph button

Tip

There are many definitions of the sad terms *widow* and *orphan* in the publishing world. In Word's world, widows and orphans are single lines that get separated from the paragraph to which they belong and become marooned alone at the top (orphan) or bottom (widow) of a page. Widows and orphans are considered aesthetically undesirable in both worlds.

Tip

Breaking manually means that when you don't like the place where Word automatically ended, or broke, a line (or a word, a column, or a page, for that matter), you can change the break yourself.

Tip

To change widow and orphan control throughout a document, change the setting for the paragraph format in the style definition.

Break Lines

1 On the Page Layout tab, click the Hyphenation button, and choose None from the drop-down menu to turn off automatic hyphenation if it's turned on.

2 On the Home tab, click the Show/Hide ¶ button if paragraph marks aren't displayed in your text. Use the Zoom Control on the status bar so that you can see the entire length of the lines of text.

3 Press Shift+Enter to create a manual line break.

4 Select an existing hyphen, and press Ctrl+Shift+hyphen (-) to create a nonbreaking hyphen that will keep a hyphenated word (or a telephone number) all on one line.

5 Click in a long word where it can be correctly hyphenated (consult a dictionary if you're not sure), and press Ctrl+hyphen (-) to create an optional hyphen. An optional hyphen appears only when the whole word won't fit on the line.

6 Select a space between two words that shouldn't be separated, and press Ctrl+Shift+Spacebar to create a nonbreaking space that will keep both words on the same line.

7 Inspect your finished result, and determine whether you need to make any adjustments or undo any of the adjustments you just completed.

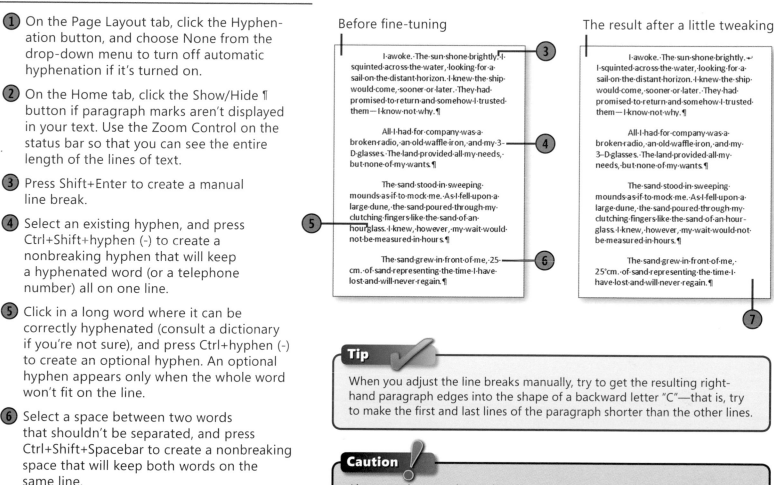

Before fine-tuning

The result after a little tweaking

Tip

When you adjust the line breaks manually, try to get the resulting right-hand paragraph edges into the shape of a backward letter "C"—that is, try to make the first and last lines of the paragraph shorter than the other lines.

Caution

Always apply manual page breaks as the very last adjustment you make to a document before you print it. Editing a document after you've applied page breaks can result in an unacceptably short page or an extra blank page. However, if you do need to edit the document after page breaking, use Print Preview to examine the page breaks.

Flowing Text into Columns

You can flow text into multiple columns on a page, like the columns in a newspaper or magazine. You can even vary the number of columns on a page by dividing the page into separate sections.

Change the Number of Columns

1. Without worrying about the layout just yet, complete the content of your document. Make sure the page orientation and the margins are set correctly for the document.

2. On the Home tab, click the Show/Hide ¶ button if it isn't already turned on.

3. Select the text that you want to flow into columns.

4. On the Page Layout tab, click the Columns button, and select the layout you want. Word makes the selected text into a separate section by inserting Continuous section breaks before and after the selected text.

5. If you want to adjust the columns, click anywhere in the section that has the columns.

6. Click the Columns button again, and click More Columns in the Columns gallery to display the Columns dialog box.

7. If you don't want even-width columns, clear this check box, and then specify the width you want for each column.

8. Select this check box if you want a vertical line centered between adjacent columns.

9. Make sure the settings are applied only to the selected text, and then click OK.

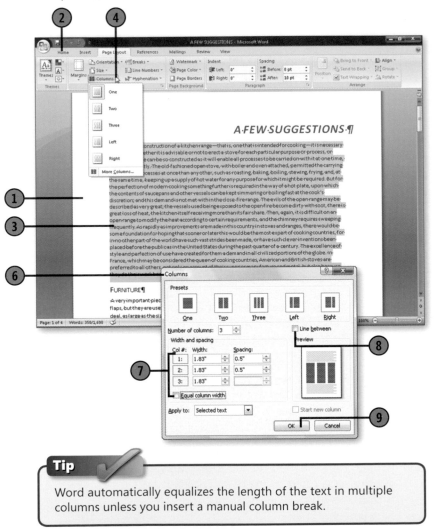

Tip

Word automatically equalizes the length of the text in multiple columns unless you insert a manual column break.

Creating Chapters

A long document is usually divided into chapters or sections, each of which should begin on an odd-numbered (right-hand, or *recto*) page. Word will start your chapters or sections on odd-numbered pages, and will create running heads to your specifications.

Start a New Chapter

1 In the document you want to divide into different chapters, place the insertion point at the beginning of the paragraph that starts a new chapter.

2 On the Page Layout tab, click the Breaks button, and click the Odd Page section-break option in the gallery. Word inserts the section break in front of the insertion point.

Change the Running Heads

1 On the Insert tab, click the Header button, and click Edit Header in the gallery. Any text in the header comes from the previous header.

2 On the Header & Footer Tools Design tab that appears, click the Link To Previous button to turn it off and to disconnect the header from any previous header.

3 Replace the old header text, if any, with the text for your new running head.

4 Click the Go To Footer button to move to the footer, and repeat steps 2 and 3 for the footer. If the document is set for a different running head on the first page, or for different running heads on odd- and even-numbered pages, repeat steps 2 and 3 for those running heads.

5 Click Close Header And Footer when you've finished.

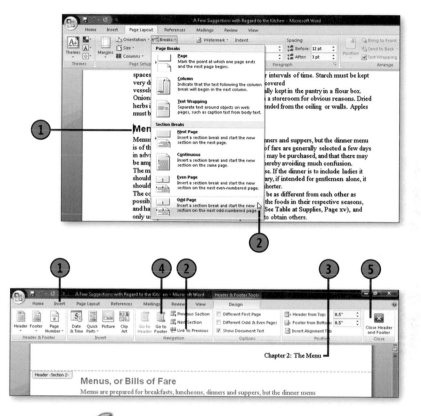

Tip

When you use an Odd Page section break to start a new chapter, note that if the previous section of your document ended on an odd-numbered page, Word will insert a blank even-numbered page so that your chapter will start on the odd-numbered page.

Creating a Table from Scratch

If you think of tables merely as containers for numbers, think again. Using a table is an efficient way to lay out and organize almost any kind of information. There are many ways to create a table, but the simplest and most versatile is to create an empty, unformatted table with a prescribed number of rows and columns. You can easily add content, and you can format and modify the table contents and layout later.

Create a Table

① On the Insert tab, click the Table button. Move the mouse pointer to select the number of rows and columns you want in your table, and then click to insert the table.

② Click in the first cell, and insert your content.

③ Press Tab to move to the next cell, and add your content. (Press Enter only to start a new paragraph inside a table cell.) Continue pressing Tab and entering content to complete your table.

④ If you've reached the end of your table but you still need to enter more items, press Tab, and Word will create a new row.

Fruit type	Choice 1	Choice 2
Apple	Red Delicious	Granny Smith
Grape	Iona	Niagara
Melon	Musk	Water

Tip

To move to the previous cell, press Shift+Tab. To insert a tab inside a cell, press Ctrl+Tab.

See Also

"Creating a Table from Text" on page 86 for information about converting existing text in paragraphs into text in a table.

Using a Predesigned Table

In the same way that you use templates for creating specialized types of documents, you can use a table template to create a specialized type of table, complete with formatting and related material—a title or caption, for example.

Choose a Table

1. Click in your document where you want the table to appear.

2. On the Insert tab, click the Table button, point to Quick Tables, and click the type of table you want.

3. Drag the mouse over the content of the table, and press the Delete key to remove the sample text.

4. Click in the top-left cell, and type your information. Use the Tab key to move through the cells, and enter the rest of your content.

Tip

Once you've created the table, you can modify its appearance by applying table styles and other formatting.

See Also

"Formatting a Table" on page 72 for information about formatting a table.

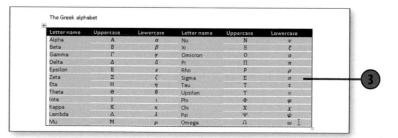

Creating a Table from Text

Many people still use tabs to create columns for a table, but doing so means that the content can get seriously messed up if you decide to reformat the document with different fonts, margins, and layouts. One way to avoid this is to convert your text into a table. That way, not only is the formatting so much simpler, but you can use the table tools to organize your information more easily.

Convert the Text

① Examine the text to make sure that the information is correctly separated by tabs, commas, paragraphs, or other marks. Delete any extra tabs (more than one tab between columns, for example) even if this affects the current alignment.

② Select all the text.

③ On the Insert tab, click the Table button, and click Convert Text To Table to display the Convert Text To Table dialog box.

④ Select the type of mark you've used to separate the columns of text.

⑤ Verify the number of columns you want. If there are more columns than you had in the text, repeat steps 1 through 4.

⑥ Click OK.

⑦ If you're not happy with the way the table looks, click the Undo button, and then repeat steps 1 through 6.

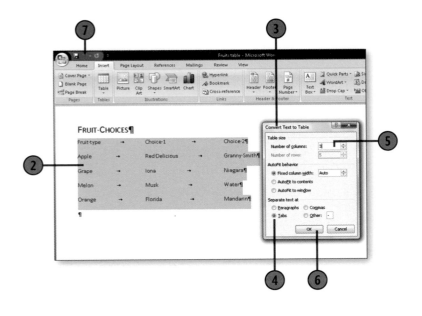

Tip

To convert text in a table to regular text, click in the table and, on the Table Tools Layout tab, click Convert To Text.

Tip

You can convert regular text to text in a table for many reasons other than just aligning columns. When the information is contained in a table, you can sort it, add or delete columns, and even do some math with it. You can also convert the text in the table back to regular text if you want to.

The Anatomy of a Table

The Move box appears when the mouse pointer is positioned over the table in Print Layout and Web Layout views.

Table cells in a row are merged into a single cell.

Different borders can be used to define areas.

The text is vertically aligned.

Some cells in a column are merged into a single cell.

There can be more than one paragraph in a cell. The text and paragraphs in one cell can have different formatting.

The text can be horizontal or vertical.

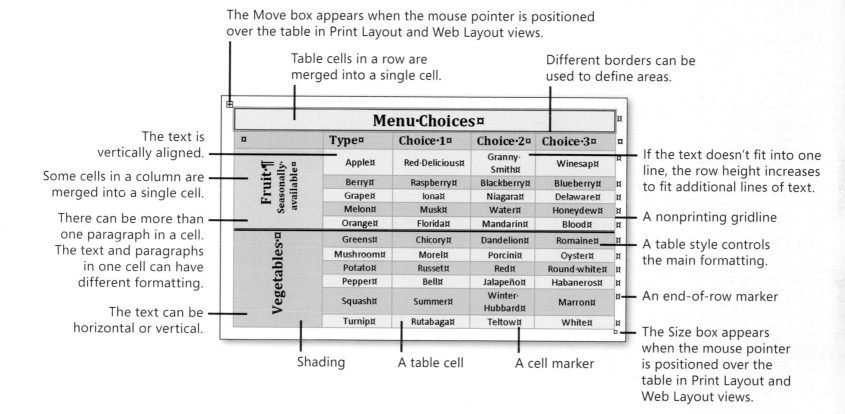

If the text doesn't fit into one line, the row height increases to fit additional lines of text.

A nonprinting gridline

A table style controls the main formatting.

An end-of-row marker

The Size box appears when the mouse pointer is positioned over the table in Print Layout and Web Layout views.

Shading   A table cell   A cell marker

Menu·Choices¤

	Type¤	Choice·1¤	Choice·2¤	Choice·3¤	
Fruit·¶ Seasonally· available¤	Apple¤	Red·Delicious¤	Granny· Smith¤	Winesap¤	¤
	Berry¤	Raspberry¤	Blackberry¤	Blueberry¤	¤
	Grape¤	Iona¤	Niagara¤	Delaware¤	¤
	Melon¤	Musk¤	Water¤	Honeydew¤	¤
	Orange¤	Florida¤	Mandarin¤	Blood¤	¤
Vegetables·¤	Greens¤	Chicory¤	Dandelion¤	Romaine¤	
	Mushroom¤	Morel¤	Porcini¤	Oyster¤	¤
	Potato¤	Russet¤	Red¤	Round·white¤	¤
	Pepper¤	Bell¤	Jalapeño¤	Habaneros¤	¤
	Squash¤	Summer¤	Winter· Hubbard¤	Marron¤	¤
	Turnip¤	Rutabaga¤	Teltow¤	White¤	¤

Adding or Deleting Rows and Columns

You can modify the layout of an existing table by adding or deleting rows and columns anywhere in the table.

Add to the Table

1. Click in the table next to where you want to add a row or column.

2. On the Table Tools Layout tab, choose what you want to add.

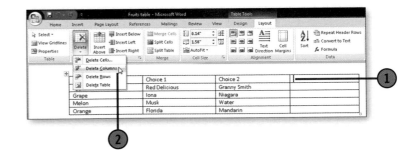

Try This!

Create a table with three columns and three rows. Click in the top-left cell. Drag the mouse to the right to select the first two cells. Click the Table Tools Layout tab, and then click Insert Left. With the new columns selected, click Insert Above. Note that the number of rows and columns that are inserted is based on the number of rows and columns in which cells were selected. Now try deleting rows and columns to revert to the size of the original table.

Tip

To delete the content of a row or column without deleting the row or column itself, select the row or column, and press the Delete key.

Caution

If you want to delete content from a row or column without deleting the row or column itself, make sure your selection doesn't extend outside the table. If it does, you'll delete whatever part of the table is selected, as well as its content.

Delete from the Table

1. Click in a table cell that's in the row or column you want to delete.

2. On the Table Tools Layout tab, click Delete, and choose what you want to delete.

Positioning Elements in a Table

You can align the text in a table in several ways. Although you can use paragraph formatting to provide some alignments, there are special tools available in a table for more varieties of alignment.

Align the Text

1 Create and format your table.

2 Click in a cell, or select all the cells to which you want to apply a specific alignment.

3 On the Table Tools Layout tab, click an Alignment button to apply the alignment you want.

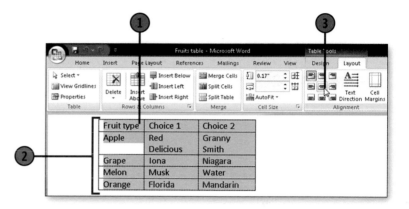

See Also

"Formatting a Table" on page 72 for information about formatting a table.

"Customizing a Table Layout" on pages 90–91 for information about changing the size of cells to accommodate sideways text.

Try This!

Select an entire column in a table that will contain decimal numbers. Select the Decimal tab stop on the ruler, and click in the horizontal ruler to place the tab stop in the column. Your numbers will be aligned by their decimal points in that column.

Set the Text Direction

 Click in a cell, or select all the cells to which you want to apply a specific text direction.

2 On the Table Tools Layout tab, click the Text Direction button. If the direction of the text isn't what you want, click the button again.

3 Adjust the text alignment and the column and row dimensions as necessary.

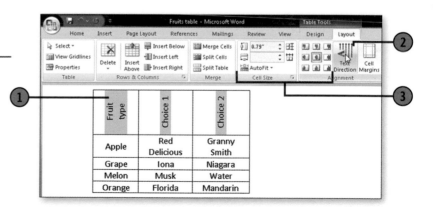

Customizing a Table Layout

A Word table can be more than just a grid of equally sized rows and columns. You can change the width of columns or the height of rows, for example, or draw new cell boundaries and erase old ones. Word gives you a great deal of flexibility in the layout of your table.

Change the Table Size

① In Print Layout view, move the mouse pointer over the table to make the Size box appear.

② Drag the Size box to change the size of the table.

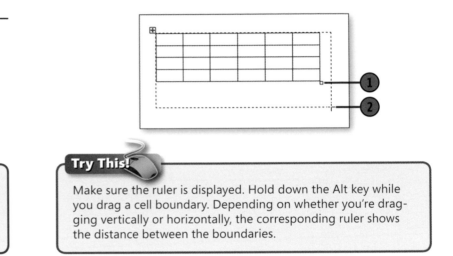

Tip

To specify precise measurements for column width and row height, enter the values on the Table Tools Layout tab. To make all the cells the same height, click in a cell, and then, on the Layout tab, click Distribute Rows.

Try This!

Make sure the ruler is displayed. Hold down the Alt key while you drag a cell boundary. Depending on whether you're dragging vertically or horizontally, the corresponding ruler shows the distance between the boundaries.

Change the Row or Column Size

① Move the mouse pointer over a vertical cell boundary until the pointer turns into a Move pointer. Drag the boundary left or right to change the size of the adjacent columns.

② Move the mouse pointer over a horizontal cell boundary, and drag the boundary up or down to change the height of the row.

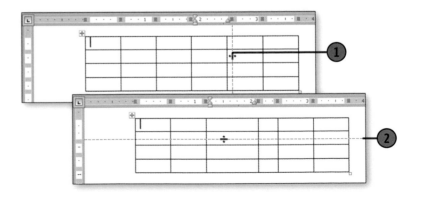

Divide One Cell into Two

1 Click in the table.

2 On the Table Tools Design tab, select the type of border, the border thickness, and the border color you want for the new boundary.

3 Click the Draw Table button if it isn't already turned on. (You'll see a little pencil pointer on your screen when the button is turned on.)

4 Drag the pencil pointer from a cell boundary to the opposite boundary. Add as many cell boundaries as you need. Click the Draw Table button to turn it off when you've finished.

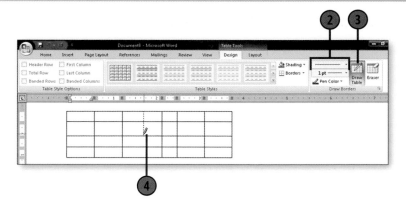

> **Tip** ✓
>
> To avoid accidentally splitting or combining cells, select the cells you want to split or combine, and then, on the Layout tab, click Merge Cells or Split Cells.

> **Tip** ✓
>
> If your table doesn't have borders and you can't see the cell boundaries, on the Table Tools Layout tab, click View Gridlines. These gridlines appear on the screen but won't be printed.

> **Caution** !
>
> When you're working on a table using the Draw Table and Eraser tools, it's difficult to achieve a high degree of precision. It's easy, for example, to accidentally add boundaries you don't want or delete those you do want. Carefully inspect your table after you add or delete a boundary. You can remedy an error by clicking the Undo button on the Quick Access toolbar.

Combine Two Cells into One

1 Click the Eraser button.

2 Click a cell boundary to delete it and merge the two cells. To delete several cell boundaries, drag the Eraser pointer to include all of them. Click the Eraser button to turn it off when you've finished.

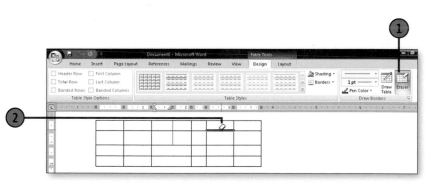

Aligning a Table

A table is usually positioned with the same alignment as the accompanying text. However, you might want to set a table off a bit by changing its horizontal position—indenting or centering it, for example. By using Word's alignment settings instead of moving the table manually, you'll ensure that the settings will remain in effect even if you change the margins or any other page-layout settings.

Set the Alignment

1. Click in the table, and then, on the Table Tools Layout tab, click the Properties button to display the Table Properties dialog box.

2. On the Table tab, click an alignment.

3. If you chose Left Alignment, specify the distance you want the table to be indented from the left margin.

4. If you want the change the default alignment settings, click Around in the Text Wrapping section, click the Positioning button, make your changes in the Table Positioning dialog box that appears, and then click OK.

5. Click OK.

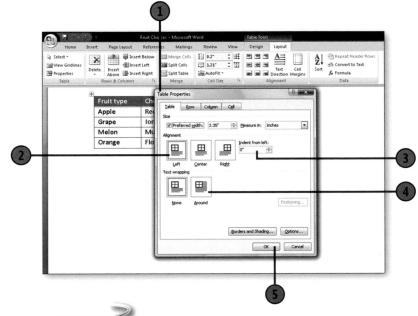

See Also

"Moving a Table" on the facing page for information about setting text to wrap around a table.

Try This!

Create two tables, one smaller than the other. Drag the smaller table and place it on top of the larger table. Note that the smaller table has become "nested" inside the larger table. Right-click in the nested table, choose Table Properties from the shortcut menu, and, on the Table tab of the Table Properties dialog box, click an alignment for the table. Click OK. Note that the alignment of the nested table is relative to the cell in which it's nested. Now click the Undo button to return the tables to their original state.

Moving a Table

If you're not happy about the position of your table, you can easily move it into a better location. When you drag a table, you can position it both horizontally and vertically on the page, just as you can position a picture on the page. When you move the table horizontally, you're also setting it to have text wrapping, so, if there's room, any text can wrap around all four sides of the table.

Move the Table

1. Switch to Print Layout view or Web Layout view if you aren't already in either view.

2. Hold the mouse pointer over the table until the Move box appears at the top-left of the table.

3. Drag the Move box, and the table, to the location you want.

4. If you can't place the table in the exact location you want, or if the text isn't wrapping in the way you want, on the Table Tools Layout tab, click Properties to display the Table Properties dialog box.

5. Specify the alignment relative to the text, and specify that you want the text to wrap around the table.

6. Click Positioning to display the Table Positioning dialog box.

7. Make any changes to the position of the table, and specify how far the table should be from any surrounding text.

8. Click OK.

9. Click OK to close the Table Properties dialog box.

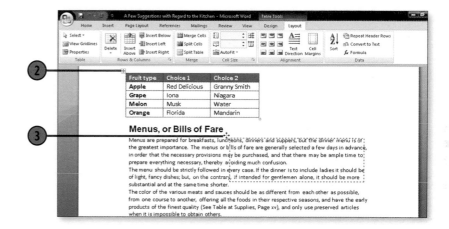

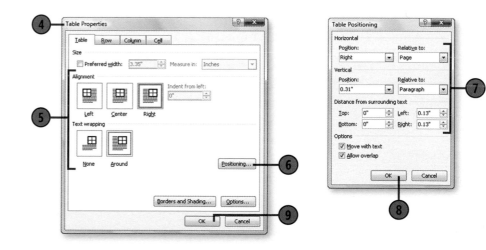

Creating a Side-by-Side Layout

A side-by-side layout is often used to present an item—a picture, a title, or a topic, for example—in one paragraph, along with a description or an explanation of the item in the adjacent paragraph. It's easy to create this type of layout using a Word table. With a table, the contents of the two paragraphs are always side by side, regardless of their size or category.

Create the Layout

1 On the Insert tab, click the Table button, and drag out a two-row-by-two-column table. Resize the columns to the size you need, and format each cell with the appropriate paragraph style.

2 On the Layout tab, click the Cell Margins button to display the Table Options dialog box.

3 Set the margins you want inside each cell.

4 Specify whether you want spacing between the cells, and, if so, specify an amount.

5 Click OK.

6 Enter your side-by-side paragraphs. To add another row, click in the last cell, press Tab, and enter your content. Repeat until you've inserted all the content.

> **Tip** ✓
>
> To set margins inside a single cell, on the Table Tools Layout tab, click Properties, and click the Options button on the Cell tab.

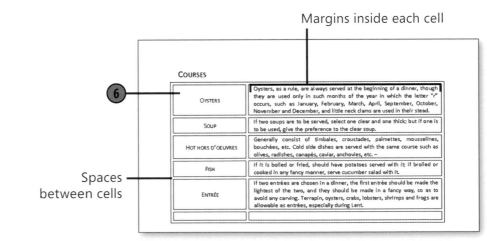

Margins inside each cell

Spaces between cells

5

Creating Specialized Documents

In this section:

- Composing Different Types of Documents
- Word's File Formats
- Writing and Publishing a Blog
- Printing Envelopes and Mailing Labels
- Mail Merge: The Power and the Pain
- Creating and Personalizing Form Letters
- Addressing Envelopes from a Mailing List
- Switching Templates
- Creating Running Heads
- Organizing Your Information
- Reorganizing a Document
- Creating a Master Document

When you need to create a specialized document—a business letter, report, contract, or memo, to name just a few document types—think "Templates!" Microsoft Office Word 2007 provides a large variety of templates, and you can download many more from Office Online. Just choose an appropriate predesigned template and replace the placeholder text with your own text. If you can't find a suitable design, you can make changes to an existing template or create your own.

This new version of Word offers some new file formats, and we'll discuss these formats briefly so that you can decide which ones work best for you. We'll also cover producing other specialized documents, including writing blog entries, printing envelopes and labels, creating running headers and footers, using Outline view to reorganize a document, and creating a master document.

And then there's the mail merge feature—a great time-saver when you need to send the same information to a few individuals or to a large group of people. You provide a *main document* and a *data source* (names and addresses, for example) and Word combines, or *merges*, the information into a new, personalized document. You can even incorporate data from Microsoft Excel and Microsoft Access into mail-merged documents.

Composing Different Types of Documents

You can use templates to quickly create all kinds of documents. Word 2007 comes with numerous templates, and you can download many more. When you start a new document based on a template, the document contains its own design elements, and the template's predefined styles ensure that all your paragraphs work harmoniously together.

Start the Document

① Choose New from the Office menu to display the New Document dialog box.

② With Blank And Recent selected in the left pane, review any templates you've used recently, and double-click the one you want.

③ If you don't see the one you want, click Installed Templates to see the Microsoft templates that were either installed on your computer or downloaded, and double-click the one you want.

④ If you still don't see the one you want, click My Templates, and, in the New dialog box that appears, double-click one of the custom templates.

⑤ If you want to download a template from Office Online, click a topic to see templates of that type that are available for download, and double-click the one you want.

⑥ If you want to use an existing document as the basis for a new document, click New From Existing, and locate and double-click the document in the New From Existing window that appears.

Preview of selected template

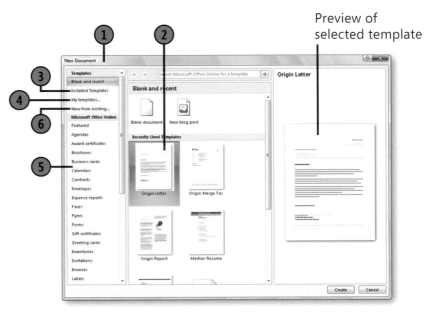

Tip

Templates are completely customizable and can come from a variety of sources, so you're likely to encounter substantial differences both in design and in ways you can complete a document based on a template. Try to choose a template that's easy to use and whose design is correct for your purposes.

Complete the Document

① If you aren't already in Print Layout view, click the Print Layout View button.

② Save the document with the file name you want, in the location you want.

③ If the Show/Hide ¶ button on the Home tab isn't already turned on, click it so that you can see all the elements in the template.

④ If information such as the date is inserted automatically, don't modify the information—it was inserted using a Word field that's automatically updated and formatted.

⑤ Click a content control—in this case, an Address content control—and replace any placeholder text with your own text.

⑥ Don't delete any of the special design elements—doing so could ruin the layout of the document.

⑦ Complete the document, and then save, print, and distribute it.

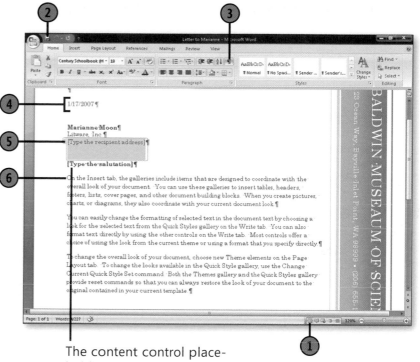

The content control place-holder text provides hints on completing the document.

Caution

A paragraph mark contains the paragraph's formatting, so don't delete a paragraph mark unless you want to remove that paragraph's elements from your document. When you delete a paragraph mark, any special formatting that was designed for that paragraph will be lost.

See Also

"Switching Templates" on page 111 for information about basing an existing document on a different template.

"Customizing a Template" on pages 200–201 for information about modifying a template.

"Designing a Template" on pages 202–203 for information about creating your own templates.

Word's File Formats

Word 2007 uses some different file formats from those of previous versions of Word, but whether or not to use them is your choice. If you decide not to use the new formats, however, be aware that you won't be able to use some of Word's very cool new features. Review the descriptions of the formats to see which work best for you. To see the list of available formats, choose Save As from the File menu, and, in the Save As dialog box, scroll through the Save As Type list.

Word's New File Formats

- **Word Document:** This is the new format that enables all of Word's new features. Documents in this format can't be opened in earlier versions of Word unless you've downloaded and installed a special translating filter program. The Word Document format has the file extension .docx and saves files in the XML (eXtensible Markup Language) format. A single Word document has multiple XML files, but Word places them in a single container.

- **Word Macro-Enabled Document:** This is the same format as the Word Document format, except that it contains macros. This special file type is a security enhancement, and it allows system managers and others to restrict the use of macros that could carry viruses and other evil things.

- **Word XML Document:** This is a plain Text file that includes all the text and the XML coding. This format is used primarily in a corporate setting where transforms are created to extract and/or reformat information that will be stored for reuse.

- **Word Template:** This new form of template also enables the new features of Word and, as in the Word Document format, stores multiple XML files in a single containing file with the .dotx file extension.

- **Word Macro-Enabled Template:** This is the same format as the Word Template format, except that it can contain macros.

There are, of course, many other existing formats you can use.

Word's Other File Formats

- **Word 97–2003 Document:** This is the binary file format used in previous versions of Word. It provides compatibility with earlier versions of Word, but saving in this format disables some of the advanced features of Word 2007.

- **Word 97–2003 Template:** This is the binary file format used in previous versions of Word. Macros, AutoText, custom toolbars, and styles are stored in this file.

- **Single File Web Page:** This format creates a Web page and stores all the graphics in the same file.

- **Web Page:** This format creates a standard HTML-format Web page whose graphics are stored in a separate folder.

- **Web Page, Filtered:** This format creates a standard HTML-format Web page, which deletes Word-specific information that isn't needed to display the Web page. Any graphics in the document are stored in a separate folder.

- **Rich Text Format:** This is a binary file that contains the text and formatting information but little else. It provides compatibility with many programs, including WordPad and earlier versions of Word.

- **Plain Text:** This text file contains only the text of the document and no formatting.

- **Word 2003 XML Document:** This format saves a document in the XML format compatible with Word 2003 XML schemas.

- **Works 6.0–9.0:** This format provides compatibility with people who use the Microsoft Works word processor.

Creating an Online Document

An effective online Word document can fully utilize the benefits of being on line—that is, using *hyperlinks* to other parts of the current document or to other documents, and including other documents or files as icons—to make it as easy as possible for readers to quickly obtain the information they want.

Create the Document

1. Create your document, format and proof-read it, and save it with a descriptive name.

2. Select the text that you want to become a link to other information.

3. On the Insert tab, click Insert Hyperlink, and use the Insert Hyperlink dialog box to link to another document or to a different part of this document.

4. To insert an entire file as an icon, click the Object button.

5. On the Create From File tab, click Browse, locate the file, and click Insert.

6. Select this check box.

7. If you want to use a different icon, click Change Icon, select a different icon or type a new caption, and click OK.

8. Click OK in the Object dialog box. Set the text wrapping for the icon, if desired. Set any document protection you want, and then save and distribute the document.

See Also

"Using Hyperlinks" on pages 150–151 for information about inserting hyperlinks.

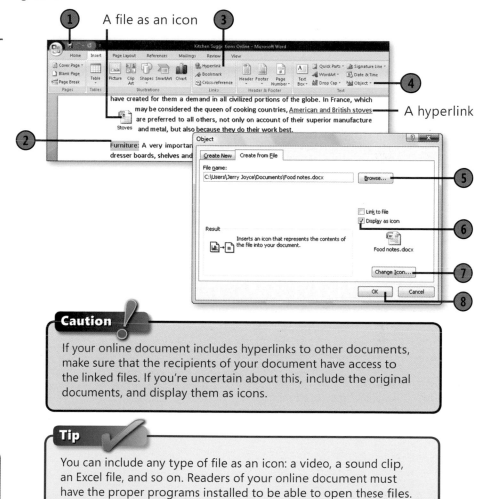

A file as an icon

A hyperlink

Caution

If your online document includes hyperlinks to other documents, make sure that the recipients of your document have access to the linked files. If you're uncertain about this, include the original documents, and display them as icons.

Tip

You can include any type of file as an icon: a video, a sound clip, an Excel file, and so on. Readers of your online document must have the proper programs installed to be able to open these files.

Writing and Publishing a Blog

A *blog*, or Web log, is a Web-based site where you post frequently updated information sequentially. You can write your entries in Word, using the spelling and grammar checkers and all of Word's formatting tools, after which you can publish the entry directly to your blog.

Set Up Your Blog

1. Choose New from the Office menu, and, in the New Document dialog box, double-click New Blog Post.

2. If this is the first time you're using Word to post to your blog, click Register Now in the Register A Blog Account dialog box. In the New Blog Account Wizard that appears, select the service you're using, and click Next.

3. Complete your account information. The details you're asked to provide will vary depending on the service you're using, but will likely require your user name and password, the URL (Web address) of your blog, and possibly the type of blog interface you're using.

4. Click the Picture Options button to display the Picture Options dialog box.

5. Specify whether you want to include pictures in your blog postings, and, if so, where you want the pictures to be stored.

6. Click OK.

7. Click OK.

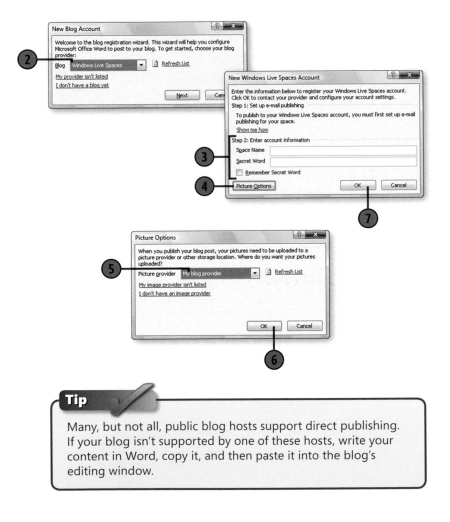

Tip

Many, but not all, public blog hosts support direct publishing. If your blog isn't supported by one of these hosts, write your content in Word, copy it, and then paste it into the blog's editing window.

Create a Blog Entry

① On the Blog Post tab, click the Post Title content control, and type the title for this blog entry. Use any of the formatting tools to format the title the way you want it.

② If you want to include a category for the entry, click the Insert Category button, enter the name and password for your account, if necessary, and then choose a category from the drop-down list that appears.

③ Click in the body of the document, and enter your text, using styles or direct formatting. Use the items on the Insert tab to insert special content, including tables, pictures, shapes, and hyperlinks.

④ Check to make sure there are no errors in the document, and then save and name it.

⑤ Click Publish to publish the entry on your blog. If you want to send the entry to your blog as a draft so that you can view it there before you publish it, click the down arrow at the bottom of the Publish button, and choose Publish As Draft from the drop-down menu.

⑥ Click the Home Page button to go to your blog site, and verify that the blog appears as you want it. If you published the entry as a draft, sign in if necessary, and use the tools on your blog site to edit and publish the draft.

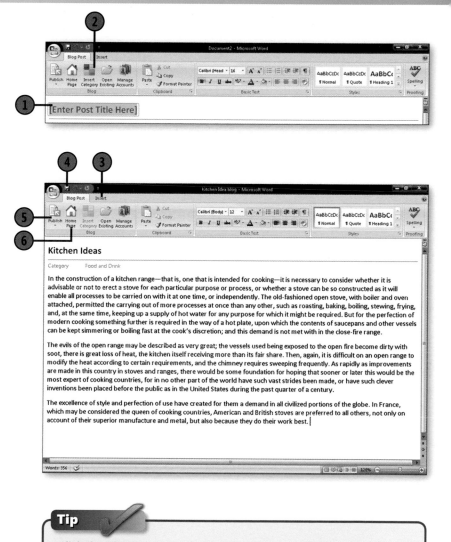

Tip

Click the Manage Accounts button to select a different blog account or to change the settings for your account. Click the Open Existing button to review your past blog postings.

Printing an Envelope

When you've taken the time and trouble to create a professional-looking letter or other document for mailing, you don't want to ruin the good impression with a hand-written envelope! Word makes it easy for you to create crisp, businesslike printed envelopes. You can easily include your return address, and, in the United States, you can add electronic postage. If you already have the delivery address in your letter, Word usually detects it and copies it to the Envelopes And Labels dialog box. You can also type the address directly in the dialog box.

Add the Address

1. On the Mailings tab, click the Envelopes button to display the Envelopes And Labels dialog box.

2. If a delivery address is displayed on the Envelopes tab, verify that it's correct.

3. If no delivery address is shown, or if you want to use a different address, type the address. If the address is in your Microsoft Outlook Contacts list, click the Insert Address button.

4. Verify that the return address is correct. If you're using an envelope with a preprinted return address, select the Omit check box so that the return address won't be printed.

5. Click Options.

6. On the Envelope Options tab, specify the envelope size and the fonts and positions for the addresses.

7. On the Printing Options tab, specify how the envelope is to be loaded and printed. Click OK.

8. If you have Electronic Postage (E-Postage) software installed, select this check box to use electronic postage.

9. If you need to make changes to your E-Postage setup, click the E-Postage Properties button.

10. Click Print to print the envelope.

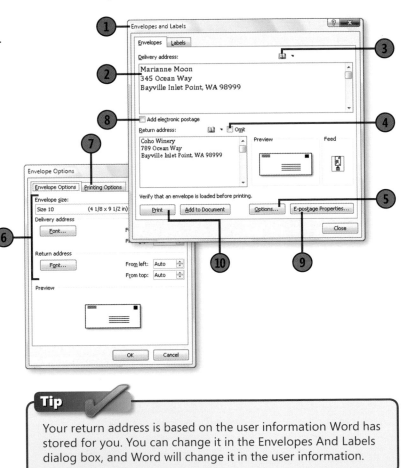

Printing a Mailing Label

Whether you need to print a single mailing label or a full page of labels, Word provides a tool that takes care of most of the details for you. All you need to do is specify the type of label you're using, the address, and the way you want the label to be printed. That's it! Word obligingly does the rest for you. You can also use this method to print other types of labels, from business card labels to CD labels.

Print a Label

1. Make a note of the manufacturer and the design number of the labels you'll be using. If you're planning to print only one label, figure out which label on the sheet of labels is the one you're going to use. Later in the process, you'll need to specify the label by row (the horizontal line of labels) and by column (the vertical line of labels). Insert the sheet of labels into your printer (usually into the manual feed tray, if there is one).

2. On the Mailings tab, click the Labels button to display the Envelopes And Labels dialog box.

3. On the Labels tab of the Envelopes And Labels dialog box, use the proposed address, type a new one, or click the Insert Address button to insert an address from your Outlook Contacts list. To insert your return address, select the Use Return Address check box.

4. If the type of label shown isn't the one you're using, click here to display the Label Options dialog box, specify the label you're using, and click OK.

5. Click the appropriate option to print a whole page of identical labels or only one label on the sheet of labels. If you want to print only one label, specify the label by row and column.

6. Click Print to print your label or labels.

Tip

If you need to print a large number of different mailing labels, consider using the mail merge feature.

See Also

"Mail Merge: The Power and the Pain" on pages 104–105, and "Creating a Form Letter" on pages 106–107, for everything you've always wanted to know about conducting a mail merge.

Mail Merge: The Power and the Pain

Mail merge is a tool that combines two different parts into a sleek and well-crafted whole: that is, a series of identical printed documents (form letters, for example) with the appropriate information (individual names and addresses) inserted automatically into each document. The two parts are the *master document* and a *data source*. The master document is the template (although not a template in the Word-document sense) that lays out your document and contains text or other items that never change. The master document also contains instructions for inserting data from a data source into each document. The data source is a uniform collection of information from one of a number of sources.

Mail merge is an almost unbelievable time-saver once you've set it up, and its power can be awesome. But—and here's the rub—you have to be willing to deal with the complexities of *fields* and *conditional expressions*. The good news is that the mail merge feature is extremely *scalable*—that is, it's easy to do a simple, basic mail merge, but the process becomes increasingly demanding as your mail merge becomes more complex. If, for example, you simply want to address a stack of envelopes to people whose addresses are contained in a Word table, a Microsoft Excel worksheet, a database table, or your Microsoft Outlook Contacts list, you can just jump in and do it with little preparation and a great likelihood of success.

If you want to go beyond the basics—for example, printing letters and envelopes that are grouped by a specific city or postal code—you'll need to venture into a bit of data management and selective merging. And if you want to get even more deeply involved—using conditional content, for example, whereby certain text is included only when some data value meets or exceeds a certain threshold—you'll find yourself wandering around Word's fields. Once you get involved in complex mail merges, you'll need to exercise caution by testing your setup. You'll want to make sure

there's no major error that will cause you to toss out all those printed letters or envelopes or, even worse, send them out, only to discover too late that the merge made a horrible mess of your intentions.

Managing the Data

In many types of mail merge there's no need for you to manipulate the data—you simply specify the data source and create the merged documents from the existing data. In other situations, however, you'll want to either sort the data according to a certain parameter (ZIP code or other postal code, for example) or exclude data that doesn't meet specific criteria (someone who didn't contribute enough money, for example).

Word can use data from many different sources. For some types of data, it's often easiest to modify the data in its original program and then do a simple mail merge in Word without worrying about data manipulation. For example, if you're using a list of addresses in Excel and you want to print envelopes grouped by city, you can sort the data by city in Excel. Or if you want to send a message to only the top contributors, and all your data is in a Microsoft Access database, you can run a query in Access and use the results of the query for your mail merge.

However, Word provides data-manipulation tools, and these are especially useful for data from sources that you can't manipulate. When you specify a data source in the Mail Merge Wizard, you can decide (in Word, rather than in the source program) which data fields you want to use, and, by sorting the data by one or more of the data fields, you can also decide how the data records are to be grouped. For example, you might want to sort all the data first by city and then by ZIP code or other postal code so that the final documents will already be sorted for you when you print them. Another way to manipulate the data is to *filter* it—that is, to specify criteria that must be met in order for the data to be included. For example, you could set the criteria to send a letter only to contributors who live in a specific city and whose contributions exceed a certain amount of money. If you're using data from an Outlook Contacts list or from a large database used for many purposes, you'll find these features particularly useful.

Setting Conditional Content

One of the real powers of mail merge is the ability it gives you to tailor the content of a document based on some data stored in your mailing list. For example, you might offer a tour of your company to individuals who have invested a large amount of money in the company, but offer only a monthly newsletter to the small investors. If you have an entry in your data file for the level of investment, you can use that data to control the content of your document.

You control conditional content by using the IF Word field. To use this field, you place it in your document where you want the conditional text to appear by clicking Rules on the Mailings tab and then clicking If...Then...Else in the list that appears. In the Insert Word Field: IF dialog box, you specify the data field that lists the value to be tested (for example, amount of investment), the comparison (Greater Than Or Equal To), and the value (for example, 5000). Then you insert the text to be used if the comparison is true ("Please call to arrange a tour.") or untrue ("Please call to receive your monthly newsletter.").

It's More than Letters

The mail merge feature can do more than create form letters and address envelopes. You can save the merged documents as a file so that you can edit them or send them by e-mail.

You can create almost any type of document by using a specific template or creating a design from scratch. All Word needs is a data document with some data fields in it. You can create mailing labels and address books, awards, parts lists, different versions of exams, and catalogs designed for specific geographical areas or demographic populations. The uses for mail merge are limited only by your creativity, your willingness to experiment with different data fields and Word fields, and your decision as to whether mail merge would be faster than manually creating individual documents.

The Pain of Mail Merge

Mail merge is undeniably powerful, but it's also a bit tricky. The tools on the Mailings tab simplify the process. However, any inconsistencies or errors in the data and any typographic or layout errors in the master document can produce some surprising results. Fortunately, the tools on the Ribbon let you preview the results of your mail merge on the screen; conduct a simulated merge, which reports any errors in the merge; or print a sampling of your documents for a visual check of the finished product.

If you do find a problem in a merge, carefully track down the source of the problem. Is it a problem in the data source, in the master document, or in the way you sorted or filtered the data? Once you've determined the source of the problem, correct it, and then test the merge again. Don't assume, however, that the merge will have no further problems. Your fix might not have completely fixed the problem or might have caused a different problem. Don't despair! Just be aware that setting up a mail merge that works perfectly might take a while. Once you've perfected it, though, you'll be amazed by the speed with which you can accomplish your mailings.

Creating a Form Letter

"Mail merge"—a dreaded phrase in the world of word processing! Not only does it conjure up an image of piles of junk mail, but associated terms such as "fields" and "conditional statements" add to the intimidation factor.

However, with just a little effort—and a lot of help from Word—when you need to send nearly identical letters to numerous people, you can create your own mail-merged documents and personalized form letters.

Set Up Your Letter

1. Create your letter as you would any other letter, leaving blank any parts of the letter you want to be completed with data from your mailing list. Save the letter.

2. On the Mailings tab, click Start Mail Merge, and choose Letters from the drop-down menu.

3. Click the Select Recipients button, and specify the type of data you want to use for your mailing list:

   - Type New List to enter your data in the New Address List dialog box.

   - Use Existing List to use data that exists in a file Word can read. To see which type of data sources you can use, open the list of file types in the Select Data Source window, and review the list.

   - Select From Outlook Contacts to use data from your Outlook Contacts list.

4. Click Edit Recipient List to display the Mail Merge Recipients dialog box.

5. Select or clear check boxes to designate whom you want to include in the mail merge.

6. Click an arrow for the field you want to sort or filter by, and select your action from the list that appears. Click OK when you've finished.

Specify the Data to Be Merged

1 In your document, click where you want to add information from your data source.

2 Click the type of information you want to insert.

3 In the dialog box that appears, specify the options you want, and then click OK. Continue adding items to the letter.

4 Click the Preview Results button to display your data in the document.

5 Use the buttons to see how your form letters will look when they're merged with the different data records.

6 Click the Edit Recipient List button if you see that the form letter you're previewing is addressed to someone you don't want to include in this mailing. In the Mail Merge Recipients dialog box, clear the check box for that individual, and click OK.

7 Click the Auto Check For Errors button, and choose to do a simulated merge to check the document for errors. Correct any errors.

8 Click the Finish & Merge button, and specify how you want your letters to be completed.

Tip

If you're familiar with conducting a mail merge using the Mail Merge Wizard that steps you through the process, and if you want to use the wizard, click the Start Mail Merge button, and choose Step By Step Mail Merge Wizard from the drop-down list.

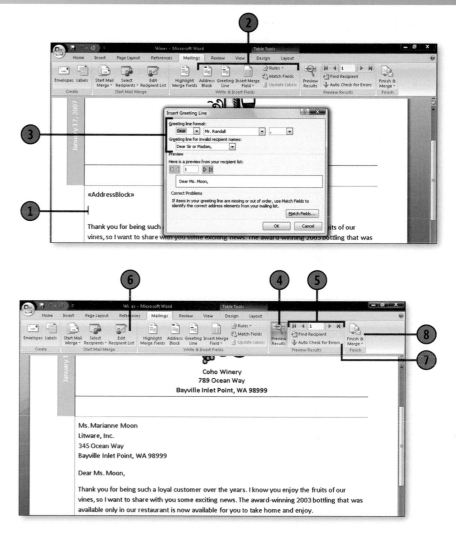

Personalizing a Form Letter

Mail merge lets you use fields in your letter so that you can place specialized information by pulling the information from your data source. You can also use a conditional field that places the information only if certain criteria are met.

Include Personal Information

1. Create your form letter, and step through the mail merge procedures to specify your data source and add such items as the address and a greeting.

2. Click where you want to add the personal information.

3. Click the down arrow on the Insert Merge Field button, and select the field you want to insert.

4. Click the Preview Results button, and step through some of the records to make sure the field is working correctly.

5. Repeat steps 2 through 4 to insert any other merge fields you want.

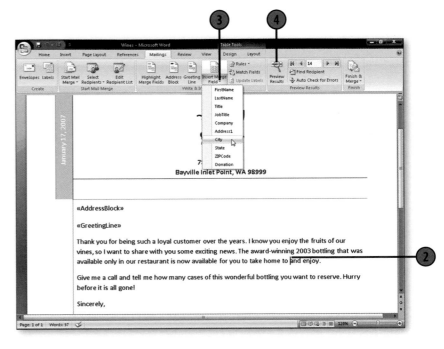

Tip

If you click the Insert Merge Field button instead of the down arrow on the button, the Insert Merge Field dialog box appears. In this dialog box, you can choose to insert address fields that aren't currently part of your data field in case you want to change or modify your data source later.

Tip

Word provides several templates designed for creating form letters and other mail-merged documents. When you open one of these templates, you'll find some fields already inserted into your document.

Add Conditional Content

1. Click where you want to add the conditional information.

2. Click Rules, and choose If...Then...Else... from the drop-down list.

3. In the Insert Word Field: IF dialog box, select the field that contains the condition you want to use.

4. Specify how you want to evaluate the condition.

5. Enter the value to be used to evaluate the condition.

6. Enter the text to be inserted if the condition is evaluated as true.

7. Enter the text to be inserted if the condition is evaluated as not true.

8. Click OK.

9. Click Preview Results, and step through some of the records to make sure the field is working correctly. When you're ready, print the merged letters.

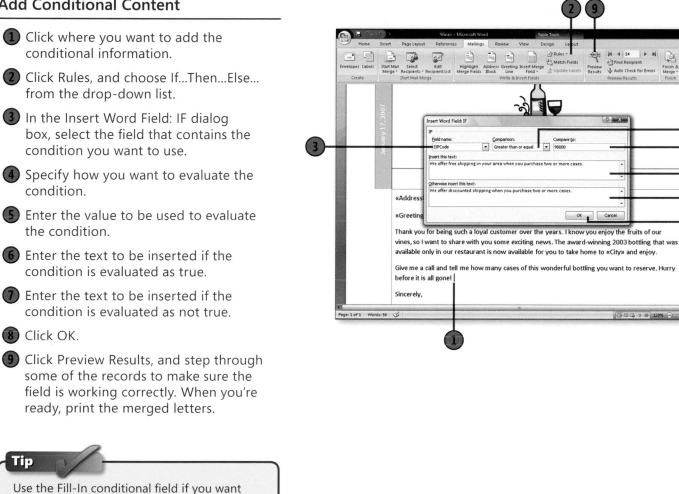

Tip

Use the Fill-In conditional field if you want to be prompted for text each time a record is merged, and use the Next Record If field or the Skip Record If field if you want to control which records are merged based on a record in the Recipients database.

Addressing Envelopes from a Mailing List

When you have a stack of envelopes to address, whether they're for a party or a corporate promotion, you can automate the process by using the mail merge feature to address and print the envelopes you need from your list of recipients.

Create the Envelope Merge

① Create and save a new, blank document. On the Mailings tab, click Start Mail Merge, and choose Envelopes from the drop-down menu. In the Envelope Options dialog box, specify envelope size, fonts to be used, and printing options. Click OK.

② Click Select Recipients, and select or create the source of your addresses.

③ To exclude certain people, click Edit Recipient List and, in the Edit Recipient List dialog box, clear the check boxes for those you want to exclude. Sort or filter the data as needed.

④ Type your return address, or leave the address area blank if you're using preprinted envelopes.

⑤ Click in the address frame.

⑥ Click the Address Block button to insert the address. In the Insert Address Block dialog box, specify what you want to include in the address. Click OK.

⑦ Click Preview Results, and inspect some or all of the merged records to verify their correctness.

⑧ Click Finish & Merge, and choose to print the envelopes. Select which records to print, and click OK. In the Print dialog box, specify your printer, and click Properties to select the paper source. Click Print to print your envelopes.

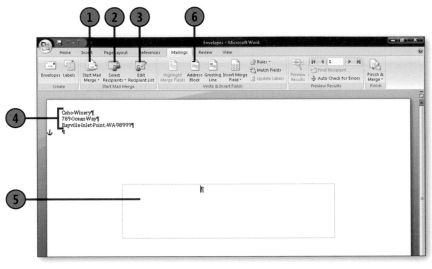

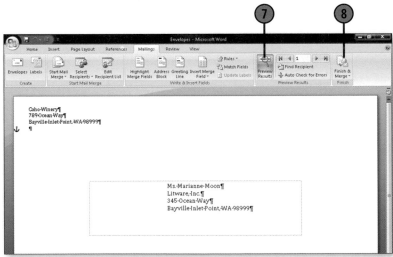

Switching Templates

Every document is based on a template. When you start a plain, blank Word document, its design is based on the Normal template. When you want to create a different type of document—a letter or a report, for example—that document is based on the template designed for that type of document.

Different templates, however, provide different styles, as well as different formatting and layouts. If you have an existing document that you want to be based on a specific template, you can simply switch templates, and Word will automatically update the styles to switch them to those of the new template.

Switch Templates

① On the Developer tab, click the Document Template button to display the Templates And Add-Ins dialog box. (If the Developer tab isn't visible, choose Word Options from the Office menu, click Personalize, select the Show Developer Tab In The Ribbon check box, and click OK.)

② In the Templates And Add-Ins dialog box, click the Attach button.

③ Use the Attach Template window to locate the template you want to use.

④ Double-click the template.

⑤ Select this check box so that the styles in your document will be updated to match the style definitions in the new template.

⑥ Click OK.

"Transferring Styles and Macros" on page 221 for information about using the Organizer to copy styles and macros from one template to another template or document.

Creating Running Heads

In addition to page numbers, a long document usually has some type of identifying text—called a *running head*—at the top or bottom of each page of the document. All you do is create the running head once, and Word places it on the pages you designate. For the sake of consistency, we're using the term *running head* for the heading itself, and the terms *header* and *footer* to indicate the running head's position on the page. Note that on the screen you can see the headers and footers on your page only in Print Layout view or in Print Preview.

Create a Header and Footer

1. On the Insert tab, click the Header button, and, in the gallery that appears, select the layout and content you want in the header.

2. If there are placeholders in the header, click the placeholder field or text, and select or type your information.

3. On the Header & Footer Tools Design tab, click the Footer button, select the layout and content you want, and enter the footer information.

4. Click the Close Header And Footer button to return to the main part of your document.

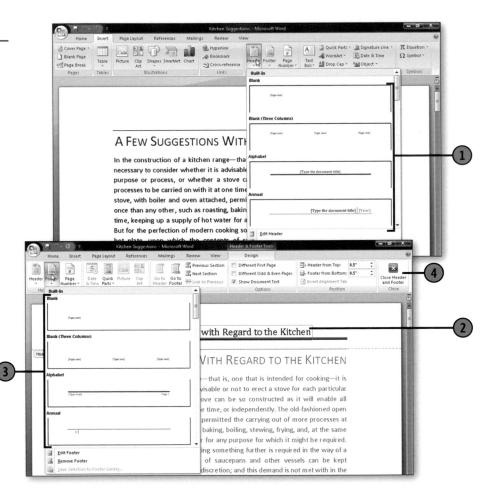

Tip

Much of the content in running heads is based on fields, and many of these fields use the properties of your document to fill in the information. When you complete the information in these fields, that information is added to your document's properties.

Create a Custom Header and Footer

① On the Insert tab, click the Header button, and then click Edit Header in the gallery.

② If there are items you don't want in the header, delete them, and then use any of the items on the Header & Footer Tools Design tab to add content and format the header. Type or add the content you want. Use tabs, paragraph spacing and alignment, and font settings to customize the layout.

③ Click the Go To Footer button.

④ Add and format the content you want in the footer.

⑤ Click the Close Header And Footer button when you've finished.

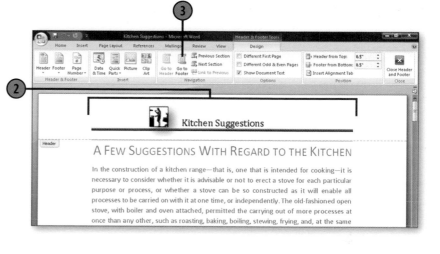

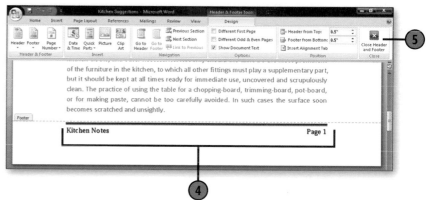

See Also

"Adding Document Properties" on pages 162–163 for information about adding the properties for your document.

"Customizing the Page Numbers" on page 207 for information about adding a page number only, with no other text.

Creating Variable Running Heads

Look through many books and you'll see that the odd- and even-numbered pages often have alternating running heads. This is a fairly standard design, especially for double-sided documents, and you can set it up quite easily in Word.

Running heads are visible on the screen when you look at your document in Print Layout view or Print Preview, and they appear on designated pages of the printed document.

Specify Different Headers or Footers

1 Press Ctrl+Home to move to the first page of your document. On the Insert tab, click the Header button, and click Edit Header in the gallery that appears.

2 On the Header & Footer Tools Design tab, select this check box to specify different running heads for odd- and even-numbered pages.

3 Select this check box for a different or blank first-page running head.

Create a First-Page Running Head

1 Either click the Header button and choose the header you want from the gallery, or create a custom header.

2 Click the Go To Footer button to move to the footer.

3 Either click the Footer button and choose the footer you want, or create a custom footer.

4 Click the Next Section button to move to the even-page footer.

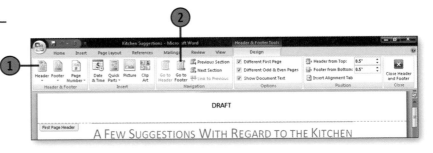

> **Tip**
>
> It's a common practice to omit the running head on the first page of a document or the first page of each chapter in a book. If you want to omit the running head, leave the first-page header and footer areas blank.

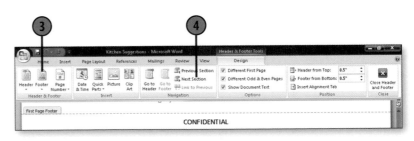

Create an Even-Page Running Head

① Either create a custom footer, or click the Footer button and choose an even-page footer from the gallery. For a custom footer, place the text on the left side so that it will appear on the outside edge of an even-numbered (left-hand, or *verso*) page.

② Click the Go To Header button to move to the even-page header.

③ Click the Header button, and either insert an even-page header or create a custom header.

④ Click the Next Section button to move to the odd-page header.

Create an Odd-Page Running Head

① Either create a custom header, or click the Header button and choose a header from the gallery. For a custom header, place the text on the right side so that it will appear on the outside edge of an odd-numbered (right-hand, or *recto*) page.

② Click the Go To Footer button to move to the odd-page footer.

③ Click the Footer button, or enter the footer information.

④ Click the Close Header And Footer button.

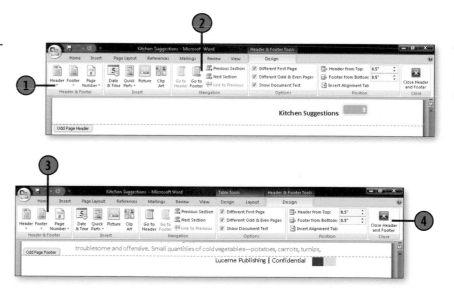

Organizing Your Information

Tables and lists are invaluable tools for presenting information briefly and clearly, and you can make them even more useful by organizing their contents as efficiently as possible. If you have a table or a list that you want to rearrange so that it's presented in alphabetic or numeric order, all you need to do is tell Word to sort it for you.

Sort a Table

① With the insertion point anywhere in the table, on the Table Tools Layout tab, click the Sort button.

② In the Sort dialog box that appears, specify whether the table will contain a header row (a row that shows the column titles).

③ Specify the title of the column you want to use to sort the table, the type of content in the column, and whether you want the information to be sorted in ascending or descending order.

④ If you want to conduct a second- or third-level sort, enter the criteria.

⑤ Click OK.

⑥ Inspect the results of the sort. If you're not happy with the results, either click the Undo button on the Quick Access toolbar or conduct another search with different search criteria.

See Also

"Creating a Bulleted or Numbered List" on pages 68–69 for information about creating lists.

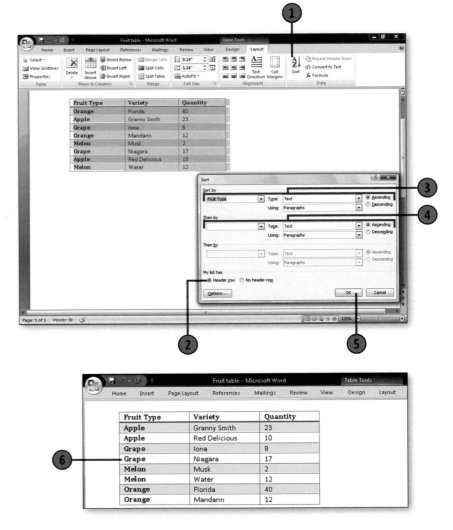

Sort a List

① Select the entire list.

② On the Home tab, click the Sort button to display the Sort Text dialog box.

③ Specify whether you want a header row for the list to be included in the selection.

④ To sort a simple list by the first letter, the number, or the date of the paragraph, in the Sort Text dialog box, specify whether you want to sort by paragraphs, the type of information that's in the list, and whether you want the information to be sorted in ascending or descending order. Click OK.

⑤ To sort a more complex list—for example, one that contains columns—click Options to display the Sort Options dialog box, specify the character to be used to separate the columns, and click OK.

⑥ Specify which column to sort by, the type of content in the column, and whether you want the information to be sorted in ascending or descending order.

⑦ If you want to do a second- or third-level sort, enter the criteria.

⑧ Click OK.

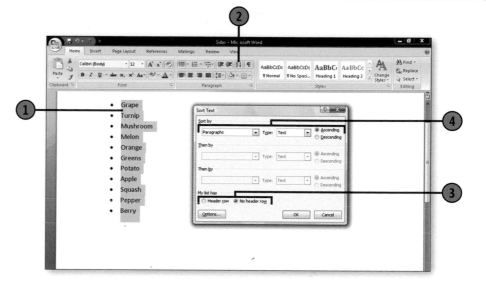

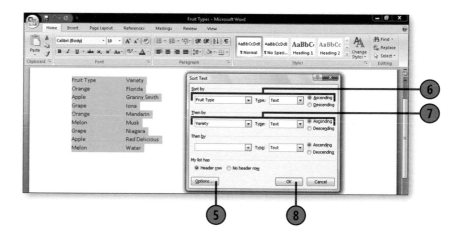

Reorganizing a Document

Outline view provides a powerful way for you to view the structure of your document and to rearrange the order of presentation of the topics in the document. The outline structure assumes that you've used specific heading and body styles to organize your document into a hierarchy of topics and subtopics.

View the Document's Outline

① Click the Outline View button at the bottom-right of your screen to switch to Outline view.

② On the Outlining tab, specify the lowest level of heading to be displayed.

③ Click to expand or collapse the content under the selected heading.

④ Click to change the outline level by promoting it one level or demoting it one level, or to change body text to a heading or a heading to body text.

Tip ✓

To quickly expand or collapse a section, double-click the plus sign next to the heading.

Try This! 🖱

Drag a topic's plus or minus sign to the left to quickly promote the topic's outline level, to the right to demote it, or to the far right to turn it into body text. Changing the outline level also changes the style that's assigned to that paragraph.

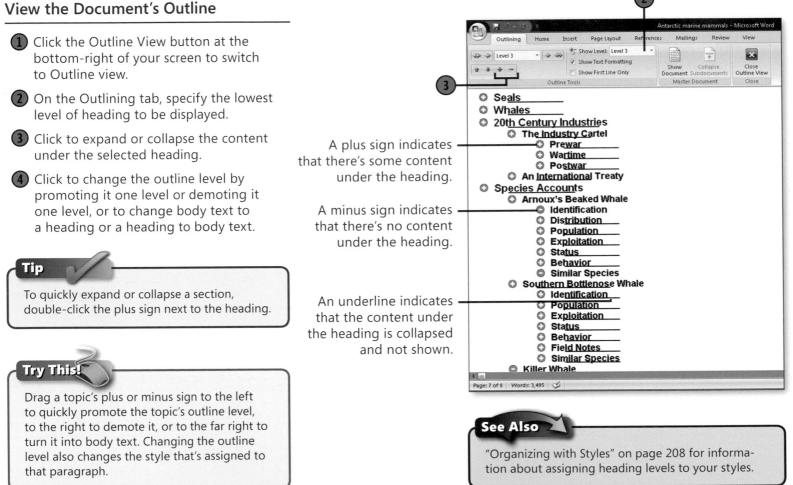

A plus sign indicates that there's some content under the heading.

A minus sign indicates that there's no content under the heading.

An underline indicates that the content under the heading is collapsed and not shown.

See Also ◢

"Organizing with Styles" on page 208 for information about assigning heading levels to your styles.

Move a Paragraph

 1 Expand the outline so that the paragraph you want to move and the area into which you want to move it are both displayed.

2 Click in the paragraph that you want to move.

3 Click to move the paragraph up or down in the document.

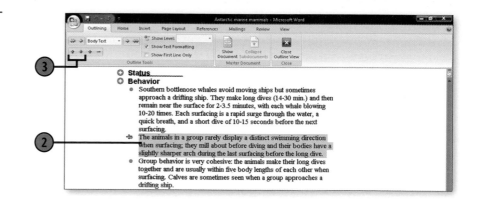

Tip

When you select and move a section, all the paragraphs in that section are moved, including those that haven't been expanded and displayed.

Tip

To quickly move a section, click the plus sign next to the heading, and then drag the heading up or down in the document.

Caution

Be very careful about editing text in Outline view. For example, if the text of a section is collapsed under its heading, you might think that you're deleting only the heading, but you're actually deleting all the text in that section.

Move a Section

1 Click a plus sign to select the section heading and all the content contained under that heading.

2 Click to move the heading and all its content up or down in the document.

Creating a Master Document

A master document is one that's assembled from multiple documents, called *subdocuments*. A master document is extremely useful when multiple authors are working independently on separate sections of a document. All the changes are coordinated, so whether you edit documents separately or as part of the master document, all the changes are saved. When the separate documents are incorporated into the master document, you can easily establish common styles and formatting and can develop pagination, cross-references, and a table of contents.

Create the Master Document

(1) Start a new document, using the template that will be used for the entire master document. Add any introductory text to the master document, save it, and switch to Outline view.

(2) On the Outlining tab, click the Show Document button.

(3) Click Insert, and use the Insert Subdocument dialog box to insert the documents that will be part of the master document. Click OK if Word informs you that the subdocument has a different template, or click Yes if there are styles with the same name.

(4) Move to the paragraph following the inserted subdocument if the insertion point isn't already there, and repeat steps 2 and 3 until all the subdocuments have been added.

(5) Edit the contents using standard editing methods in any view you want. Save and close the master document when you've finished.

(6) Open any of the documents separately, and edit and save them. The next time you open the master document, you'll see any editing changes that have been made to these documents.

Expand or collapse topics using the outlining tools.

> **Tip**
>
> To open a subdocument as a separate document directly from the master document, click Collapse Subdocuments, and then hold down the Ctrl key and click the link to the document.

> **Tip**
>
> If you open the master document and all you see are the links, click Show Document and then click Expand Subdocuments.

6

Adding Graphics to Your Documents

In this section:

- Inserting a Picture
- Changing the Size of a Picture
- Adding Clip Art and Shapes
- Editing a Picture
- Wrapping Text Around a Graphic
- Formatting a Shape
- Arranging Multiple Graphics
- Positioning Graphics on the Page
- Combining Graphics
- Creating Stylized Text
- Inserting a Relational Diagram
- Creating a Chart
- Inserting an Excel Chart

Putting graphics—photographs, clip art, drawings, charts, and diagrams—into your documents is one of the most exciting ways to use today's technology. Using the power of Microsoft Office Word 2007, you can create complex illustrated documents with little effort or time, and the results can be spectacular!

As you might expect, Word gives you the ability to do much more than just plop those graphics into your documents. You can modify your graphics by changing their size or cropping out the parts you don't want. You can make changes to the brightness or contrast of a picture, place a border around it for a finished look, or, for a really professional touch, wrap text around it in various configurations. You can add special effects—color, soft edges, glow, 3-D formats, and so on—and turn words into art with WordArt. You can combine graphics of different types in several ways—layer them on top of each other, use a grid to align them in specific ways, or combine them into a group on a *drawing canvas*. Then, if you don't like your creation, simply click the Reset Picture button, and *voilà!* There's your original, untouched picture again. Word also provides a new diagramming system for tracking projected workflow or creating organization charts. And, if you use Excel data to create charts or graphs, you'll see how simple it is to insert them into your Word documents.

Inserting a Picture

You can add different types of picture files to a single document—photographs and drawings, for example— provided the pictures are in any of the many different file formats Word can use.

Insert a Picture

1. Click in your document where you want to insert the picture.

2. On the Insert tab, click the Picture button to display the Insert Picture window.

3. Navigate to the folder that contains the picture you want, and select the picture file from the list.

4. Click the down arrow next to the Insert button, and click one of the following:

   - Insert to copy the picture and store it in the Word document.

   - Link To File to connect to the picture file without increasing the file size of your Word document. (The source picture file must be available for the picture to be displayed.)

   - Insert And Link to copy the picture, store it in the Word document, and update the picture automatically whenever the source picture file changes.

See Also

"Adding Clip Art" on page 124 for information about inserting pictures that you've cataloged using the Clip Organizer.

"Editing a Picture" on page 126 for information about modifying a picture or its placement.

Tip

If you have lots of pictures, use a picture manager to manage and categorize your pictures, and then drag a picture you want into your document. Microsoft Office Picture Manager, which comes with most versions of Microsoft Office; and Windows Photo Gallery, which comes with Windows Vista, both provide great ways to work with your pictures.

Changing the Size of a Picture

Your inserted picture doesn't always look exactly right—the subject might be too far to one side, or the picture is too big or too small in proportion to the page. You can easily fix both problems: You can crop the picture to keep only the content you want, and you can decrease or increase the size of the picture.

Trim It

1. Click to select the picture if it isn't already selected and to activate the Picture Tools Format tab.

2. On the Picture Tools Format tab, click the Crop button.

3. Place the cropping mouse cursor over a cropping handle, and drag the sides, top, or bottom of the picture to crop off the parts you don't want.

4. Click the Crop button again to turn off cropping.

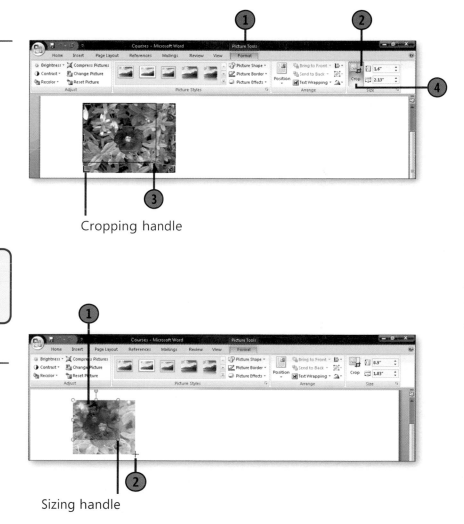

Cropping handle

Tip

When you drag a Sizing handle, your picture can become distorted. To change its size but keep its original aspect, adjust the picture's size in the Size section of the Ribbon.

Size It

1. Click to select the picture if it isn't already selected.

2. Drag a Sizing handle on the picture to modify the size of the picture.

Sizing handle

Adding Clip Art

When you're looking for just the right piece of clip art to illustrate your story or article, you can hunt through different categories or conduct a search using keywords. When you add a picture to a document, the picture becomes part of the document.

Find and Insert Clip Art

(1) Click in your document where you want to place the clip art.

(2) On the Insert tab, click the Clip Art button.

(3) In the Clip Art pane, type a keyword or keywords to describe the type of picture you want.

(4) In the list, click the clip-art collection you want. To select only certain categories, expand the list under the collection, and select the check box for each category you want to look through.

(5) Specify the type of clip you want.

(6) Click Go to view the items that match your criteria.

(7) Click to insert the picture into your document. Add any other clip art you want, and close the Clip Art pane when you've finished.

See Also

"Changing the Size of a Picture" on page 123 for information about cropping and resizing the clip art, and "Editing a Picture" on page 126, for information about modifying the clip art.

"Adding or Removing Word Components" on page 232 for information about installing the Clip Organizer if it isn't already installed.

Adding Shapes

Shapes are drawing objects that you can manipulate in many ways to create unusual and eye-catching effects. You can also use shapes as containers for text, which allows you to create callouts, pull quotes, advertising blurbs, and so on, producing all sorts of interestingly shaped special effects.

Draw a Shape

1. Click in your document where you want to insert the shape.

2. On the Insert tab, click Shapes, and choose the shape you want from the gallery that appears.

3. Hold down the left mouse button, and drag out the shape.

4. Adjust the shape by dragging

    • The Sizing handles to change the size of the drawing.

    • The Adjustment handle to reshape the drawing.

    • The Rotation handle to rotate the drawing.

5. Drag the shape to place it where you want it.

6. Use the tools on the Drawing Tools Format tab to customize the appearance of the shape.

See Also

"Formatting a Shape" on page 130 for information about modifying the appearance of a shape.

"Arranging Multiple Graphics" on page 131 for information about combining multiple shapes for special effects.

"Adding a Sidebar or a Pull Quote" on page 153, and "Creating Custom Text Boxes" on pages 154–155, for information about customizing the text and text layout in a text box.

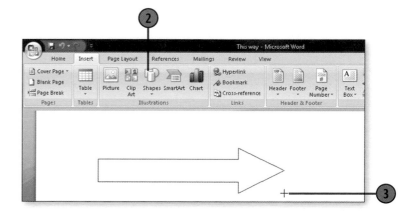

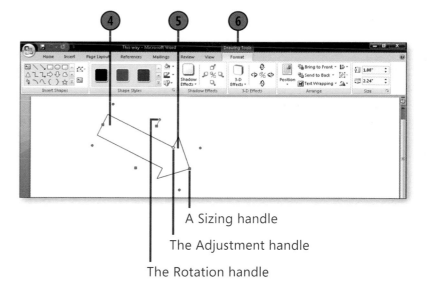

A Sizing handle

The Adjustment handle

The Rotation handle

Editing a Picture

After you've placed a picture in your document, you can make substantial changes and can add many different effects to the picture to make it look exactly the way you want.

Change Its Appearance

(1) Click to select the picture if it isn't already selected, and click the Picture Tools Format tab if it isn't already displayed.

(2) Click the Brightness, Contrast, and Recolor buttons in turn, and drag your mouse through each gallery that appears to see how the settings affect the picture. Click the settings to produce the effects you want.

> **Tip**
>
> When you edit a picture, you're editing only the copy of it that you've inserted into your Word document. If you want to change the original picture file, you'll need to edit it in a separate program—for example, in the Windows Photo Gallery that comes with Windows Vista.

Rotate It

(1) Click to select the picture if it isn't already selected.

(2) Drag the Rotation handle to rotate the picture.

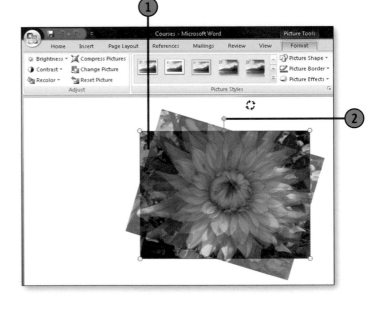

Add an Effect

(1) Move your mouse though the different styles in the Picture Styles section of the Ribbon to see how your picture looks when you apply that style, and then click the style you want.

(2) Click Picture Border, and move your mouse through the gallery to see the effects of a different picture border color, weight, or pattern. Click any effects you want.

(3) Click Picture Effects to add or change the 3-D rotation, shadow, reflection, glow, or soft edges.

(4) If, after all that hard work, you don't like the result, click Reset Picture to reset the entire picture to the way it looked when you first inserted it.

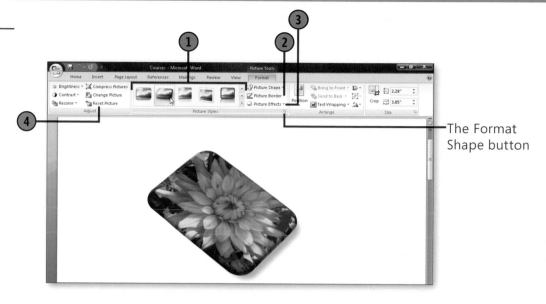

The Format Shape button

Tip

If you want to set precise values for brightness, contrast, shadows, or 3-D settings, including rotation, click the Format Shape button. To rotate a picture 90 or 180 degrees, click the Rotate button in the Arrange section of the Ribbon.

Caution

The Reset Picture button resets all the changes you've made, including any cropping or sizing. If you want to undo only one or two changes, use the Undo button on the Quick Access toolbar.

Wrapping Text Around a Graphic

Wrapping text around an item can add another level of polish to the professional look of your document. However, using one of the standard text-wrapping configurations doesn't always produce the desired effect. As you might expect, you can customize the way Word wraps the text.

Set the Text Wrapping

1. Click the graphic to select it.

2. On the appropriate Format tab for that item (for example, the Picture Tools Format tab or the Drawing Tools Format tab), click the Text Wrapping button, and specify the text-wrapping option you want.

3. Drag the picture to set its position in the paragraph and the way the text wraps around it.

4. If the text wrapping still doesn't look the way you want, click the Text Wrapping button again, choose More Layout Options from the menu, and make your custom layout settings in the Advanced Layout dialog box. Click OK when you've finished.

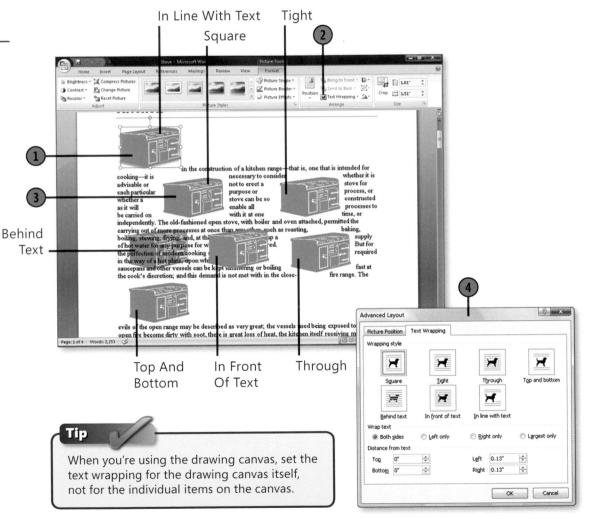

In Line With Text

Square

Tight

Behind Text

Top And Bottom

In Front Of Text

Through

Tip

When you're using the drawing canvas, set the text wrapping for the drawing canvas itself, not for the individual items on the canvas.

Change the Wrapping Shape

① Click to select the item to be wrapped if it isn't already selected.

② Click the Text Wrapping button, and choose either Tight or Through text wrapping. Click the Text Wrapping button again, and choose Edit Wrap Points from the menu.

③ Drag a wrapping point to change the wrapping outline. Continue moving wrapping points, or drag the line to create a new wrapping point.

④ Click outside the item to deselect it.

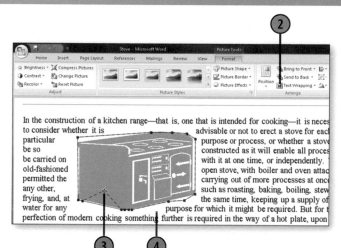

Wrap Part of an Item

① Click at the point where you want to stop the wrap.

② On the Page Layout tab, click the Breaks button, and click the Text Wrapping option.

Try This!

Set an item with Behind Text wrapping, move the item so that the text runs over it, and try to select the item. No luck? Click the Select button on the Home tab, choose Select Objects from the menu, and drag a selection rectangle around the item. Now you can move the item or change its wrap. Click the Select button again, and click Select Objects to turn it off.

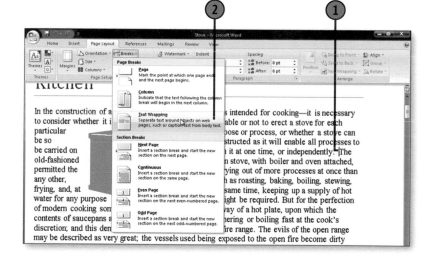

Formatting a Shape

Shapes are useful tools for illustrating your content. However, you can often add a lot more impact to a document by creating a formatted shape rather than using a plain black-and-white-outlined shape.

Format the Shape

1. Click to select the shape if it isn't already selected.

2. Point to different shape styles, and click the style you want.

3. Click the Shape Fill button if you want to customize the color of the fill.

4. Click the Shape Outline button if you want to customize the color, thickness, and style of the outline.

5. Use the Shadow or 3-D Effects galleries to add any special effects you want.

6. If you want to add text to the shape, click Edit Text to insert a text box, and then enter your text. Note, however, that all the Callouts shapes automatically contain a text box.

7. To add special effects, such as a fill pattern, fill transparency, or arrow styles, adjust the properties of the text box, or, for other advanced customizations, click the Advanced Tools button to display the Format AutoShape dialog box.

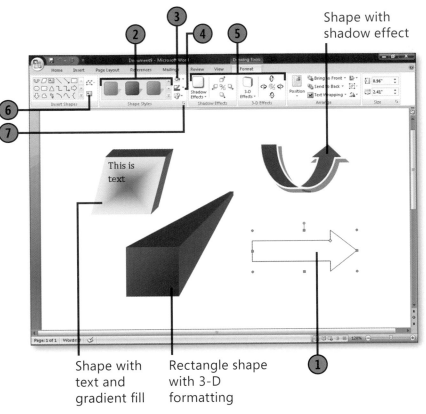

Shape with shadow effect

Shape with text and gradient fill

Rectangle shape with 3-D formatting

See Also

"Arranging Multiple Graphics" on the facing page for information about combining several shapes into a single graphic.

"Positioning Graphics on the Page" on page 132 for information about adjusting the position of the shape.

Arranging Multiple Graphics

When you have more than one graphic (or type of graphic) in your document—for example, pictures, clip art, and/or shapes that are meant to appear together—you can arrange them in whatever configuration you want.

Arrange the Graphics

1 Click a picture, a shape, or a piece of clip art to select it, click the Text Wrapping button on the Picture Tools Format tab, and choose In Front Of Text from the gallery that appears. Continue setting the same text wrapping for all the pictures and/or clip art that you want to group.

2 Drag the graphics to where you want them positioned in the document.

3 To *layer* the graphics, click a graphic, and then use the Bring To Front or Send To Back button. Repeat as needed to arrange the graphics as you want them.

4 To combine multiple shapes—but not pictures or clip art—into a single graphic, select all the shapes by holding down the Ctrl key when you click them, click the Group button, and then choose Group from the drop-down menu.

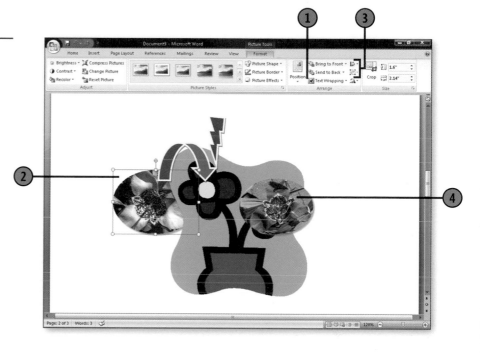

See Also

"Combining Graphics" on page 133 for information about combining different types of graphics into a single object.

Positioning Graphics on the Page

No matter how dazzling or relevant your graphics, placing them haphazardly on the page will diminish their impact and undermine your message. Word provides you with some handy tools so that you can get all your artwork laid out properly.

Align to the Page

1 Click to select a picture or a drawing, if it isn't already selected. On the Picture Tools Format tab or the Drawing Tools Format tab, click the Align button, and choose View Gridlines to display a nonprinting layout grid on the page.

2 Click the Align button again, and specify whether you want the graphic to align relative to the edge of the paper or to the margin.

3 Click the Align button again, and click where you want to place the graphic on the page.

4 To fine-tune its position, drag the graphic to where you want it, using the grid to align the graphic to other items.

Align to Each Other

1 Position the pictures or drawings in the approximate location you want, and then select the ones you want to align by holding down the Ctrl key as you click each one.

2 Click the Align button, and, with the Align Selected Objects check box selected, specify the way you want the objects to align to each other.

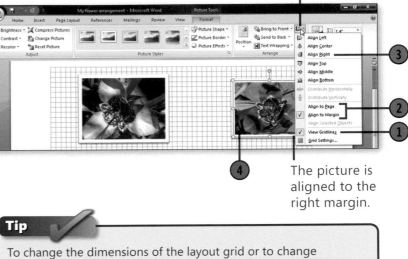

The Align button

The picture is aligned to the right margin.

> **Tip**
>
> To change the dimensions of the layout grid or to change whether the graphics will automatically align to the gridlines, click the Align button and choose Grid Settings.

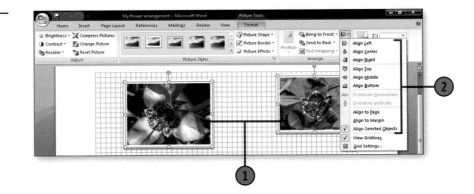

Combining Graphics

Sometimes you might have several graphics—a picture and a piece of clip art, or some drawings, for example—that you want to keep together, separately from the text. You can do this by placing the graphics on a single drawing canvas. You can even format the canvas to get the look you want.

Gather Your Graphics

① On the Insert tab, click the Shapes button to display the Shapes gallery, and click New Drawing Canvas.

② Use the Insert tab to insert pictures, clip art, drawings, or WordArt. Size, crop, format, and arrange each item as you want.

③ Drag the boundaries of the canvas to the size you want.

④ Use the tools on the Drawing Tools Format tab to format the canvas, including setting the text wrapping. If necessary, adjust the position of the drawing canvas in relationship to your text.

Tip

When you place graphics on a canvas, your formatting options are limited. When you try to insert a chart, only the older style charts used in previous versions of Word are available.

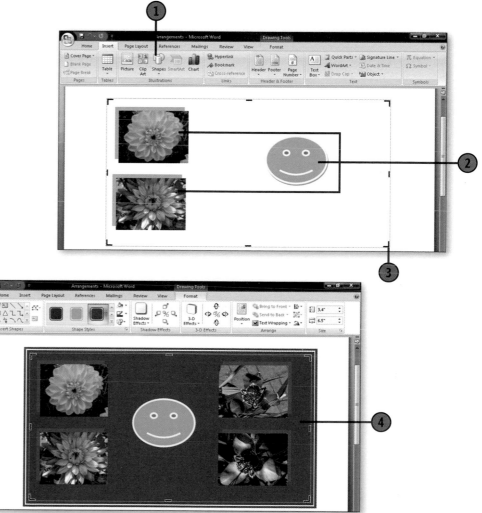

Creating Stylized Text

You can achieve some spectacular effects by creating text as art. WordArt lets you twist your text into weird and wonderful shapes and three-dimensional configurations, and then inserts the result into your document as an object. Try it. But heed our warning—it's highly addictive!

Create Some WordArt

1 On the Insert tab, click the WordArt button to display the WordArt gallery.

2 Click the WordArt style you want.

3 In the Edit WordArt Text dialog box, specify a font, a font size, and any character emphasis you want. The same formatting will apply to all the text in this piece of WordArt.

4 Type your text. Note that WordArt text doesn't wrap automatically; you press Enter to start a new line. (To transform existing text into WordArt, select the text before you click the WordArt button.)

5 Click OK.

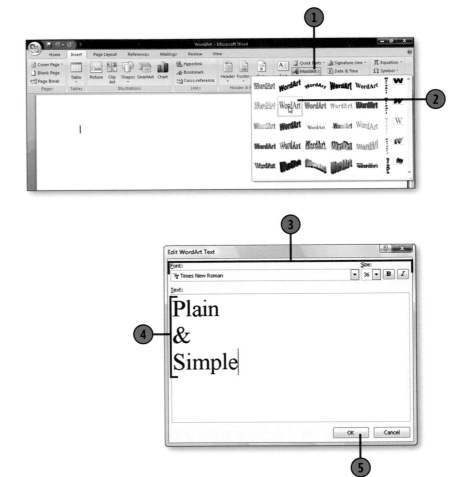

Try This!

Create some WordArt, select it, and then use the tools on the WordArt Tools Format tab to change the shape, character spacing and height, and text alignment. Use the WordArt Styles gallery to apply a three-dimensional effect. Use the 3-D Effects tools to change the color, depth, direction, lighting, surface type, and 3-D angle. Amazing, isn't it? And so much fun!

Fine-Tune the Result

1. Click to select the WordArt if it isn't already selected, and use the Sizing handles to change the size of the WordArt.

2. If you want to arrange the WordArt in relationship to your text, on the WordArt Tools Format tab, click Text Wrapping, and specify the way you want the text to wrap around the WordArt.

3. Point to different WordArt styles, and click the style you want.

4. Use the text tools to edit the WordArt text, change the font, modify the letter spacing, and change the text orientation and alignment.

5. Use the Shape Fill or the Shape Outline button to customize the color of the fill effects or the outline thickness.

6. Click the Change Shape button, and select the type of shape you want the text arranged in.

7. Add any shadow or 3-D effects.

8. Use the Rotation and Adjustment handles if you want to modify the angle or shape.

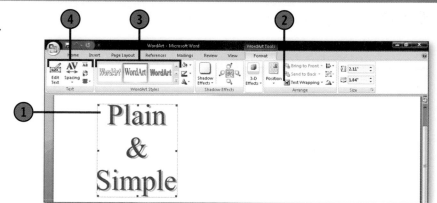

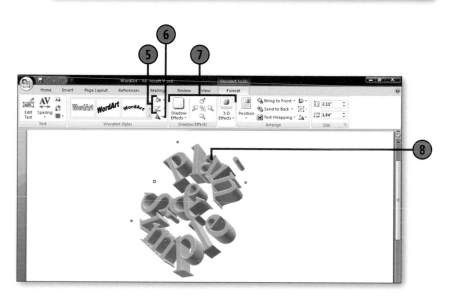

Tip

To change the colors of dual-colored or multicolored WordArt, on the WordArt Tools Format tab, click the down arrow on the Shape Fill button, point to Gradient in the gallery, click More Gradients, and modify the colors on the Gradient tab of the Fill Effects dialog box.

Inserting a Relational Diagram

The new diagramming system in Word provides a great opportunity for you to describe your topic visually, whether your diagram illustrates the command structure at your workplace, the flow diagram of a project, or the interrelationship among different activities. After you've inserted a diagram, you'll find that it's extremely customizable.

Create a Diagram

1 On the Insert tab, click the SmartArt button to display the Choose A SmartArt Graphic dialog box.

2 Select the type of diagram you want.

3 Click a diagram design, review the information about that diagram, and click OK to create the diagram.

4 Click the first item in the Text pane, and type the text for that item. If the Text pane isn't displayed, click Text Pane on the SmartArt Tools Design tab.

5 Continue entering text, doing any of the following:

- Press the Tab key to make the entry a subentry of the previous item (or click Demote); or Press Shift+Tab to elevate the entry one level (or click Promote).

- Press Enter to finish the current item and insert a new line for text.

- Press the Down arrow key to move to the next item.

- Press Delete to remove entries you don't want.

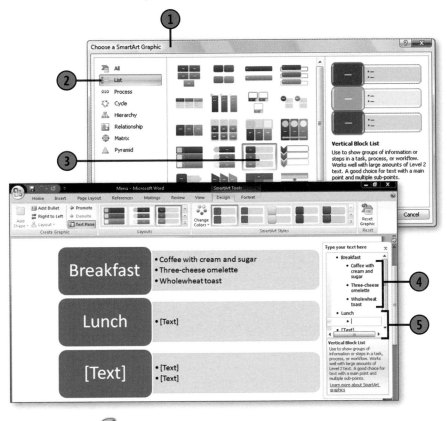

Tip

You can't create SmartArt graphics in a Word 97–2003 format document. When you save a document that contains SmartArt in the Word 97–2003 format, the SmartArt is converted into a picture that you can't modify.

Modify the Diagram

① On the SmartArt Tools Design tab, point to different layouts and click the one that works best for your content.

② Point to different SmartArt Styles and click the one you want.

③ Click an item in the diagram to select it.

④ On the SmartArt Tools Format tab, point to the different Shape Styles, and click the one you want.

⑤ Click the Shape Fill, Shape Outline, and Shape Effects buttons to modify the fill color, modify the outline color and style, or add special effects, such as a shadow or a glow.

⑥ Point to different WordArt Styles to see how the text in the shape is affected. Click a style you like if you want to use WordArt.

⑦ Drag a selected shape to move it into a new location, or use the Sizing or Rotation handle to change the dimensions or rotation of the diagram.

⑧ Click the frame of the diagram, and use a Sizing handle to change the diagram's size.

Try This!

Create a list in your document. Select the text and copy it (press Ctrl+C). Insert a SmartArt diagram. Click in the Text pane, and press Ctrl+V to paste your copied text. Edit the text, setting any levels you want. Point to different layouts to see which layout works best with your content.

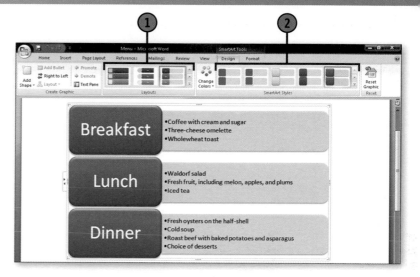

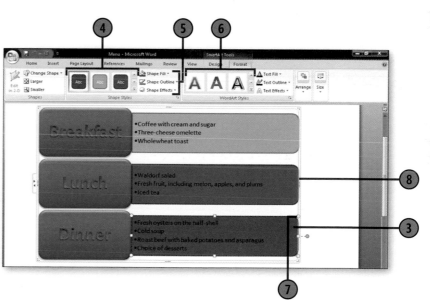

Creating a Chart

If you want to present some data as a chart, you can easily create the chart directly from Word while still using the power of Excel to create a professional-looking graphic.

Create a Chart

1. On the Insert tab, click the Chart button to display the Insert Chart dialog box.

2. Select a chart type.

3. Double-click the chart design you want.

4. In the Excel worksheet that appears, edit the sample data so that only your data is shown.

5. Close the worksheet when you've finished.

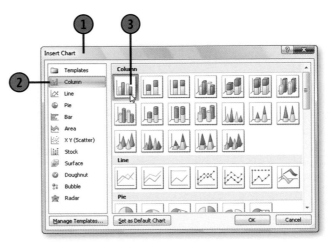

Tip

If you don't have Excel installed on your computer, Microsoft Graph will start when you click the Chart button on the Insert tab. Microsoft Graph works much like Excel, although it has fewer features.

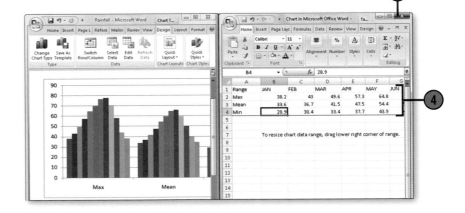

See Also

"Inserting an Excel Chart" on page 140 for information about inserting a chart that's based on complex or existing data.

Format the Chart

1. Click in the chart to select it if it isn't already selected.

2. If you need to modify which data is shown and how it's organized, on the Chart Tools Design tab, click the Edit Data button, and make your modifications in the worksheet that appears.

3. Use the tools on the Chart Tools Design tab to change the chart type, the data, the layout, and the overall appearance of the chart.

4. Use the tools on the Chart Tools Layout tab to add annotations, labels, and other elements.

5. Use the tools on the Chart Tools Format tab to format individual items in the chart.

6. Save the document to save the data and the design of the chart.

Tip

Although the Excel worksheet looks like a standard worksheet, it's actually a special Excel object that's stored in your Word file. All your chart information and data are stored in the Word file, so you don't need to access the Excel file to view or modify the chart in Word.

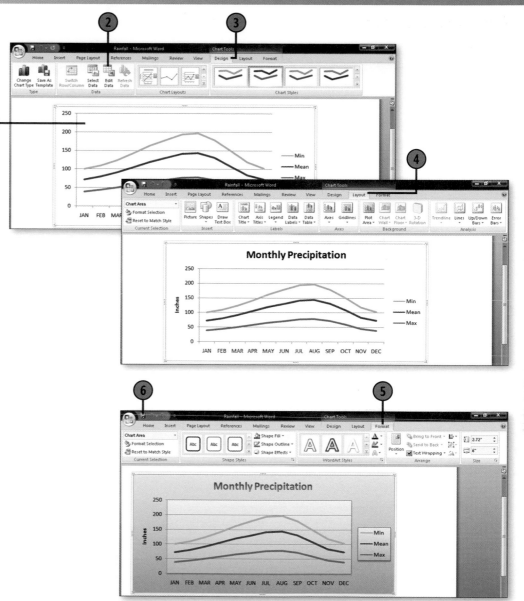

Inserting an Excel Chart

If you have the final results of your data in an Excel worksheet but you want to display the data as a chart, you can copy the chart into your Word document. After you've done so, the chart resides in Word, so you can edit it as necessary, and you no longer need the original Excel workbook.

Insert a Chart

1. In Excel, create and format your chart. Select the chart and copy it.

2. In Word, on the Home tab, click the Paste button to insert the chart.

3. Click the Paste Options Actions button that appears, and click an option to specify the way you want the chart to be inserted:

   - Chart (Linked To Excel Data) if you'll need to edit the data and you have access to the original Excel file

   - Excel Chart (Entire Workbook) to incorporate all the Excel data so that you can edit the data in Word without access to the original Excel file

   - Paste As Picture if you're not going to edit the chart and its data

See Also

"Creating a Chart" on page 138 for information about creating and formatting a chart from an Excel worksheet.

Tip

Excel provides many powerful data-management tools, so make sure you've arranged, sorted, and filtered the data the way you want it before you create the chart and copy it into Word.

Caution

If you're linking to the Excel chart, make sure you've named and saved the Excel file before you insert it.

7 Adding Specialized Content

In this section:

- Inserting a Cover Page
- Numbering Headings and Lines
- Creating an Equation
- Inserting Excel Data
- Using Hyperlinks
- Inserting Special Characters
- Adding a Sidebar or a Pull Quote
- Creating a Dropped Capital Letter
- Creating Footnotes, Endnotes, and Cross-References
- Inserting a Watermark
- Adding Captions to Tables and Figures
- Creating a Table of Contents
- Creating an Index

This section of the book deals with the special content required in certain types of documents. If your document needs a cover page, you'll find that Microsoft Office Word 2007 provides a wide selection of predesigned cover pages that you can use as is or customize to your needs.

It's a common practice to number the heading levels, and often the individual lines, in scientific and legal documents for convenience when the documents are being reviewed, and it's a snap to do in Word. We'll also discuss inserting and working with equations; inserting special symbols or characters, such as © and € or £, that don't exist on many keyboards; creating attractive dropped capital letters; and using text boxes to create sidebars and pull quotes. If your document needs footnotes or endnotes, Word not only numbers them automatically but updates the numbers if you add or delete a note, and figures out their exact placement on the page. We'll also discuss using cross-references in your papers; adding captions to tables and figures; and creating a table of figures, a table of equations, and even a table of tables (not to mention a table of contents), an index with main entries and subentries, and a bibliography. If all this sounds daunting, you'll be pleasantly surprised by how easy it is to achieve really professional-looking documents.

Inserting a Cover Page

First impressions count! A well-designed cover page can provide the incentive that makes your readers want to see what's inside your document.

Insert a Cover Page

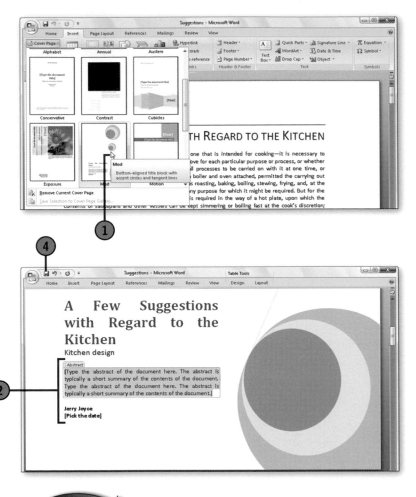

1 On the Insert tab, click the Cover Page button, and click the cover page design you want in the gallery that appears.

2 Switch to Print Layout view if you aren't already in that view, press Ctrl+Home to move to the beginning of your document, click in an area that needs to be completed, and type the required information. Repeat for all the other areas that need to be completed.

3 If you're not happy with the design of the cover page,

- On the Insert tab, click Cover Page, and choose another design.

- On the Page Layout tab, click Themes, and choose a different theme.

- Add a picture, a drawing, fields, text, or other items to customize the page.

- On the Insert tab, click Cover Page, and choose Remove Current Cover Page to delete the cover page.

4 Save your document.

Tip

Most of the information on the cover page is part of the document's properties. Some information, such as the file name, might be automatically inserted from existing properties.

See Also

"Creating a Custom Cover Page" on pages 194–195 for information about personalizing a cover page.

Numbering Headings

It's a commonly accepted practice to number each heading level in certain long documents so that when the document is being reviewed or is under discussion at a meeting, it's easy to refer to the relevant sections. Word uses the outline-level setting for each style as the basis for the numbering hierarchy.

Number the Headings

① Verify that you've applied the correct styles to all the headings.

② Click in the first heading paragraph.

③ On the Home tab, click the Multilevel List button, and click one of the heading-numbering schemes.

④ Verify that your document headings are numbered correctly. If you don't like the look of the numbering scheme, click the Undo button on the Quick Access toolbar.

The Multilevel List button

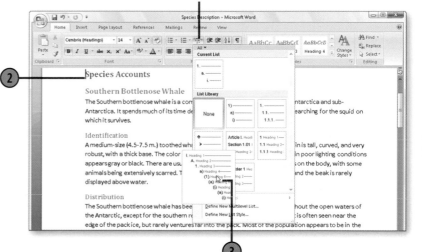

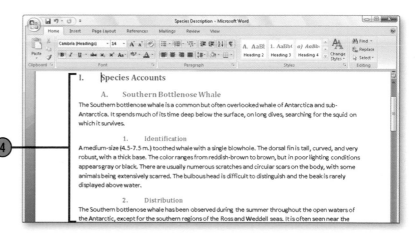

See Also

"Adding Line Numbers" on page 144 for information about numbering all the lines in a document.

"Customizing a Multilevel List" on page 206 for information about modifying the numbering scheme.

"Organizing with Styles" on page 208 for information about setting outline levels.

Adding Line Numbers

Numbering lines is a convenient—and sometimes required—way to provide references in a document that is going to be reviewed. Word will automatically number the lines for you and will also skip the numbering of any lines that you don't want numbered.

Number the Lines

1 On the Page Layout tab, click the Line Numbers button, and choose the type of line numbering you want from the drop-down menu.

2 If you want to change the starting number or the interval at which line numbers are shown (every fifth line, for example), click Line Numbers again, choose Line Numbering Options from the menu, and, on the Layout tab of the Page Setup dialog box, click the Line Numbers button to display the Line Numbers dialog box.

3 Select this check box, if it isn't already selected, to turn on line numbering.

4 Specify the options you want.

5 Click OK, and then click OK in the Page Setup dialog box.

6 Select any paragraph that you don't want to be numbered.

7 Click the Paragraph button to display the Paragraph dialog box.

8 On the Line And Page Breaks tab, select the Suppress Line Numbers check box.

9 Click OK.

The Paragraph button

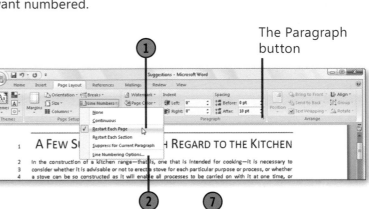

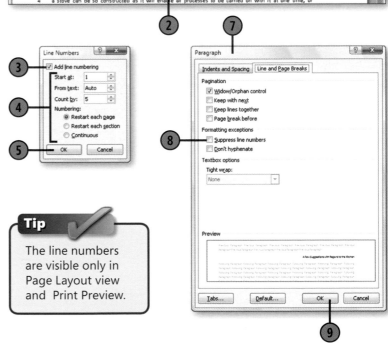

Tip

The line numbers are visible only in Page Layout view and Print Preview.

Inserting an Equation

Few things have been as difficult as displaying mathematical equations in a document—until now. Word 2007 provides powerful equation-writing tools that allow you to insert a prepackaged equation as is or modify one any way you want it to appear. Remember, however, that any equation you insert is the equation in its current form only; Word is unable to do any math with that equation.

Insert an Equation

1. Click in the document where you want to insert the equation.

2. On the Insert tab, click the down arrow at the right of the Equation button, and, in the gallery that appears, click the equation you want.

3. Use normal editing techniques, such as formatting text size and emphasis, or use the tools on the Equation Tools Design tab to insert different symbols, letters, or numbers or to change the equation into a linear form or to plain text.

4. Click outside the equation when you've finished working with it.

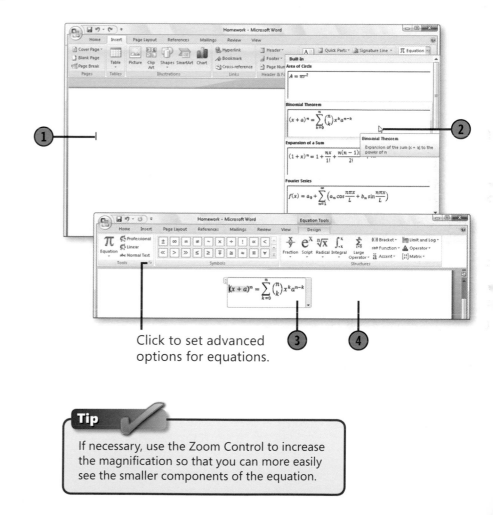

Click to set advanced options for equations.

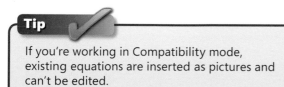

Tip

If you're working in Compatibility mode, existing equations are inserted as pictures and can't be edited.

Tip

If necessary, use the Zoom Control to increase the magnification so that you can more easily see the smaller components of the equation.

Creating an Equation

Word provides a number of common equations that you can insert into your document with just a click of the mouse.

However, if you often work with less-common or specialized equations or formulae, you can create the equations yourself.

Build an Equation

1 On the Insert tab, click the Equation button to insert an Equation content control. (A *content control* is an object used in Word to hold special content and to keep that content as one unit. Click the content to display the control; click outside the control to resume working on standard non-equation text.)

2 Start constructing your equation. Use the items in the Structures section to develop the beginning structure of the equation. If necessary, insert structures inside other structures to create nested components.

3 To insert a symbol, click the symbol; or click the More button to open the Symbols gallery, and click the symbol you want. If the symbol isn't shown, click the symbol-set name, and choose a different symbol set to find and insert the correct symbol.

4 If you want to include standard text in the equation, click Normal Text, type your text, and then click Normal Text again to turn off the option.

5 Use the mouse or the arrow keys to continue moving through the equation, adding structures and content. Click outside the equation when you've finished.

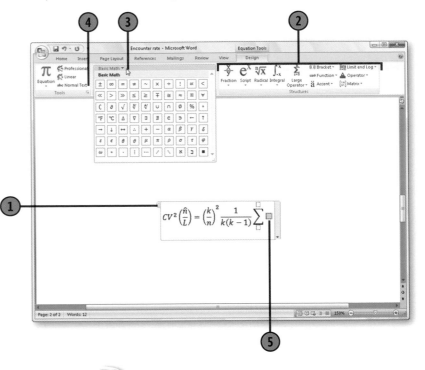

 Try This!

Click the Office button, and then click the Word Options button. Click the Proofing category, and click the AutoCorrect Options button. On the Math AutoCorrect tab, note all the codes that produce math symbols. If you want to use any of these codes in normal text as well as in a math expression, select the check box for using the Math AutoCorrect rules outside the math regions. Click OK.

Finalize the Equation

(1) Click to select the equation if it isn't already selected.

(2) To modify a multi-lined equation so that it's all expressed on a single line (one-dimensional), click Linear on the Equation Tools Design tab.

(3) To modify the equation from a linear to a multi-lined equation (two-dimensional), click Professional.

(4) To modify the size or spacing of an element in the equation, click it to select it, right-click it, and then choose the change you want from the shortcut menu.

(5) Click Equation Options on the equation's content control, point to Justification, and choose the alignment you want for the equation.

(6) If you want to add the equation to the Equations gallery for later use, click Equation Options again, choose Save As New Equation from the menu, and complete the information in the Create New Building Block dialog box that appears.

See Also

"Correcting Text Automatically" on pages 34–35 for information about adding your own entries to AutoCorrect.

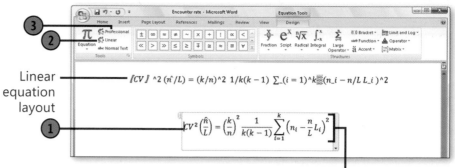

Linear equation layout

$$[CV] \char94 2 \, (\acute{n}/L) = (k/n)\char94 2 \; 1/k(k-1) \; \Sigma_-(i=1)\char94 k (n\_i - n/L \, L\_i)\char94 2$$

$$CV^2\left(\frac{\hat{n}}{L}\right) = \left(\frac{k}{n}\right)^2 \frac{1}{k(k-1)} \sum_{i=1}^{k}\left(n_i - \frac{n}{L}L_i\right)^2$$

Professional equation layout

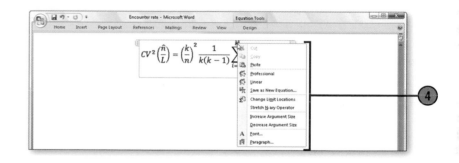

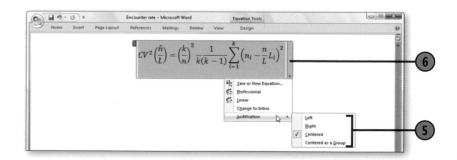

Inserting Microsoft Excel Data

Microsoft Excel is a great tool for collecting and analyzing data, but the information contained in an Excel worksheet is often more easily understood when it's presented along with some explanations or supplemental information. To that end, you can integrate Excel information into a Word document by copying the data from Excel into the Word document. You can include the Excel data in one of several ways. If the Excel information is static—that is, your data collection is complete and the numbers won't change—you can insert the data into a Word document as a table or as text. If your data collection and analysis are still in progress and the information might change, you can link the data to the original Excel file so that any changes to the Excel data will appear in the Word document. If, however, the data or analysis might change but you won't be able to access the original Excel file, or you don't want the original Excel file to be changed or played around with by anyone else who has access to it, you can copy the entire Excel worksheet into your Word document, where you can still use the worksheet features to adjust the data.

Copy the Data

1. In the Excel worksheet, select and copy the cells you want.

2. On the Home tab in Word, click the Paste button to insert the data.

3. Click the Paste Options Actions button, and specify how you want the data to be inserted.

Tip

If you want to link to the original Excel file, make sure that you name and save the file before you copy and link to it.

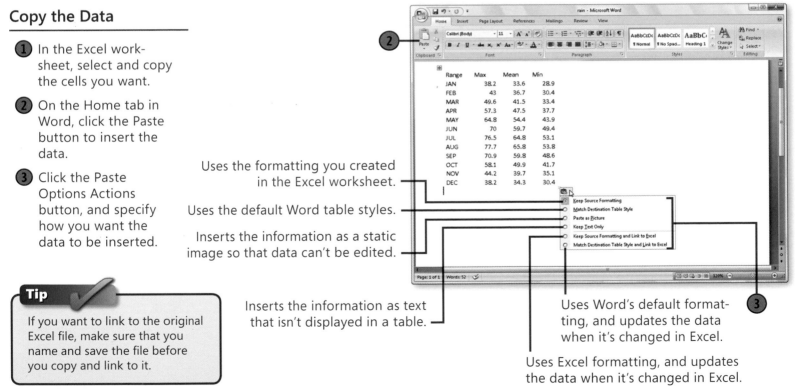

Uses the formatting you created in the Excel worksheet.

Uses the default Word table styles.

Inserts the information as a static image so that data can't be edited.

Inserts the information as text that isn't displayed in a table.

Uses Word's default formatting, and updates the data when it's changed in Excel.

Uses Excel formatting, and updates the data when it's changed in Excel.

Insert All the Data

1. In the Excel worksheet, select and copy the cells you want.

2. On the Home tab in Word, click the down arrow on the Paste button, and choose Paste Special from the menu to display the Paste Special dialog box.

3. With the Paste option selected, double-click the Excel object.

4. Double-click the inserted table to edit the data.

5. Click outside the inserted table, and continue working on your document.

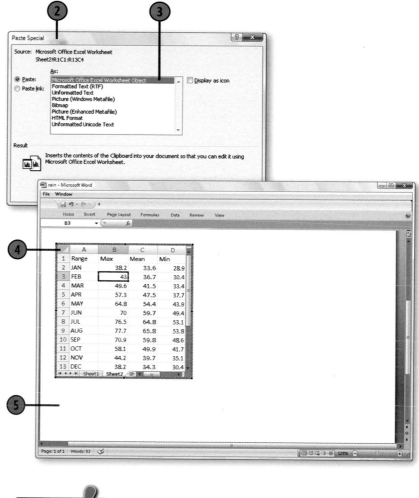

Try This!

Insert the Excel object. Click it to select it, and drag a Sizing handle. Note that the size of the text increases. Double-click the object to activate it, and drag a Sizing handle. Note that the number of rows and columns that are displayed has changed. Click outside the object to deactivate it.

Tip

To work with the entire worksheet in Excel instead of in the Word window, with the table *not* selected, right-click the table in your Word document, point to Worksheet Object on the shortcut menu, and choose Open from the submenu. In Excel, after you've worked with the data, choose Update from the Office menu, and then close Excel.

Caution

When you edit the Excel data, make sure that you return to the correct tab of the worksheet when you've finished. Otherwise, you might end up displaying a blank table or chart instead of the data.

Using Hyperlinks

A hyperlink, often called a *link* or a *jump*, creates a connection to different parts of your document, to other Word documents, or to other types of files in an online document.

Link to an Item in Your Document

(1) Type or select the text you want to use as a hyperlink.

(2) On the Insert tab, click the Hyperlink button to display the Insert Hyperlink dialog box.

(3) Click Place In This Document to see the headings and bookmarks that are contained in the document.

(4) Click the heading or bookmark you want to link to.

(5) Click the ScreenTip button, type a short description of the link that will appear when someone points to the hyperlink, and then click OK.

(6) Click OK.

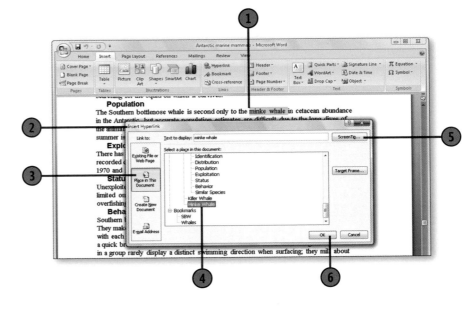

"Inserting a Bookmark" on page 159 for information about creating a bookmark.

"Creating a Custom Table of Contents" on pages 196–197 for information about creating hyperlinks in a table of contents.

Tip

In many instances, Word can automatically insert hyperlinks—for example, when you create a table of contents, a table of figures, a table of equations, or a table of tables; or when you create cross-references, footnotes, and a master document. Take a look through this book to find examples of these automatically inserted hyperlinks.

Link to a Different Document

1. Type and select the text you want to use as a hyperlink.

2. On the Insert tab, click the Hyperlink button.

3. In the Insert Hyperlink dialog box, click Existing File Or Web Page.

4. Click a category to locate the file you want to link to:

   • Current Folder for a file in your default document folder, or to locate a file in another folder on your computer or network

   • Browsed Pages for Web pages you've visited or files you've opened

   • Recent Files for files you've used recently

5. Use the Browse tools to locate a Web page or to move to the correct folder if the file is in a different folder.

6. Click the file or the Web page you're linking to.

7. Click ScreenTip, type a short description of the link, and click OK.

8. Click OK.

Tip

Unless you enter some descriptive text in the ScreenTip dialog box, the ScreenTip will display the entire path and file name of the document, which usually isn't useful and doesn't describe the content.

Tip

By default, you must hold down the Ctrl key and click a hyperlink to use the link. Requiring the use of the Ctrl key to follow a hyperlink prevents unintended jumps and simplifies selecting a hyperlink for editing. If you prefer to follow a hyperlink without using the Ctrl key, click the Office button, click the Word Options button, and, in the Advanced category of the Word Options dialog box, clear the Use CTRL+Click To Follow Hyperlink check box.

Inserting Special Characters

With at least 101 keys at your fingertips, you'd think that every character you could possibly need would be available on your keyboard. But what about the accented characters in other languages? Different currency symbols? Mathematical symbols? You'd need a keyboard with thousands of keys! As you can see in the illustration, Word gives you a huge assortment of symbols and special characters, and provides several ways to insert them into your documents.

Insert a Character

1 On the Insert tab, with the insertion point located where you want to insert the symbol into your document, click the Symbol button to display the Symbols gallery. If the character you want is displayed, click it. Otherwise, click More Symbols to display the Symbol dialog box.

2 If the symbol you want is displayed, select it, and then skip to step 6.

3 Click Normal Text to insert a character from the font you're currently using, or click a specific font. Click one of the symbol fonts for nonstandard characters.

4 Click the character's category if it's displayed.

5 Select the character you want to use.

6 Click Insert. To add more characters, click in your document to activate it, click where you want to insert each special character, and then select and insert the character.

7 To insert a typographic character, click the Special Characters tab, and double-click the character you want to insert.

8 Click Close after you've inserted the special characters and symbols you want.

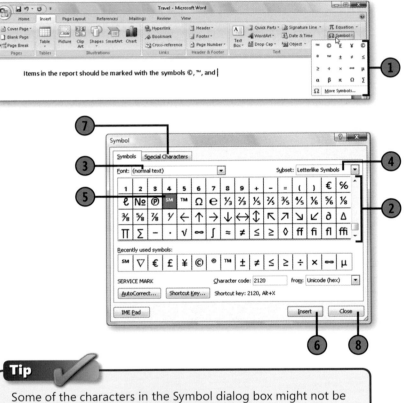

Tip

Some of the characters in the Symbol dialog box might not be supported by all fonts and printers. If you see an empty box instead of a symbol in your document, try using a different font. If you see the symbol on your screen but it doesn't print, try using only the TrueType fonts that came with Word.

Adding a Sidebar or a Pull Quote

Sidebars and pull quotes are useful features that add interest to a design and break up the sea of text on a page while drawing attention to special pieces of information. Word provides a variety of predesigned text boxes to use for sidebars and pull quotes.

Insert a Predesigned Text Box

(1) Switch to Print Layout view if you aren't already in that view.

(2) On the Insert tab, click the Text Box button, and, in the gallery that appears, click the text-box design you like.

(3) Select any sample text in the text box, and paste or type your replacement text.

(4) Click the outer boundary of the text box, and drag it to the location you want.

(5) Use any of the tools on the Text Box Styles and Text Box Tools Format tabs to modify the text box itself, or use the formatting tools on the Home tab to modify the text.

(6) Click outside the text box to resume working on the main content of your document.

See Also

"Creating Custom Text Boxes" on pages 154–155 for information about creating your own customized text box and flowing text between two or more text boxes.

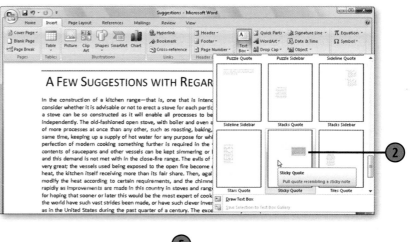

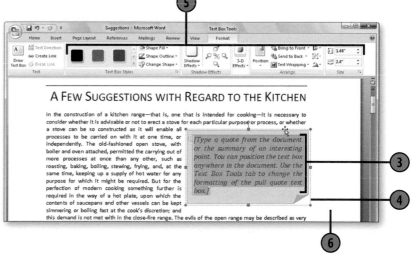

Creating Custom Text Boxes

You can use text boxes to put certain text wherever you want it, in just about any design you can come up with. You can draw attention to content that you want to stand out and be noticed, whether it's a note, a sidebar, a pull quote, a sideways heading, or even just a decoration. You can also create a series of text boxes where the text flows from one box to the next.

Create a Text Box

1. On the Insert tab, click the Text Box button, and click Draw Text Box in the gallery.

2. Hold down the left mouse button and drag out a text box to approximately the size you want.

3. Use the tools on the Text Box Tools Format tab to format the text box, and to set the text wrapping and text direction.

4. Type or paste the text you want. Use the tools on the Home tab to format the text.

5. Drag the Sizing handles to fine-tune the shape of the text box.

6. Click the Position button to position the text box at an exact location, or drag the text box to the location you want.

7. To save the formatted text box for future use, select it, click Text Box on the Insert tab, choose Save Selection To Text Box Gallery, and use the Create New Building Block dialog box to save the text box.

Tip

If you try to format or save a text box but your options are grayed (unavailable), you've probably selected the text area instead of the whole text box. Click the outside border of the text box to select the whole text box.

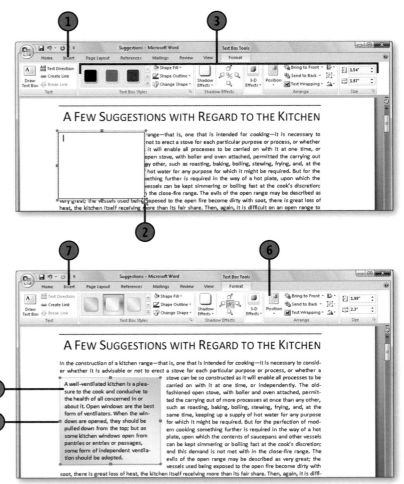

Link Text Box Text

1 Create, format, and position the text boxes into which you want to flow your text. Some or all of the text boxes can be contained in shapes if you want to create special effects.

2 Click the first text box to select it, and type or paste the text you want.

3 On the Text Box Tools Format tab, click the Create Link button.

4 Click inside the text box into which you want to flow the text.

5 Add line breaks or blank paragraphs to control the way the text flows from one text box to another.

6 Adjust the size and position of each text box if necesssary.

7 If you want to link additional text boxes, select the last linked box and repeat steps 3 and 4.

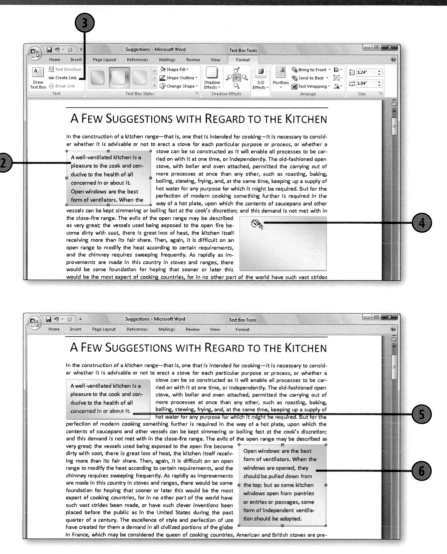

See Also

"Formatting a Shape" on page 130 for information about using a text box with a shape to create special effects with your text.

Tip

To select all the text in all the linked text boxes, click in one of the boxes and press Ctrl+A.

Creating a Dropped Capital Letter

A *drop cap,* sometimes called a *fancy first letter,* adds style and interest to a document and attracts the reader's eye to the page. Drop caps are typically used at the beginning of chapters or sections, as in this book.

Create a Drop Cap

1. Click at the right of the first letter of your paragraph.

2. On the Insert tab, click the Drop Cap button, and point to the different choices to see the effect. Click the type of drop cap you want.

3. If you want to change the font, the number of lines over which the drop cap extends, or the distance between the drop cap and the text, click Drop Cap again, and click Drop Cap Options in the gallery to display the Drop Cap dialog box.

4. Do any of the following to customize the drop cap:

   • Specify a different font.

   • Specify a different number of lines over which you want the drop cap to extend.

   • Specify an increased or decreased horizontal distance between the drop cap and the text.

5. Click OK.

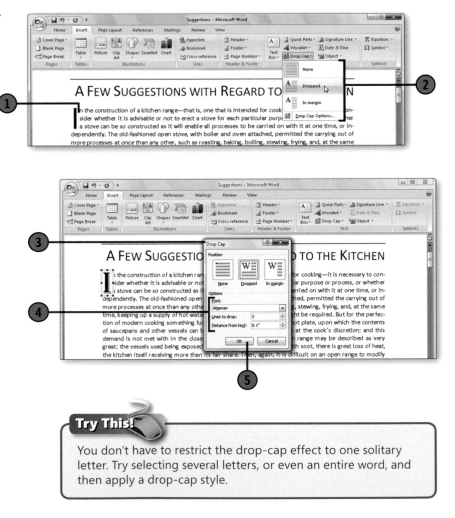

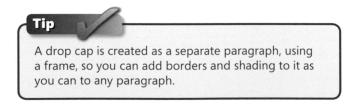

Tip

A drop cap is created as a separate paragraph, using a frame, so you can add borders and shading to it as you can to any paragraph.

Try This!

You don't have to restrict the drop-cap effect to one solitary letter. Try selecting several letters, or even an entire word, and then apply a drop-cap style.

Creating Footnotes and Endnotes

Word makes it so easy to add footnotes and/or endnotes to a document! Endnotes are just like footnotes, except that endnotes appear all together at the end of a document (or a section) instead of at the foot of each page. Word numbers the footnotes in one number series and the endnotes in a different series or format. If you add or delete a footnote or an endnote, Word automatically renumbers the appropriate series. Word also estimates how much space is required for the footnote and, if a footnote is too long for the page, automatically continues it on the next page.

Insert a Footnote or an Endnote

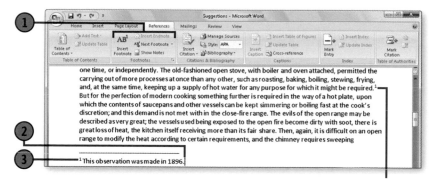

1. On the References tab, with the insertion point located where you want the footnote or endnote reference mark to appear in your document, click the Insert Footnote button for a footnote or the Insert Endnote button for an endnote.

2. Type your footnote or endnote text.

3. Double-click the footnote or endnote number to return to the place in your document where you inserted the footnote.

The footnote mark

Tip

You enter footnote/endnote text directly on the page in Print Layout view. In Web Layout, Outline, and Draft views, you enter the text in a Footnote pane that appears at the bottom of the window when you insert the mark.

Change the Reference Mark

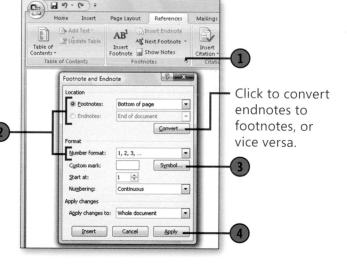

1. On the References tab, click the Footnote & Endnote button.

2. Specify where you want the footnotes or endnotes to appear, and click the numbering series you want.

3. Click to display the Symbol dialog box, choose a symbol for the footnote or endnote mark, and click OK.

4. Click Apply.

Click to convert endnotes to footnotes, or vice versa.

Creating Cross-References

Cross-references are valuable tools in a long and informative document, but you have to be *extremely* well organized if you're planning to insert them manually, especially if you do a lot of editing and rewriting. It's much easier to let Word do the work for you! Word will keep track of all your cross-references and will keep all the information current. Word can even insert your cross-references as hyperlinks in an online document.

Create a Cross-Reference

① Type the beginning text of your cross-reference.

② On the References tab, click the Cross-Reference button to display the Cross-Reference dialog box.

③ Specify the type of item to be cross-referenced.

④ Specify the type of cross-reference to be inserted.

⑤ Select this check box if you want to create a hyperlink to the section of the document being cross-referenced. (A hyperlink is useful only when a document is being read on line.)

⑥ Select the cross-reference.

⑦ Click Insert.

⑧ Continue using the Cross-Reference dialog box to insert cross-references. Click Close when you've finished.

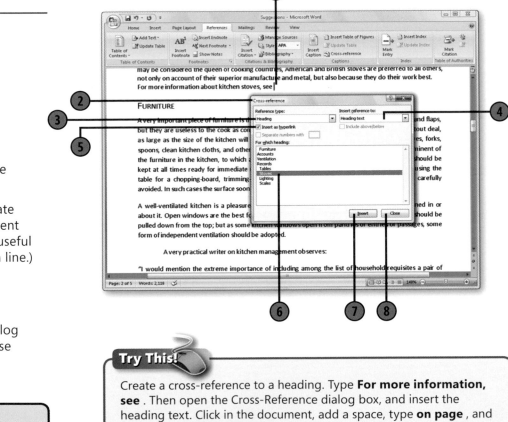

See Also

"Inserting a Bookmark" on the facing page for information about creating a bookmark.

Try This!

Create a cross-reference to a heading. Type **For more information, see** . Then open the Cross-Reference dialog box, and insert the heading text. Click in the document, add a space, type **on page** , and use the Cross-Reference dialog box to insert the page number for the heading. (Insert a space after *see* and *page*.)

Inserting a Bookmark

Bookmarks are useful reference markers in your document that you can use for such tasks as creating cross-references, creating an index, inserting hyperlinks, or just jumping around in your document.

Create a Bookmark

① Click in your document where you want to insert the bookmark, or select all the text you want to include in the reference.

② On the Insert tab, click the Bookmark button to display the Bookmark dialog box.

③ Type a unique name to describe the bookmark. Don't include any spaces or punctuation marks in the name.

④ Click Add.

In a document containing bookmarks, on the Home tab, click the down arrow at the right of the Find button, and choose Go To from the drop-down menu. On the Go To tab of the Find And Replace dialog box, click Bookmark in the Go To What list, select a bookmark you want to go to, and click Next. Continue selecting different bookmarks and clicking Next. Click Close when you've finished.

Tip

You can use the Bookmark dialog box for more than just creating bookmarks. For example, if you don't know what an existing bookmark is marking, select it, and then click the Go To button to find the content in your document that's marked by that bookmark. Then, if you decide that you don't need that bookmark, select it in the list, and click Delete. Close the dialog box when you've finished.

Inserting Information with Smart Tags

Word searches through your document for certain text that it recognizes (names, phone numbers, stock symbols, and so on) and, when it finds that text, attaches a *smart tag* to it. You use the smart tag to obtain additional information about an item or to perform some type of action. Because smart tags are add-ins, there are many different types available, depending on which ones are installed on your computer.

Use the Tags

 Look through your document for text with the purplish-red dotted underline that indicates a smart tag.

 Point to the text and wait for the Smart Tag Actions button to appear.

 Click the Smart Tag Actions button.

 In the drop-down list that appears, click the action you want to take. The actions listed depend on the type of data represented by the text (an address or a name, for example) and the type of smart tag being used.

Try This!

Click the Office button, and then click the Word Options button to display the Word Options dialog box. Click the AutoCorrect Options button in the Proofing category. On the Smart Tags tab, select the check boxes for the smart tags you want to use and clear the check boxes for the tags you don't want to use. Make sure the Label Text With Smart Tags check box is selected. Click More Smart Tags to see if there are other tags you want to use. In the Word Options dialog box, click Recheck Document, and then click OK.

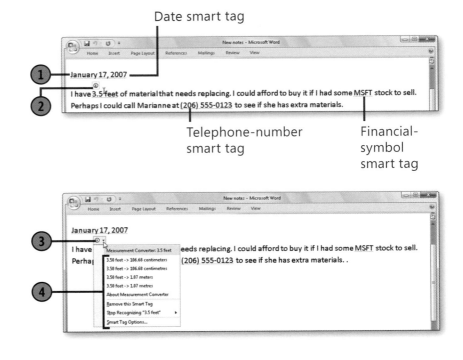

Date smart tag

Telephone-number smart tag

Financial-symbol smart tag

Tip

Note the difference between smart tags and Actions buttons. A smart tag identifies a certain type of text. An Actions button lists the actions you can perform. Some Actions buttons, such as the AutoCorrect and Paste Options buttons, aren't associated with smart tags.

Inserting a Watermark

A *watermark* is some text or a picture (a company logo, for example) that sits "behind" the main text. It appears on every printed page as if it were part of the paper. You can create a picture watermark or a text watermark, but you can't have both on the same page.

Create a Watermark

1. On the Page Layout tab, click the Watermark button, and choose the watermark you want from the gallery that appears.

2. If none of the existing watermarks is what you want, click Custom Watermark in the gallery to display the Printed Watermark dialog box.

3. To create a text watermark, select Text Watermark, select or type your text, choose your formatting options, and click OK.

4. To create a picture watermark, select Picture Watermark, locate and select the picture file you want to use, choose your formatting options, and click OK.

5. If you decide you don't want a watermark after all, click the Watermark button on the Page Layout tab, and click Remove Watermark in the gallery.

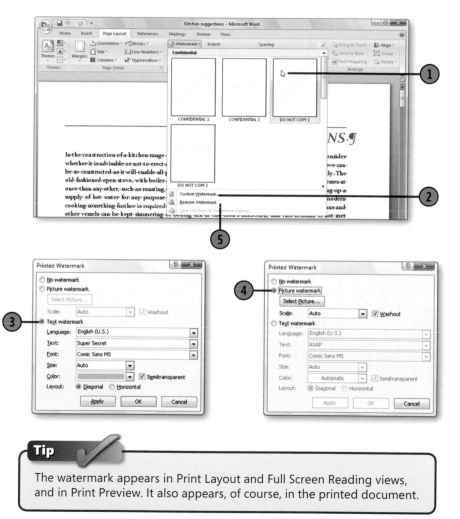

Tip ✓

To have the same watermark automatically appear in every document that you create using a particular template, create the watermark in that template. To have it available to all your documents, add it to the Watermark gallery.

Tip ✓

The watermark appears in Print Layout and Full Screen Reading views, and in Print Preview. It also appears, of course, in the printed document.

Adding Document Properties

Document *properties* are information fields about your document: for example, author, document name, subject, title, and so on. You can place many of these fields directly into your document to insert this information or, if it's missing, to enter it. You can also review the document properties, complete missing information, and even create custom properties. These properties are useful for many other purposes too, including filing, classifying, searching, and identifying documents.

Add Properties to Your Document

① Click in the document where you want the property to appear.

② On the Insert tab, click the Quick Parts button.

③ Point to Document Property on the drop-down menu, and click the property you want to insert.

④ Word inserts a content control that contains the property information.

⑤ If there is no information for that property, or the information is incorrect, type it in. That information will automatically be added to the document property.

⑥ Click outside the content control to see only the content, not the control.

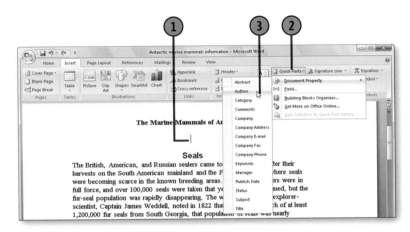

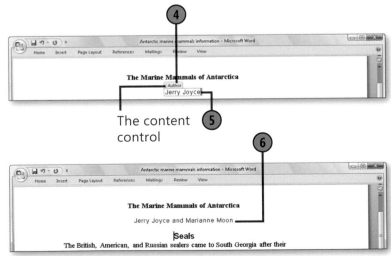

The content control

> **Tip**
>
> If you want the information you've inserted not to change even if the property information does change, right-click the content control, and choose Remove Content Control from the shortcut menu.

Add Properties to the File

(1) Open the Office menu, point to Prepare, and, in the gallery that appears, click Properties to display the Document Properties Information Panel.

(2) Complete and/or correct any missing or incorrect information.

(3) If you want to add more properties, click Document Properties, and choose Advanced Properties from the drop-down menu to display the Properties dialog box.

(4) On the Custom tab, select a property or type a new property.

(5) Complete the information.

(6) Click Add.

(7) Repeat steps 4 through 6 for any other properties.

(8) Click OK.

(9) Click Close.

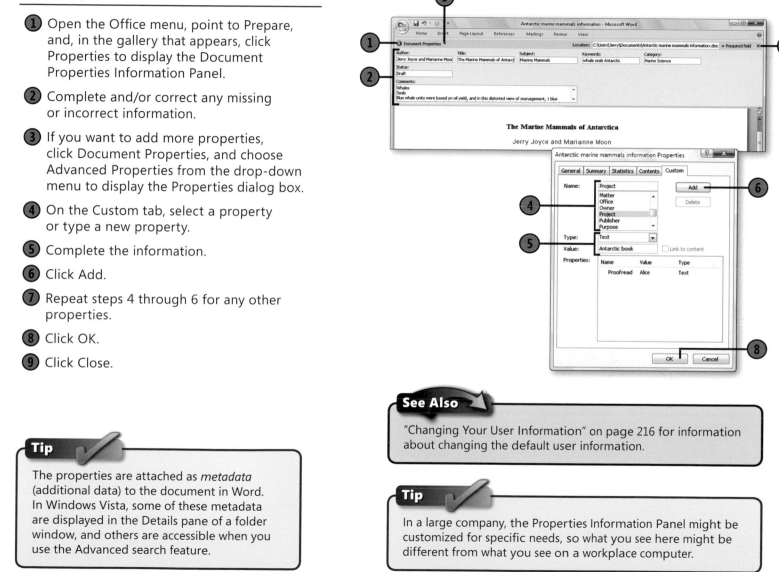

See Also

"Changing Your User Information" on page 216 for information about changing the default user information.

Tip

The properties are attached as *metadata* (additional data) to the document in Word. In Windows Vista, some of these metadata are displayed in the Details pane of a folder window, and others are accessible when you use the Advanced search feature.

Tip

In a large company, the Properties Information Panel might be customized for specific needs, so what you see here might be different from what you see on a workplace computer.

Having Word Insert Information for You

To include in a document some information that might change—the number of words, for example, or the number of the current section of the document—you can insert a *field*. A field is a bit of code that's used to insert some information or to execute a task automatically. Word often inserts fields automatically when you use elements such as captions, cross-references, dates, page numbers, and tables of contents. However, you have more choices and more options for customizing the way a field works when you insert it directly—and there are, in fact, some fields that can be used *only* when you've inserted them directly.

Insert a Field

1 Click in the document where you want the field to appear. On the Insert tab, click the Quick Parts button, and choose Field from the menu to display the Field dialog box.

2 Click a category in the list, or click All to browse through all the field names.

3 Click a field name.

4 Specify any information or select an available option to customize and format the field result. The Field Properties list varies depending on the field name you selected.

5 Select or clear check boxes, or select available options for the results you want. Not all fields provide options, and the options that are provided vary by field.

6 Select this check box if you want any direct formatting of the field result to be preserved when the field is updated. Clear the check box if you want the field result to always use the specified paragraph formatting.

7 Click OK.

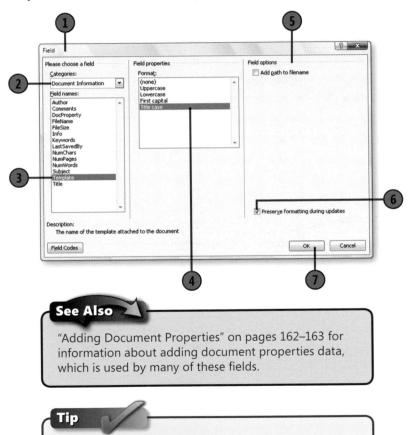

See Also

"Adding Document Properties" on pages 162–163 for information about adding document properties data, which is used by many of these fields.

Tip

Word usually updates fields when you open or print a document.

Adding Captions to Tables and Figures

Figures, tables, equations, and other similar elements in a technical document often need captions that number these elements consecutively and provide identifying, qualifying, and explanatory text. Word can label and number these items and can keep track of the numbering so that if you add or delete an item in the sequence, Word will automatically renumber the entire sequence.

Create a Caption

1 Select the item to be captioned.

2 On the References tab, click the Insert Caption button to display the Caption dialog box.

3 Specify a label or a category for the caption.

4 If there isn't an appropriate label in the list, click New Label, type the label name you want, and click OK.

5 Specify a location for the caption.

6 Type the caption text. Don't change the caption label or number.

7 Click OK.

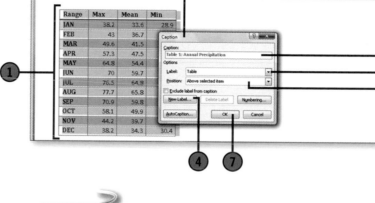

Tip

Click the AutoCaption button if you want Word to automatically number certain types of items, such as Excel charts or bitmap pictures, when you insert them into your document. If you do use the AutoCaption feature, be sure to check your document carefully to verify that each item you want to have a caption actually has one.

Try This!

After you've added all the captions to your graphics and tables, click the Select Browse Object button below the vertical scroll bar, and select to browse by Graphics. Press Ctrl+Home to move to the beginning of your document. Click the Next Graphic arrow (or press Ctrl+Page Down) to find the first graphic in your document, and verify that it has the correct caption. Continue searching for graphics and verifying that their captions are correct. When you reach the end of your document move back to the beginning, select to browse by Tables, and verify that all the captions for your tables are correct.

Creating a Table of Figures, Equations, or Tables

A technical document often contains a table that lists all the figures or illustrations that appear in the document, a separate list if equations are included, and yet another list if the document has numerous tables. If you've inserted captions for these items, Word can generate a table of figures, equations, and/or tables for you.

Create the Table

① With captions added to all your figures, click in your document where you want the table of figures to appear.

② On the References tab, click the Insert Table Of Figures button to display the Table Of Figures dialog box.

③ Select these check boxes if you want page numbers included, and specify how you want them to be aligned.

④ Select this check box if you want hyperlinks included when the document is viewed in Web Layout view.

⑤ Select the type and style of the table you want.

⑥ Select the type of list to be compiled (Equation, Figure, or Table).

⑦ Clear this check box if you want the caption, but not the number of the item, to appear.

⑧ Click OK.

Tip

If you created a new category when you added captions, you can create a table based on that category.

See Also

"Adding Captions to Tables and Figures" on page 165 for information about adding captions to your figures.

"Creating a Custom Table of Tables or Figures" on page 198 for information about modifying the design of a table and creating a table without using Word's caption feature.

Creating a Table of Contents

Provided your document is organized by styles or you have assigned outline levels to your heading paragraphs, it's a snap to have Word create a well-organized table of contents for you. Word comes with predesigned table of contents layouts. The table is inserted as a field in a content control, so after you've created the table, you can change its layout by choosing a different design. You can also update the table if you change the content of your document.

Set the Outline Text

① In Outline view, scroll through the document, verifying that any paragraph you want to appear in the table of contents has a style that uses the appropriate level 1, level 2, or level 3 outline level, and that any paragraph you don't want to include has either an outline level of 4 or below or a Body Text outline level. If a paragraph you want to include doesn't have a style with the appropriate outline level assigned to it, click in the paragraph and apply the appropriate style.

② If you want to include or exclude a paragraph but don't want to change its style, click the Add Text button on the References tab, and click the outline level you want to apply.

③ Switch to Print Layout view, and click in the document where you want the table of contents to appear.

④ On the References tab, click the Table Of Contents button, and select the style and type of table of contents you want to insert.

Tip

To update the table of contents after you've made changes to your document, click the Update Table button on the References tab.

See Also

"Creating a Custom Table of Contents" on pages 196–197 for information about modifying which styles are used for the table of contents, the number of levels used in the table, and the numbering format.

"Organizing with Styles" on page 208 for information about assigning outlining levels to styles.

Inserting a Citation

When your writing references outside sources and/or works by other people, including books, articles, legal decisions, or whatever other items you reference, you'll need to cite them. Word provides a rich environment for entering, compiling, formatting, and inserting citations into your documents. If you're working in a company, a school, or an agency that frequently creates documents that include citations, you probably already have the data entered in bibliographies, ready to be dropped in. However, if you don't have access to existing bibliographies, you can enter the data once and then save it for future use.

Add Existing Citations

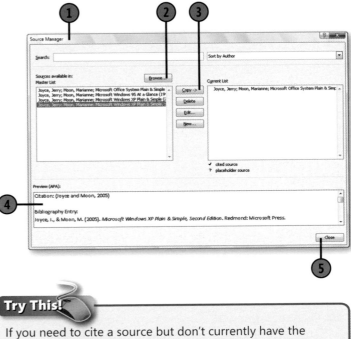

1 On the References tab, click the Manage Sources button to display the Source Manager dialog box.

2 If the default source file isn't the one you want, click Browse. Use the Open Source List window to locate the source file you want, and then click OK. You can use numerous source files to copy citations into your document.

3 If citations exist in the source file that aren't already in your document, and you'll eventually want to add them, select the citations you want, and click Copy. Use the Sort and Search tools if you need to find citations in a large source file, and add those you want to your document.

4 Select any citation you're not sure of to inspect the information, and then decide whether or not to add it to your document.

5 Click Close when you've finished.

Tip

All citations are tagged as fields, and you can easily modify their styles by changing the Citations & Bibliography Style on the References tab.

Try This!

If you need to cite a source but don't currently have the citation information, don't worry. Just click in the document where you want to place the citation, click the Insert Citation button on the References tab, and choose Add New Placeholder from the menu. When you eventually have the information, click the placeholder, click the Citation Options down arrow at the bottom-right of the content control, and choose Edit Source from the drop-down menu. Enter the information in the Edit Source dialog box that appears.

Insert a Citation

(1) Select the citation style you want for all of your citations.

(2) Click in your document where you want the citation to appear.

(3) On the References tab, click the Insert Citation button, and, if the citation you want is listed, click it.

(4) If the citation isn't listed, click Add New Source to display the Create Source dialog box.

(5) Select the type of citation you want.

(6) Enter the information for the citation.

(7) Either use the proposed citation tag name or enter a unique name.

(8) Click OK.

Select this check box if you want to include additional bibliographic information.

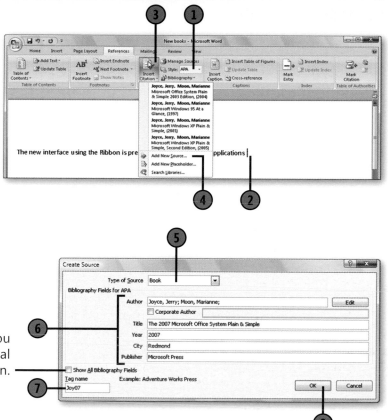

Tip

The citation is placed inside a content control in your document. To edit the citation or the source, or to convert the citation into static text that can be edited but will no longer be automatically updated if the citation changes, point to the content control, click the Citation Options down arrow that appears, and choose what you want to do from the drop-down menu.

Inserting a Bibliography

A bibliography is a list containing the relevant information for all the sources that were cited in a document. Using the Bibliography tool, you not only automatically generate the list, but you can make sure that only the references cited in your document are included. The bibliography will automatically be updated when you add citations to your document, or when you add sources to or remove them from the Source Manager dialog box.

Insert a Bibliography

1 On the References tab, click the Manage Sources button to display the Source Manager dialog box.

2 Select any item marked as a placeholder.

3 Click Edit to display the Edit Source dialog box. Complete the information for that citation, and click OK. Continue editing and completing all placeholders.

4 Select any item that isn't marked as being cited in the document, and click Delete to remove it from the list. Click Close when you've finished.

5 Click in your document where you want the bibliography to appear.

6 Select the style you want to use for both your citations and the bibliography.

7 On the References tab, click the Bibliography button to preview the Bibliography and the Works Cited lists, based on your selected style. If you don't like the appearance of either, change the style.

8 Click to insert the Bibliography or the Works Cited list when it looks the way you want.

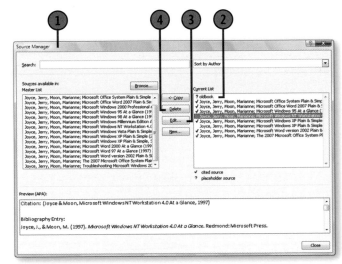

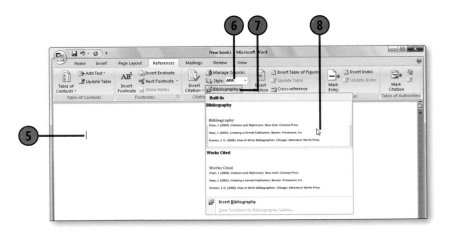

Creating a Table of Authorities

Tables of authorities are used to cite precedents, laws, rules, regulations, and other terminology and language peculiar to the legal world. You need to mark the citations in your document and provide the short form of the citation as well. Once the document has been marked up, you can assemble one or more tables of authorities, as needed.

Tag and Compile the Citations

The Insert Table Of Authorities button

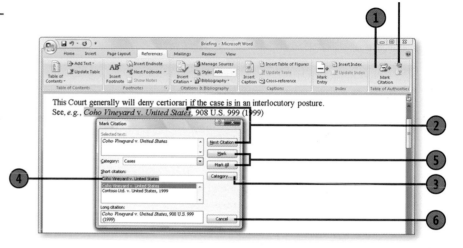

1 With your document completed and containing the citations you want, on the References tab, click the Mark Citation button.

2 In the Mark Citation dialog box that appears, do either of the following:

- Click Next Citation to direct Word to find and highlight the next citation in your document.

- Click in your document, and select the text of a citation.

3 In the Mark Citation dialog box, click Category, and, in the Edit Category dialog box, select a category for the citation. Click OK.

4 Edit the text of the short description for the citation.

5 Click either Mark to insert a field marking this entry or Mark All to insert fields marking every instance of this citation in your document.

6 Repeat steps 2 through 5, if necessary, to mark all the citations in your document. Click Close when you've finished.

7 With the insertion point where you want the table of authorities to appear in your document, click the Insert Table Of Authorities button.

8 In the Table Of Authorities dialog box, select the category to be included in the table.

9 Select your formatting options, and then click OK to insert the table.

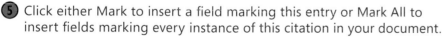

Creating an Index

If you're not blessed with the expertise of a professional indexer, Word is the next best thing. It simplifies and automates the complex and arduous mechanics of indexing. Word places a hidden-text tag next to each indexed item, so no matter how the page numbers change, the index is kept current. Your index can include multiple levels, cross-references, and even a range of pages when an indexed item extends beyond a single page.

Tag the Entries

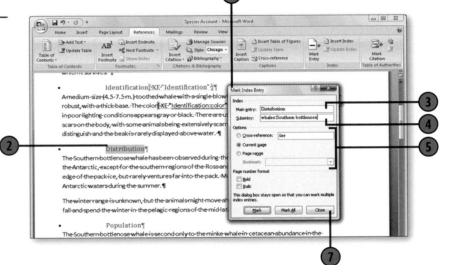

1. On the References tab, click the Mark Entry button to display the Mark Index Entry dialog box.

2. In your document, select the text you want to index.

3. Click the Mark Index Entry dialog box to make it active. The text you selected appears in the Main Entry box.

4. Type any subentries. To specify more than one level of subentry, separate subentry levels with colons.

5. Specify options as follows:

   • Click Cross-Reference, and type the topic to be cross-referenced.

   • Click Current Page to list the page number next to the entry.

   • Click Page Range, and select the bookmark that marks the entire text of the entry. The text must be bookmarked before it can be included as an entry.

6. Click in the document, select your next index entry, and repeat steps 3 through 5.

7. When you've finished, click Close, and save the document.

See Also

"Inserting a Bookmark" on page 159 for information about bookmarking text.

Compile the Index

1. Press Ctrl+End to move to the end of the document.

2. On the References tab, click the Insert Index button to display the Index dialog box.

3. Select the type of index you want.

4. Specify the number of columns the index will occupy on the page.

5. Clear this check box to have the page numbers placed immediately next to the entry, or select the check box to have Word insert a tab and align the page numbers to the right edge of each column. If you selected the check box, choose the type of tab leader you want between the index entry and the page number.

6. Specify the format you want for the index. If you chose From Template, click the Modify button to change the styles used for the index.

7. Click OK.

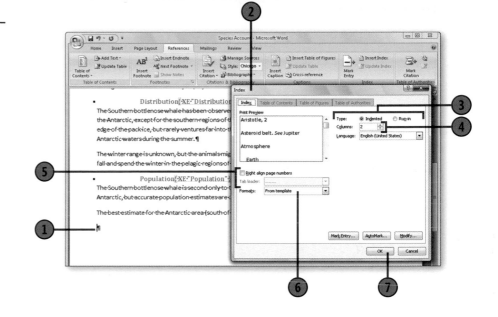

Try This!

To cross-reference a related entry but still include a page number, tag the entry twice—once using "See also" in the Cross-Reference box, and again with the Current Page option selected.

Tip

The Mark All button in the Mark Index Entry dialog box finds every instance in your document of the text you've selected, and marks each instance with the tag information you entered in the dialog box. The AutoMark button in the Index dialog box lets you specify a document that contains a list of items you want Word to mark automatically for your index. If you use either of these automated techniques, you'll need to go through your document and carefully verify these index entries.

8

Reviewing and Finalizing

In this section:

- Marking Changes in a Document
- Comparing Changes in a Document
- Combining Reviews
- Comparing Documents Side by Side
- Comparing Different Parts of a Single Document
- Standardizing the Formatting
- Proofreading in Another Language
- Checking the Word Count
- Checking the Compatibility
- Finalizing Your Document

If you send out a lot of writing to be reviewed, edited, or commented on by your peers or coworkers, you'll find that Microsoft Office Word 2007 provides just the tools you need to simplify the work that faces you when all those separate reviews are returned. Word's Track Changes feature keeps track of the changes made by each reviewer, and you can then accept or reject those changes. If your reviewers haven't used the Track Changes feature, don't despair! You can use Word's Compare feature to compare the original version with the edited version, and you can specify which elements of the document you want marked to show changes. You can also use the Window Split bar to compare different sections of the same document on your screen. When you've reviewed all the reviews and accepted or rejected the changes, you can then merge all the disparate pieces into one final document. Word also helps you find and fix formatting inconsistencies.

If you sometimes use other languages in your work, provided you have the appropriate dictionaries and spelling and grammar checkers installed, Word can proofread your foreign-language document. And, when you need to stay within a certain word count or page count in your writing, Word obligingly keeps track so that you can see when you've exceeded your limit.

Marking Changes in a Document

When your document needs to be reviewed, edited, or changed in any way, you can use Word's Track Changes feature to mark the changes that you and your coworkers have made. With Track Changes turned on, Word marks all additions, deletions, moves, and even formatting changes. If you need to, you can also add comments. When you're reviewing the edited document, you can accept or reject any change or comment, view the changes made by individual reviewers, and even view the document as it was before any of the changes were made. You can also view the document as it would look if you accepted all the changes.

Review a Document

1. Open the document to be reviewed.

2. On the Review tab, click the Track Changes button if it isn't already selected.

3. Click Final Showing Markup to see your changes.

4. If you want to monitor your changes, click the Reviewing Pane button.

5. Edit the content as usual. Note that text you insert is underlined, text you delete has strikethrough formatting, text you move to a location has a double underline, and text you move from a location has a double strikethrough.

6. To insert a comment, select the text you want to comment on, and click New Comment.

7. Type your comment in the balloon that appears or in the Reviewing pane, depending on your settings.

8. Switch to Final view, review the document for any errors, and then save and close it.

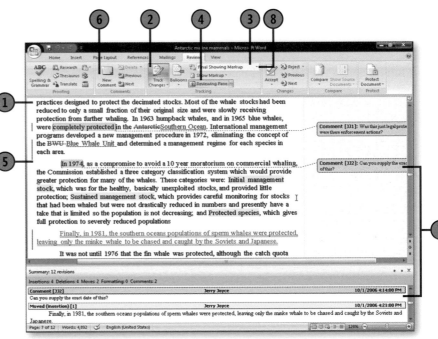

Tip

In Draft view, all the changes are marked in the document, and any descriptions and comments are displayed in the Reviewing pane on the left side or at the bottom of the window. In Page Layout view, click the Balloons button to specify what content is placed in the balloons.

Review a Review

1. Open a document that has been reviewed and edited. If it's marked as Read-Only, save it using a different name.

2. On the Review tab, click the Track Changes button, if it's selected, to turn it off.

3. Switch to Final Showing Markup view if it isn't already selected.

4. Click Show Markup, and specify the types of changes you want to be displayed. If you don't want to see the markup from every reviewer, specify which reviewers' changes you do want to see.

5. Click Next to locate a change. Click Accept to include the change or Reject to delete the change. Continue choosing Accept or Reject to review and incorporate changes. To accept all the changes, click the down arrow on the Accept button and choose Accept All Changes In Document from the drop-down menu. To reject all changes, click the down arrow on the Reject button, and choose Reject All Changes In Document.

6. When you've finished, switch to Final view, review the document for any errors, and then save and close it.

Tip

To highlight text without adding a comment, click the Highlight button on the Home tab, and drag the mouse pointer over the content you want to highlight.

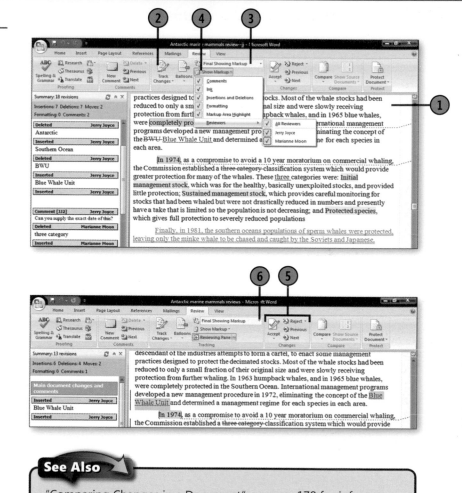

See Also

"Comparing Changes in a Document" on page 178 for information about comparing two versions of the same document and marking the changes.

"Combining Reviews" on page 180 for information about combining separate files that contain marked changes by different reviewers.

Comparing Changes in a Document

If you have two versions of the same document, and changes have been made but not marked in one of them, how do you know what changes were made? Using Word's Compare feature, you can compare the original with the revised document and have Word mark all the changes.

Set Up the Comparison

1 On the Review tab, click the Compare button and, in the gallery that appears, choose Compare to display the Compare Documents dialog box.

2 Specify the original document by clicking either the down arrow to see a list of recently used documents or the Browse button to locate and select the document.

3 Specify the revised document.

4 If you want to change the name assigned to a reviewer's changes—to Reviewer 1, for example—enter the new name.

5 If the More button is displayed, click it to show the options for the comparison. (When the More button has been clicked, it's replaced by the Less button.) Clear the check boxes for any items you don't want to be marked, and select the check boxes for the items you do want to be marked.

6 Specify how and where you want the changes to be shown.

7 Click OK.

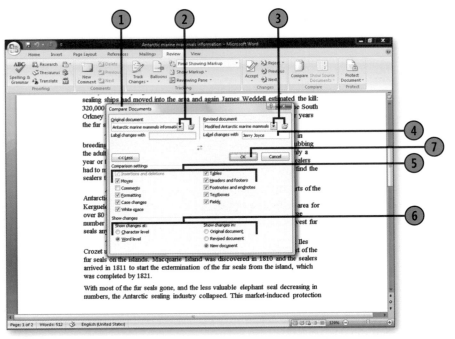

Tip

You can use this method of comparison to create legal black-lining in contracts or agreements so that each party can see how the original document was revised.

Review the Changes

1. On the Review tab, click the Show Source Documents button, and specify whether you want to see the source documents. If so, specify which ones you want to see.

2. Click the Reviewing Pane button to show or hide the Reviewing pane. Click the down arrow at the right of the Reviewing Pane button to change the location of the Reviewing pane.

3. Scroll through the main document, noting the changes. As you scroll, the source documents, if shown, are simultaneously scrolled so that the same parts of the documents are shown in all windows.

4. Save the main document with the marked changes.

5. Review the main document, using the same methods you normally use when you're reviewing any document that contains marked changes.

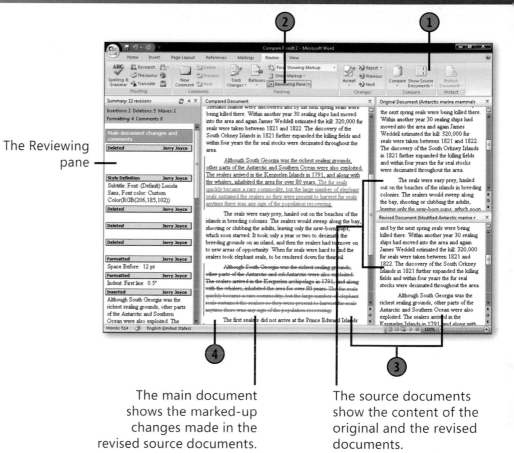

The Reviewing pane

The main document shows the marked-up changes made in the revised source documents.

The source documents show the content of the original and the revised documents.

Combining Reviews

When you send a document out for review, you'll usually receive several separately reviewed and/or edited copies of the document. How do you combine all those separate changes into one document? Provided your reviewers used Word's Track Changes feature, you can combine all their changes and comments by merging the separate documents into a single document so that you can easily create a final version.

Merge the Documents

1. On the Review tab, in any document, click the Compare button and, in the gallery that appears, choose Combine to display the Combine Documents dialog box.

2. Specify the document that contains the first set of reviews as your original document, and the document that contains additional reviews as the revised document.

3. Click the More button if you want to modify which changes are displayed and in which document. (When the More button has been clicked, it's replaced by the Less button.) Select the check boxes for the items you want to be marked as changed.

4. Specify whether you want each character or each word change to be noted, and specify where you want the changes to be shown.

5. Click OK, and then save the merged document.

6. Repeat steps 1 through 5 to merge the other reviews into the combined final document. Use standard reviewing methods to review the changes in the document.

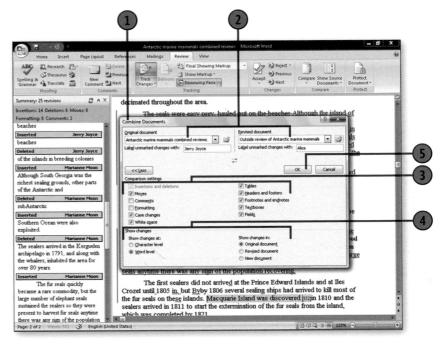

Tip

When you combine two documents, you can include the formatting changes from only one of the documents. It's a good idea, therefore, to clear the Formatting check box if you want to keep the formatting changes marked in the original document; otherwise, you can end up with only the formatting changes made in the revised document.

Comparing Documents Side by Side

When you want to look at two documents simultaneously to compare their content, Word will place the documents in adjacent windows. If the documents are similar enough, you can have Word scroll through both of them at the same time, or you can scroll through the documents one at a time.

View the Documents

1. Open the two documents you want to view and compare.

2. On the View tab, in one document, click the View Side By Side button.

3. If a dialog box appears and asks you which document you want to view, select the document you want, and click OK.

4. If you don't want the documents to scroll together, on the View tab, click the Window button to expand the window section (if it's collapsed), and click Synchronous Scrolling to turn off the scrolling. Click Synchronous Scrolling again to resume the coordinated scrolling.

5. Scroll through the documents. When you've finished, click the Window button again, and click the View Side By Side button to turn off that view.

Tip

If the two windows don't start at the same part of the document when you start scrolling through them, turn off Synchronous Scrolling, scroll through one window until it displays the same top line as the other window, and turn Synchronous Scrolling back on.

Tip

To review more than two documents at one time, open all the documents you want to review and close any that you don't want to include in your review. In any one of the open documents, click Arrange All on the View tab.

Comparing Different Parts of a Single Document

Sometimes, especially in a very long document, you want to see two different parts of the document at the same time.

You can do this by splitting the Word window horizontally and scrolling through the separate panes independently.

Split the Window

1 With the document you want to review open and set to the view you want to use, drag the Window Split bar into the position you want.

2 Scroll through the active pane to the part of the document you want to see.

3 Click in the other pane to make it active, and scroll through that pane to the part of the document you want to see.

4 Edit or format the content in either pane.

5 When you've finished, double-click the Split bar to remove the split and return to a single window.

The Window Split bar

See Also

"Comparing Documents Side by Side" on page 181 for information about comparing two documents side by side.

Standardizing the Formatting

A document can quickly develop a chaotic look when you apply various types of direct formatting to your text. Word provides several tools that can help you keep track of the formatting, that can indicate where small but significant changes to the formatting exist, and that can allow you to quickly change one style or type of formatting to another.

Find Formatting Inconsistencies

1. Choose Word Options from the Office menu, click the Advanced category in the left pane of the Word Options dialog box, and select the Keep Track Of Formatting and the Mark Formatting Inconsistencies check boxes, if they're not already selected. Click OK.

2. Right-click any text that's marked with blue squiggles.

3. From the shortcut menu, choose

   - The suggested fix to standardize the formatting.

   - Ignore Once to keep the existing formatting for this one instance.

   - Ignore Rule to keep the existing formatting for all instances in the document.

4. Continue reviewing the document for inconsistencies.

Try This!

In Draft view, on the Home tab, click the Styles button in the Styles section of the Ribbon. Click the Style Inspector button in the Styles pane. Click the Reveal Formatting button in the Style Inspector pane. Choose Word Options from the Office menu, and, in the Display section of the Advanced tab, specify the size of the style area. Click OK. Now move around in your document, and select text to see what information you can get from the style area and the various panes.

Proofreading in Another Language

Word speaks many languages. Using the Microsoft Office language tools, Word can automatically identify which paragraphs are in which language. With the proper dictionaries and the spelling and grammar checkers installed, Word can check a multilingual document, using the correct proofing tools for each language. If your document contains only a few scattered words in another language, you can identify those words as being in another language so that they'll be checked correctly. If the proofing tools for a particular language aren't installed, you can identify the words in that language to Word and it will skip them to avoid adding unnecessary spelling and grammar squiggles to the document.

Turn On Office Language Detection

1. Choose Word Options from the Office menu, and, with the Popular category selected, click the Language Settings button to display the Microsoft Office Language Settings 2007 dialog box.

2. On the Editing Languages tab, select a language you want Word to detect, and click Add. Repeat for additional languages.

3. Select the default editing language.

4. Click OK, and then click OK again to close the Word Options dialog box. Close Word and any other open Office programs to implement the settings.

5. Start Word, and open your document. On the Review tab, click the Set Language button in the Proofing section of the Ribbon to display the Language dialog box, and select this check box if it isn't already selected.

6. Click OK to activate language detection.

Tip
If you enable a different language keyboard in Windows, that language is automatically enabled in Word.

Work in Different Languages

1 Type a paragraph in any enabled language other than your default editing language. Word should recognize the different language when you press Enter.

2 Click in the paragraph you just typed, and look at the status bar to confirm that Word properly identified the language.

3 If Word didn't detect the correct language for the paragraph, select the paragraph.

4 On the Review tab, click the Set Language button to display the Language dialog box.

5 Specify the language of the selected text so that Word can check it for spelling and grammar.

6 Click OK.

7 Repeat steps 2 through 6 for any individual words or paragraphs that aren't in your default language and whose language isn't detected by Word.

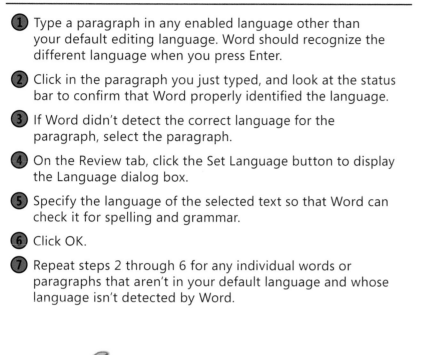

Tip

The languages for which you've installed proofing tools display spelling icons next to their names in the Language dialog box. If you don't see a spelling icon, you'll know that text in that language won't be checked for spelling or grammatical errors.

Tip

The language of the text at the insertion point is identified on the status bar, provided the Language indicator on the status bar is turned on.

See Also

"Show or Hide Items on the Status Bar" on page 212 for information about displaying the Language indicator on the status bar if it isn't currently displayed.

Checking the Word Count

Journalists, students, and even technical writers live by word, line, or page count. Ask an editor or a teacher what's required, and the first words you'll hear are "A 500-word article about...".

Word makes it easy to keep track of how many words you've written by displaying the current word count on the status bar, but you can get additional information just by asking.

Check the Counts

1. Look at the status bar and note your current word count.

2. Click the word count on the status bar to display the Word Count dialog box.

3. Examine the statistics that show the number of pages, words, characters, paragraphs, and lines.

4. Select this check box if you want any text in footnotes and endnotes to be included in your count.

5. Click Close.

Click the Word Count button on the Review tab if the word count isn't visible on the status bar.

Try This!

Create your document. At the end of the document, type **words:**. On the Insert tab, click the Quick Parts button, and then click Field. Click Document Information in the Categories list box, select NumWords, and click OK. Right-click the number, and choose Update Field from the shortcut menu. Now you'll know the number of words in your document (although the count includes the one extra word you just typed).

See Also

"Having Word Insert Information for You" on page 164 for information about inserting fields.

"Show or Hide Items on the Status Bar" on page 212 for information about displaying the word count on the status bar if the word count isn't currently displayed.

Checking the Compatibility

The Word 2007 format and some of its features aren't fully compatible with earlier versions of Word. Although people running earlier versions of Word will be able to open a Word 2007 file using a converter (provided they've installed it), some features and content might be changed or lost. To see which Word 2007 features aren't fully compatible and will be changed or lost, run the Word Compatibility Checker before you distribute the document.

Run the Check

(1) With your document completed and saved, click the Office button.

(2) On the Office menu, point to Prepare, and choose Run Compatibility Checker to display the Microsoft Office Word Compatibility Checker dialog box.

(3) Scroll through the list of items that will be changed or lost.

(4) Click OK.

(5) If you're not sure whether the changes are acceptable, point to Save As on the Office menu, and choose Word 97–2003 Document from the gallery that appears. In the Save As dialog box, enter a different name for the document, and click Save. If the Microsoft Office Word Compatibility Checker dialog box appears, click OK. Scroll through your document and examine the changes to see whether they're acceptable. If they are, distribute your original document; if they aren't, edit the document to eliminate the incompatibilities.

Tip

If you select the check box for checking compatibility in the Microsoft Office Word Compatibility Checker dialog box, this check will be run automatically any time you save a Word 2007 document in the Word 97–2003 format.

Finalizing Your Document

If you've ever released what you thought was the final version of a document, only to find that there were still changes marked on it or that it contained information you didn't want others to see, you know that you don't want to do that again! And if you've ever released a document whose wording made you cringe because someone had edited it without your permission, you don't want that to happen again either. Fortunately, Word provides tools to prevent such embarrassing *faux pas*.

Prepare Your Document

1. Click the Office button, point to Prepare on the drop-down menu, and, in the gallery that appears, click Inspect Document to display the Document Inspector dialog box.

2. Clear the check boxes for the items you want to keep in the document, select the check boxes for the items you don't want to appear in the document, and then click Inspect.

3. In the Document Inspector dialog box, click the Remove All button for each type of item you want to remove. Close the dialog box when you've finished.

4. If you don't want other people who have access to your document to edit it, open the Office menu, point to Prepare, and choose Mark As Final from the submenu. Click OK to confirm that you want to mark the document as final.

5. Close and distribute the document.

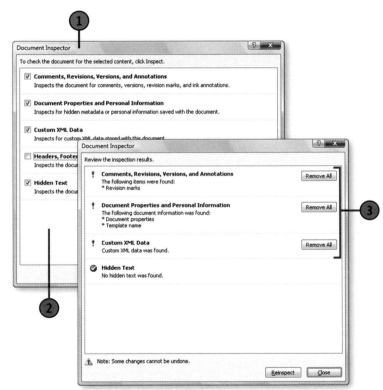

See Also

"Protecting a Document with a Password" on pages 228–229 for information about using additional security settings to prevent changes to your document.

Tip

To edit a document that has been marked as Final, choose Mark As Final again from the Prepare submenu.

9

Customizing Your Content

In this section:

- Creating Your Own Styles
- Creating a Table Style
- Creating a Quick Style Set
- Customizing a Cover Page
- Customizing a Table of Contents
- Customizing a Table of Figures
- Saving Your Customized Table Design
- Customizing a Template
- Designing a Template
- Customizing a List
- Customizing a Multilevel List
- Customizing Page Numbers
- Organizing with Styles

Styles are crucial to the look of any document, and you'll find that Microsoft Office Word 2007 provides a multitude of styles for just about any type of document (or part thereof) that you might need to create, including tables, lists, cover pages, tables of contents, tables of figures, page numbers, and more.

If you need to create a document quickly and have neither the time nor the inclination to do any customizing, you can use the existing styles just as they are to create a professional-looking document with minimal time and effort. If you enjoy the creative aspects of playing around with styles and formatting, you can modify and customize the existing styles to achieve just the look you want. If you still aren't satisfied with the results, you can create your own styles. Whichever way you do it, the great thing is that you need to create a particular style only once; then you can save it and reuse it for all documents of that type.

Word also supplies many generic templates that you can use for memos, letters, reports, and so on, and, as with styles, you can modify and save the templates for future use. If you can't find the right template, you can simply create an original document using the styles you want, and then save that document as a template, which you can then reuse whenever you need it.

Creating Your Own Styles

Styles are critical to creating a professional-looking, consistently formatted document. Microsoft Word provides many styles, but, if you can't find one that's just right for your document, you can create your own style. After you've created it, you can save the style and use it over and over again.

Create a Style

1 Format the text and/or paragraph the way you want, using the tools on the Home tab, and, if necessary, in the Paragraph, Font, Tabs, and Borders And Shading dialog boxes. Select the formatted text if you want to create a character style, or select the entire paragraph if you want to create a linked style or a paragraph style.

2 On the Home tab, click the More button to display the Quick Style gallery, and click Save Selection As A New Quick Style to display the Create New Style From Formatting dialog box.

3 Enter a name for the style.

4 If the style is exactly the way you want it and you'll be using it only in this document, click OK. Otherwise, click Modify.

5 In the expanded Create New Style From Formatting dialog box, make any changes you want to the name, style type, base style, following style, and formatting. Specify whether the style is to be available in just this document or in all documents based on this template, and add any special formatting you want.

6 Click OK.

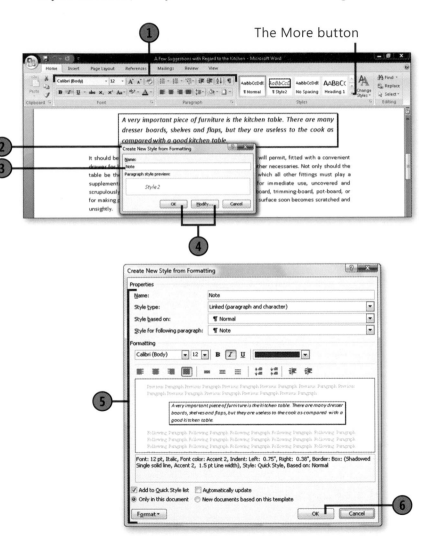

The More button

Modify a Style

1 In the Quick Style gallery, right-click the style you want to modify, and choose Modify from the shortcut menu to display the Modify Style dialog box.

2 Type a new name for the style if you want.

3 Click the style that you want to be automatically applied to the paragraph that follows a linked style or a paragraph style.

4 Use the formatting tools to change any formatting.

5 Select this check box if you want the style to be modified automatically when you apply direct formatting to a paragraph that's using the style. Clear the check box if you want to sometimes use direct formatting without changing the style.

6 Specify whether you want the changes to apply only in the current document or in any document created using the current template.

7 Click to display the dialog boxes you need if you want to apply additional formatting, including text in another language, numbering, borders, and so on.

8 Click OK.

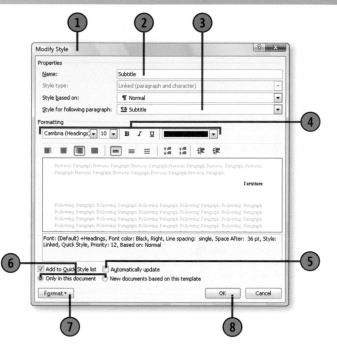

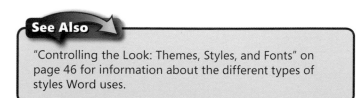

See Also

"Controlling the Look: Themes, Styles, and Fonts" on page 46 for information about the different types of styles Word uses.

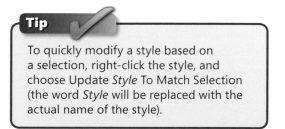

Tip

To quickly modify a style based on a selection, right-click the style, and choose Update *Style* To Match Selection (the word *Style* will be replaced with the actual name of the style).

Creating a Table Style

Tables in Word can look really sophisticated when you apply one of Word's table styles. However, if you can't find an existing table style that you like, you can create your own.

The easiest way to do this is to create a table, apply an existing table style to it, and then modify the formatting to create your own style.

Create a Table Style

1 Create a table, and, on the Table Tools Design tab, apply the table style that's closest to what you have in mind.

2 Click the More button to display the Table Styles gallery, and click Modify Table Style to display the Modify Style dialog box.

3 Enter a new name for your style.

4 Click Whole Table in the drop-down list.

5 Use the formatting tools or click the Format button to specify any formatting that will be common to all the elements of the table—the font, for example. Click another element in the list, and use the formatting tools or click the Format button to redefine the formatting for that element. Continue clicking elements and changing their formatting as necessary.

6 Specify whether you want to have this style available in only this document or in all documents based on the current style.

7 Click OK.

The More button

Creating a Quick Style Set

When you create or modify several styles that you want to use over and over again, you can save the whole group as a single Quick Style set. That way, you can keep all the styles you use in one place and, if you want to, you can remove the styles that you never use.

Create a Quick Style Set

1. Create and/or modify the styles you want in your set, and make sure they're added to the Quick Style gallery.

2. Right-click any styles that you don't want in your style set, and choose Remove From Quick Style Gallery.

3. Click Change Styles to open the gallery, point to Style Set, and choose Save As Quick Style Set from the submenu.

4. In the Save Quick Style Set window that appears, type a name for your style set.

5. Click Save.

6. In a document in which you want to use your new style set, click Change Styles, point to Style Set, and, on the submenu, click the style set you created.

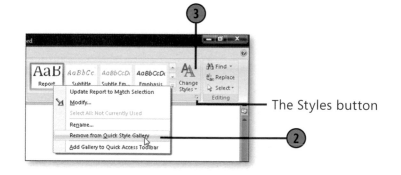

The Styles button

See Also

"Creating Your Own Styles" on pages 190–191 for information about creating and modifying styles.

Tip

To add an existing style to the Quick Style gallery, click the Styles button in the Styles section of the Home tab, right-click the style you want to add, and choose Add To Quick Style Gallery from the shortcut menu.

Creating a Custom Cover Page

Your document's cover page is the first thing your readers see, and it's what makes them want to turn the page and discover what's inside. Word provides many cover-page styles, but if you can't find one that appeals to you, you can create your own cover page that includes the content and the look and feel that properly represents you and your work. Building a cover page isn't exactly simple if you want to incorporate numerous elements, but you'll only need to do it once, and it's a great way to practice all the skills you've been reading about (and trying out, we hope!) throughout this book.

Modify an Existing Cover Page

① On the Insert tab, in a document that's formatted with the theme you'll be using for most of the documents that will use this cover page, click the Cover Page button. In the gallery that appears, click a cover-page design that looks most like the one you want to create.

② Click one of the graphics elements, and, on the Page Layout tab, click the down arrow next to the Group button, and choose Ungroup from the drop-down menu. Each time you click a graphics element, use the Ungroup command to make sure that you'll be able to select the individual elements when you want to.

③ Select and remove any elements you don't want, such as graphics and text boxes that contain text or content controls.

④ For an element you want to keep but whose location you want to change, select the element, and, on the Page Layout tab, click the Position button. Select one of the positions in the gallery that appears; or click More Layout Options, and use the Advanced Layout dialog box to set the alignment and the absolute or relative position of the element.

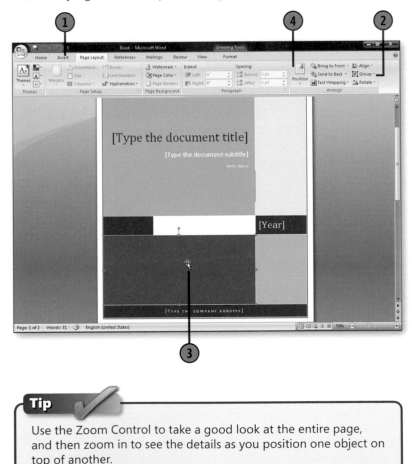

Tip

Use the Zoom Control to take a good look at the entire page, and then zoom in to see the details as you position one object on top of another.

Add Your Content

1 On the Insert tab, click the Shapes button, and select a shape. Drag out the shape on your cover page, and format it as you want. Add any other shapes to enhance your composition.

2 On the Insert tab, click the Text Box button, and choose a text box from the gallery that appears; or click Draw Text Box at the bottom of the gallery, and draw the text box you want.

3 With the text box selected, insert your content, including text, fields, pictures, or any other content that isn't a shape, and format the text box as you want. Insert additional text boxes to hold content that you want located in other areas of the cover page.

4 On the Text Box Tools Format tab or the Drawing Tools Format tab, arrange the elements on the page, using the Arrange tools, the Text Wrapping settings, and the Position settings. Group the elements as you complete them. When you've finished, make sure that all the elements are grouped together.

5 On the Insert tab, with your cover page selected, click the Cover Page button, and choose Save Selection to Cover Page Gallery to display the Create New Building Block dialog box.

6 Name the cover page, and, with Gallery set to Cover Pages and Options set to Insert Content In Its Own Page, click OK.

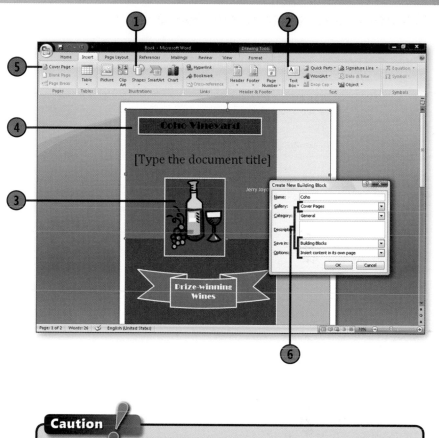

Caution

When you close your documents and Word asks you if you want to save your changes to the Building Blocks, be sure to click Yes—otherwise, you'll lose all your changes.

See Also

"Arranging Multiple Graphics" on page 131 for information about grouping and arranging items.

Creating a Custom Table of Contents

You can create a standard table of contents with just a click of the mouse. However, if you don't want all the styles of a certain outline level included; or if you want to base the table on styles to which you haven't assigned outline levels; or if you want to change the number of sublevels you've used in the outline, you can easily create a custom table of contents.

Set Up a Table of Contents

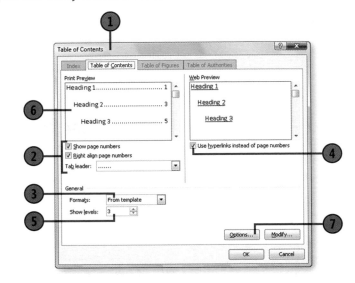

 On the References tab, with the insertion point located in your document where you want the table of contents to appear, click the Table Of Contents button, and click Insert Table Of Contents in the gallery to display the Table Of Contents dialog box.

2 Select the check boxes to display the page numbers either next to corresponding entries in the table of contents or aligned at the right side of the page. If you want the page numbers to be right-aligned, specify a style for the tab leader that's placed between the entry and the page number.

3 Specify the style you want for the table of contents.

4 Select this check box to display links in Web Layout view, or clear the check box if you want the page numbers to be displayed.

5 Specify the lowest outline level you want to be included in the table of contents. The paragraphs whose style has been assigned an outline level within this range will appear in the table.

6 Use the preview to confirm the layout. If it looks the way you want, click OK.

7 To change which paragraphs are used and at what level, click Options.

Tip

A table of contents is inserted into your document as a field. If you have a final table of contents that you want to edit, and if you want to make sure that it doesn't automatically update itself, select the entire table of contents, and press Ctrl+Shift+F9 to keep the text but remove the field.

Select the Content You Want to Include

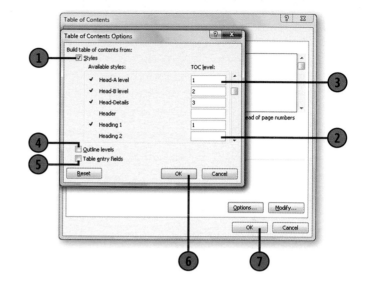

① In the Table Of Contents Options dialog box that appears when you click Options in the Table Of Contents dialog box, select this check box if you want to base what's included in your table of contents on certain styles.

② For any style you don't want to include that has a TOC Level number, select the number and press the Delete key.

③ For any style that you do want to include, click in the TOC Level text box, and type the level you want to assign to that style. You can assign the same level to more than one style if you want.

④ Clear this check box if you don't want to include paragraphs to which you've assigned outline levels.

⑤ Select this check box only if you've manually marked paragraphs with the TC field and want to include those paragraphs, or the assigned text for those paragraphs, in the table of contents.

⑥ Click OK.

⑦ Inspect all your settings, verifying that the values in the Show Levels box in the Table Of Contents dialog box match the levels you assigned in the Table Of Contents Options dialog box, and then click OK to create the table of contents.

"Organizing with Styles" on page 208 for information about assigning outline levels to styles.

Tip

The TC field is rarely used; it's much more tedious to use than using styles or outline levels to designate table-of-contents entries.

Creating a Custom Table of Tables or Figures

If you've created a long scientific or technical document or report, you'll probably want to create one or more tables listing any tables and/or figures contained in the document. If you've included these types of items without using Word's captioning feature, you can still have Word create the tables for you. Word will also update the page numbers in the tables if the pagination of the document changes. Because the table is built on a style you identify, you can use this method to create a table for any types of items, whether they're equations, graphs, quotes, or notes.

Create the Table

1 In your document, for each type of item for which you want to create a table, create a new style, and use it to format the title for each item (Figures or Tables, for example). The title will appear in the table of figures.

2 On the References tab, click the Insert Table Of Figures button to display the Table Of Figures dialog box.

3 Choose the settings you want to use to format the table.

4 Click Options to display the Table Of Figures Options dialog box.

5 Select the Style check box.

6 Select the style you assigned to the title of the item (the figure title, for example).

7 Click OK.

8 Click OK to create the table.

9 Repeat steps 2 through 8 to create additional tables for the different types of items you want listed.

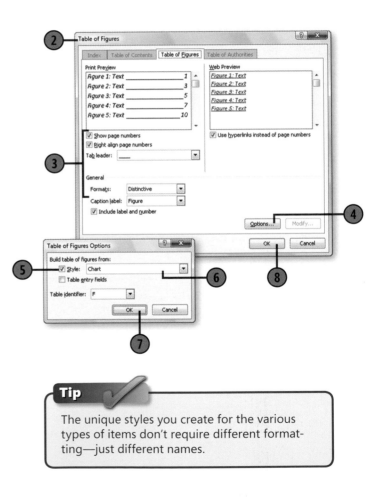

See Also

"Adding Captions to Tables and Figures" on page 165 for information about creating a table of figures using Word's captioning feature.

Tip

The unique styles you create for the various types of items don't require different formatting—just different names.

Saving Your Custom Table Design

When you create documents that contain information that's likely to change over time and that you want to list in a table—an inventory, a class list, or a meeting schedule, for example—you might eventually need to create several different versions of the table to include the changed content. Instead of formatting each table separately, you can build your table format and standard content once, save it, and then insert it into any document with just a couple of mouse-clicks.

Create a Quick Table

1. Create and format a table with the number of rows and columns you want. Add any text that you want to appear in all the tables.

2. Select the entire table. (A quick way to do this is to move the mouse over the table and then click the Move box at the top-left corner of the table.)

3. On the Insert tab, click the Table button, point to Quick Tables in the gallery, and click Save Selection To Quick Tables Gallery in the Quick Tables gallery that appears.

4. Enter an identifying name for the table.

5. Enter a description if you want one. (The description will appear in the ScreenTip when you point to the table in the Quick Tables gallery.)

6. With Gallery set to Tables, with Save In set to Building Blocks, and with Options set to Insert Content In Its Own Paragraph, click OK.

7. When you want to use the table in any document, just choose it from the Quick Tables gallery.

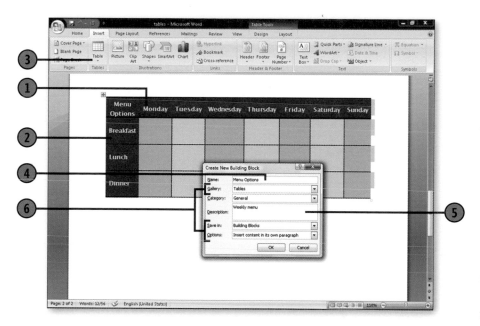

Caution

When you close all your Word documents, Word will ask you whether you want to save the changes you've made to the Building Blocks. You should click Yes—otherwise, you'll lose any quick tables you created in this session.

Customizing a Template

Microsoft Word 2007 provides templates that are useful for many different purposes. However, they're generic templates that might not include every element you need. If you use a particular template frequently, you can create a highly personalized document—and save lots of time—by creating a new, customized template based on the existing template.

Open the Template

1. Choose New from the Office menu to display the New Document dialog box.

2. Click either Installed Templates or My Templates.

3. Click the template you want to modify.

4. Click Template in the Create New section.

5. Click Create.

Tip

If you want to make changes to a template that's either stored on a company Web site or available from Office Online, you won't be able to open the template as a template. Instead, you'll need to open it as a document, make your modifications, and then save the document as a template on your computer.

See Also

"Designing a Template" on pages 202–203 for information about designing your own template.

Modify the Template

1. Click the Save button on the Quick Access toolbar, type a unique and descriptive file name for your new template, and click Save. The template will be saved in your personal Templates folder and will appear in the New dialog box when you choose New from the Office menu and click My Templates.

2. On the Home tab, click the Show/Hide ¶ button if it isn't already turned on.

3. Replace the placeholder text with any text that will be common to all documents based on this new template.

4. Add any new text or other page elements.

5. Redefine or create your own paragraph styles and character styles.

6. Save and close the template.

7. Choose New from the Office menu, click My Templates, and create a document based on the modified template to verify that the template is correct.

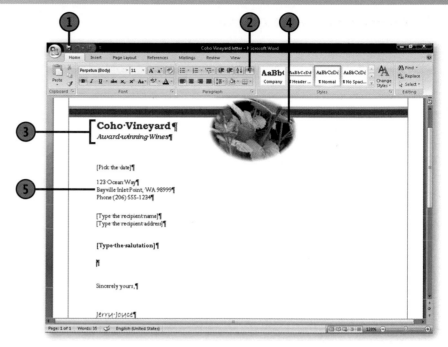

"Composing Different Types of Documents" on pages 96–97 for information about starting a document based on a template.

Designing a Template

Sometimes an existing template just doesn't do the job for you, no matter how much you modify it. If that's the case, you'll want to create a template from scratch. The easiest way to do this is to use an existing document and set it up as a template. If you don't have an existing document that incorporates all the special elements you need, create one, and then save it. Review the entire document to determine whether the design really works, and then close the document. You'll be using a copy of the document as the basis for your template's design, so if you don't like the resulting template, you can simply delete it and then revise it using the same document.

Create the Design

(1) Choose New from the Office menu to display the New Document dialog box.

(2) Click New From Existing, and, in the New From Existing Document dialog box that appears, locate the document you want to use, and create a new document based on it.

(3) On the Office menu, point to Save As, and click Word Template in the gallery that appears.

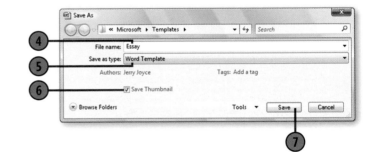

(4) Type a unique and descriptive file name.

(5) Verify that Word Template is shown in the Save As Type list.

(6) Select this check box to save a thumbnail image of the template.

(7) Save the template.

Customize the Content

1 On the Home tab, click the Show/Hide ¶ button if it isn't already turned on.

2 Edit the document so that it contains the items you'll want to appear in every document you'll create from this template.

3 Delete the text, but leave the placeholder paragraph marks where they are so that any text that's inserted into the document will have the correct styles applied automatically.

4 Use document properties and other fields in headers or footers to insert information that will be updated automatically.

5 Click the Save button on the Quick Access toolbar.

6 Close the template when you've finished.

7 Choose New from the Office menu, click My Templates, and create a document based on the new template to verify that the template is correct.

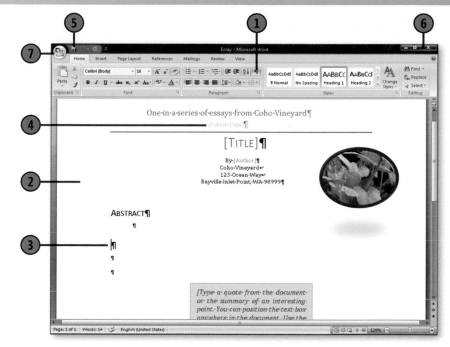

Tip

To include the date and time in the template and to have Word update both each time you create a new document, click the Date And Time button on the Insert tab, click the format you want to use, select the Update Automatically check box, and click OK.

Tip

To locate the fields in your template while you're designing it, or to see the fields in documents based on the template so that you don't accidentally delete them, choose Word Options from the Office menu, click the Advanced category, and, in the Show Document Content section, specify whether you want fields to be shaded when they're selected or always to be shaded. Click OK to close the Word Options dialog box.

Customizing a List

Although standard bullets or numbers will suffice for most lists, you might want to add some pizzazz to a special document with decorative bullets, or you might need to change your numbering format to conform to certain document specifications. Whatever the reason, you can customize the bullets and the numbering scheme for your lists.

Change the Bullets

1. Select the entire list if it's completed, or click in your document where you want to start a list.

2. On the Home tab, click the down arrow at the right of the Bullets button to display the Bullets gallery. If none of the available bullets is exactly what you want, click Define New Bullet at the bottom of the gallery to display the Define New Bullet dialog box.

3. To use a text symbol, or *dingbat,* as a bullet, click Symbol.

4. In the Symbol dialog box, select the font and the symbol you want, and click OK.

5. To modify the size, color, or any other aspect of the symbol, click the Font button, make your changes in the Font dialog box, and click OK.

6. To use a clip-art picture bullet, click Picture.

7. In the Picture Bullet dialog box, select the bullet you want.

8. If you don't see a bullet you like, select the Include Content From Office Online check box, click Go, and then select the bullet you want. Click OK.

9. Select the alignment of the bullet in relation to the table text, and click OK.

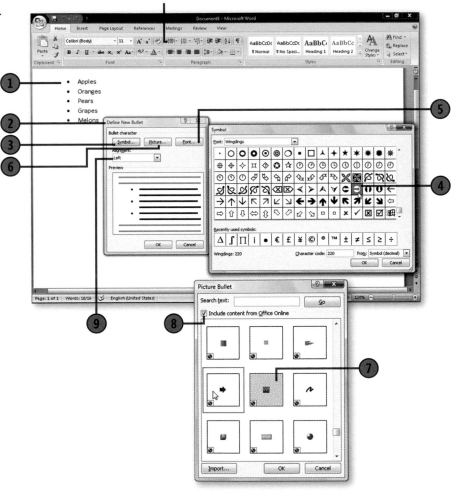

The Bullets button

Change the Numbering Scheme

The Numbering button

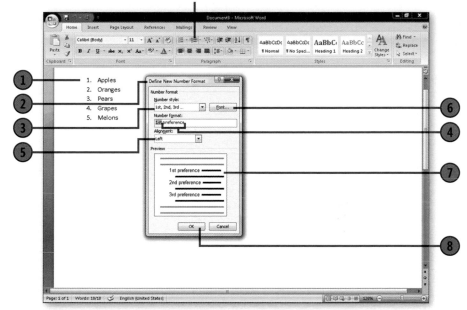

(1) Select your entire list if it's completed, or click in your document where you want to start a list.

(2) On the Home tab, click the down arrow at the right of the Numbering button to display the Numbering gallery. If none of the available numbering formats is what you want, click Define New Number Format near the bottom of the gallery to display the Define New Number Format dialog box.

(3) Select the numbering style you want.

(4) Add any text that you want to be included in the numbering.

(5) Select the alignment of the numbering in relation to the table text.

(6) If you want to modify the font, size, color, or any other aspect of the numbering and any added text, click the Font button, make your changes in the Font dialog box, and click OK.

(7) Use the preview to see the effect of the alignment and any changes you've made to the font settings.

(8) Click OK.

Tip

Word assigns the List Paragraph style to bulleted or numbered lists when you click the Bullets or Numbering button. If you want Word to use the Normal style by default, choose Word Options from the Office menu, click the Advanced category, and, in the Editing Options section, select the Use Normal Style For Bulleted Or Numbered Lists check box. Click OK to close the Word Options dialog box.

Customizing a Multilevel List

A multilevel list is a powerful tool for presenting your information in an organized, hierarchical way. The multilevel lists that are available in the List Library provide some structure, but you might need to develop your own structure to present the information in exactly the way you want.

Create a List Structure

1 Click the down arrow at the right of the Multilevel List button, and click Define New Multilevel List near the bottom of the gallery to display the Define New Multilevel List dialog box. Click the More button, if it's displayed, to see all the settings. (The Less button is displayed when the More button has been clicked.)

2 Click a list level that you want to modify.

3 Define your numbering format. Add or edit any text that you want to use with the number; then specify the numbering style and the number with which that list level starts; when the list resets to the start number that you specified; and whether you want the number to include the number from the preceding higher list-level entry.

4 Set the position of the numbering in relation to the text.

5 Specify whether these changes apply to the entire list or only part of it.

6 Specify which style you want to use with this level and what level you want assigned to this style when it's included in a list.

7 Click OK.

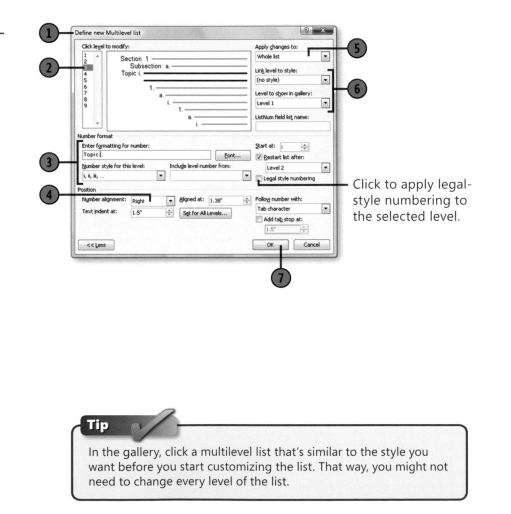

Click to apply legal-style numbering to the selected level.

> **Tip**
>
> In the gallery, click a multilevel list that's similar to the style you want before you start customizing the list. That way, you might not need to change every level of the list.

Customizing the Page Numbers

Word no longer limits you to a plain old number at the top or bottom of the page. You'll find a wide selection of designs that allow you to place the page number inside a graphic at the top, bottom, or side of the page. And, as with most of Word's design elements, if you can't find the right one, you can create your own page-number design, and you can make it as dramatic or evocative as you like.

Customize the Page Numbers

① On the Insert tab, click the Page Number button, point to the location you want for the page number, and, in the gallery that appears, click a page number in the With Shapes category that's the closest to the look you want.

② On the Insert tab, click the Header button, and click Edit Header in the gallery.

③ Click the page number wherever it is on the page.

④ On the Text Box Tools Format tab, click the down arrow at the right of the Change Shape button, and, in the gallery that appears, click the shape you want.

⑤ Format the shape, and then drag it to the location on the page where you want it to appear.

⑥ On the Insert tab, with the number selected, click the down arrow at the right of the Page Number button, point to the type of page number you created, and, at the bottom of the gallery that appears, click Save Selection As Page Number to display the Create New Building Block dialog box.

⑦ Name the page-number style you created, leave the other settings as they are, and click OK. Your page-number design will be listed in the Page Number gallery for future use.

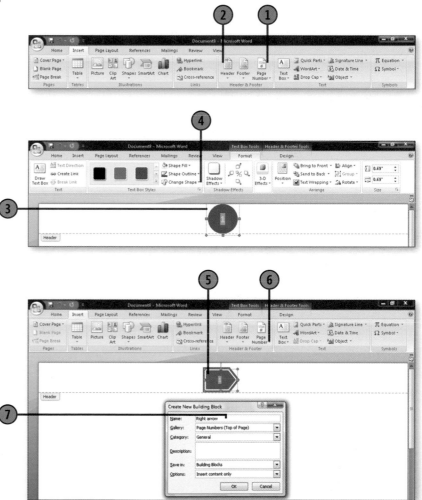

Organizing with Styles

Paragraph styles do more than quickly apply formatting to your paragraphs; they also assign an outline level to each paragraph in a document. Word uses these outline levels to understand the way you're organizing the document—which paragraphs are headings, which are subheadings, and which are text. The outline level also affects the way Word creates a table of contents and the way it organizes the document in Outline view.

Set the Outline Level

1. Start Word, and open your document if it isn't already open.

2. Click in a paragraph that has a style to which you want to assign an outline level.

3. On the Home tab, right-click the style for your paragraph in the Quick Style list, and choose Modify from the shortcut menu.

4. In the Modify Style dialog box, click the Format button, and choose Paragraph from the list that appears.

5. In the Paragraph dialog box, select the outline level you want for this style, and click OK.

6. In the Modify Style dialog box, specify whether you want this change to apply only in this document or in all documents based on this template. Click OK.

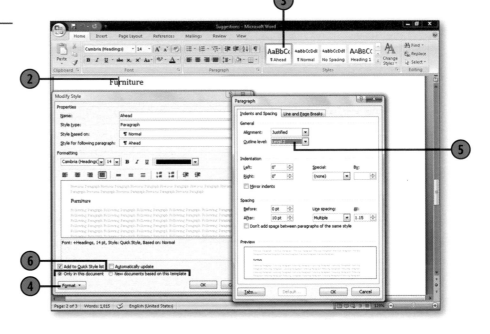

See Also

"Reorganizing a Document" on pages 118–119 for information about using Outline view to look at your heading hierarchy.

"Creating Your Own Styles" on pages 190–191 for information about creating your own styles.

Tip

To see the style names for all your paragraphs as you work, in Draft view, choose Word Options from the Office menu, click the Advanced category, and, in the Display section, enter a measurement (0.7", for example) in the Style Area Pane In Draft And Outline Views text box. Click OK to close the Word Options dialog box.

10

Customizing and Securing Word

In this section:

- Customizing the Quick Access Toolbar
- Customizing the Window
- Creating Keyboard Shortcuts
- Changing Your User Information
- Creating Macros
- Safeguarding a Document
- Restricting Access and Changes to a Document
- Digitally Signing a Document
- Protecting a Document with a Password
- Controlling Macros, Add-Ins, and ActiveX Controls
- Fixing Word
- Adding Or Removing Word Components

You might want to use Microsoft Office Word 2007 just as it comes, without making changes to any of its components. However, if you want to customize Word, there's practically no limit to the changes you can make. You can put as many items on the Quick Access toolbar as you like, customize Word's color scheme, show or hide items on the status bar, and make the Ribbon appear and disappear. You can create your own keyboard shortcuts, tailor the way Word checks your documents for spelling and grammar errors, and create custom spelling dictionaries for uncommon scientific or technical terms. You can create time-saving *macros* to automate actions that you conduct repeatedly. And Word provides methods to reduce the chance that you'll ever lose any of your work. You can prevent people from accessing or making changes to your documents, and you can sign documents with a *digital signature*. If you don't need all of Word's components, you can install the ones you want and remove those you don't want.

Word also provides a very high level of protection against malicious programs and other items that can harm your computer and damage your security. If Word doesn't seem to be working properly, you can run an automated series of diagnostics to find out what's wrong and learn how to fix the problem.

Customizing the Quick Access Toolbar

The Quick Access toolbar, as its name suggests, is the place to keep the items that you not only want to access quickly but want to be immediately available regardless of which of Word's tabs you're working on. If you put so many items on the Quick Access toolbar that it becomes too big to fit on the title bar, you can move it onto its own line.

Add or Remove Items Common to the Quick Access Toolbar

① Click the down arrow at the right of the Quick Access toolbar.

② On the Customize Quick Access Toolbar menu, click any unchecked items that you want to add to the toolbar.

③ Click any checked items that you want to remove from the toolbar.

④ Right-click any item anywhere on the Ribbon that you want to add to the toolbar, and choose Add To Quick Access Toolbar from the shortcut menu.

⑤ If the toolbar becomes too large to fit on the title bar or if you want easier access to it, click the down arrow at the right of the toolbar, and click Show Below The Ribbon on the menu.

The Quick Access toolbar on its own line

See Also

"Show or Minimize the Ribbon" on page 213 for information about minimizing the Ribbon when you don't need it.

Control the Customization

1 Click the down arrow at the right of the Quick Access toolbar, and, on the Customize Quick Access Toolbar menu, click More Commands to display the Word Options dialog box with the Customize category selected in the left pane.

2 Specify where you want to save the changes to the toolbar.

3 Specify the category of commands you want to select from.

4 Click a command you want to add to the toolbar.

5 Click Add.

6 To remove a command you don't use, select it and click Remove.

7 To change the order in which commands will appear on the toolbar, click a command, and use the up or down arrow to move the command.

8 Repeat steps 3 through 7 to make any further customizations to the Quick Access toolbar; click OK when you've finished.

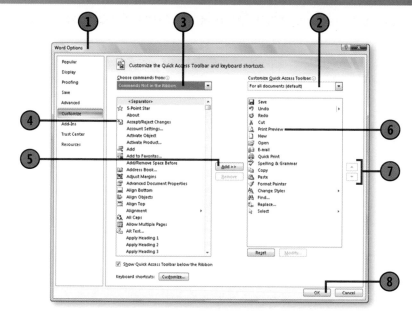

> **Tip**
>
> You're not limited to "standard" Word commands. You can include styles, fonts, and macros on the toolbar.

> **Tip**
>
> When you add or delete items using the Customize Quick Access Toolbar menu or the shortcut menu on the Ribbon, you'll see that version of the toolbar in all your documents. If you want to see that version of the toolbar in the current document only, use the Word Options dialog box to specify that you want to save these changes in the current document only.

Customizing the Window

The Word window is where you do your work, so you'll probably want to customize it to fit your work habits and working style. You can show or hide items on the status bar, set the Ribbon to appear only when you need to use it, change the overall color scheme for the window, and so on.

Show or Hide Items on the Status Bar

1. Right-click anywhere on the status bar.

2. Review the information on the Customize Status Bar menu.

3. To show an item that isn't currently displayed on the status bar, click the item.

4. To hide an item that's currently displayed, click the item.

Change the Window's Color Scheme

1. Click the Office button, and choose Word Options from the menu to display the Word Options dialog box.

2. With the Popular category selected in the left pane, specify the color scheme you want.

3. Click OK.

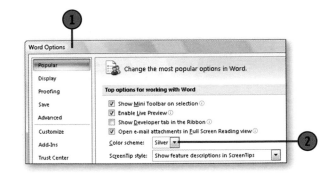

Show or Minimize the Ribbon

① With the Ribbon displayed, click the down arrow at the right of the Quick Access toolbar, and, on the Customize Quick Access Toolbar menu, click Minimize The Ribbon.

② When you want to use the Ribbon, click the tab you want, and the Ribbon for that tab will appear and will remain displayed until you click a command, choose an option on the Ribbon, or click in the document.

③ To have the Ribbon always displayed, click the down arrow at the right of the Quick Access toolbar, and click Minimize The Ribbon again.

Try This!

With the Ribbon in its displayed state, double-click the active tab to minimize the Ribbon, and then click any tab to display the Ribbon temporarily. Click in your document to minimize the Ribbon again. Double-click the active tab to have the Ribbon always displayed. Press Ctrl+F1 to hide the Ribbon, and press Ctrl+F1 again to always display the Ribbon.

Creating Keyboard Shortcuts

It's quick and easy to use a keyboard shortcut for an action you do repeatedly. Many commands already have keyboard shortcuts assigned to them, but you can specify your own assignments—either to make the keyboard shortcut easier to remember or to add keyboard shortcuts to items that don't already have them.

Assign a Keyboard Shortcut

1. Click the Office button, choose Word Options to display the Word Options dialog box, click the Customize category in the left pane, and click the Customize button.

2. In the Customize Keyboard dialog box, specify in which open template or document you want to save the changes you're going to make. (Specify Normal to make the changes available to all documents.)

3. Click the category for the item or command to which you're assigning the keyboard shortcut, or click All Commands to see all the available commands.

4. Select the item or command you want.

5. Note whether there's already a keyboard shortcut assigned to the item or command.

6. Click in the box, and type the keyboard shortcut you want.

7. Verify that the keyboard shortcut you chose isn't assigned to another item or command. If it is, press Backspace, and type another keyboard shortcut.

8. Click Assign to assign the new keyboard shortcut to the selected item. Click Close, and then click Close in the Word Options dialog box.

Tip

Even if you don't have the time or inclination to assign any new keyboard shortcuts, take a look at the existing ones. It's a great way to remind yourself about all the things you can do with keyboard shortcuts.

Specifying What You Want Word to Display

In Word, you generally choose to see all or none of the formatting marks in your document by turning the Show/Hide ¶ button on or off on the Home tab. However, you can be as choosy as you like, telling Word to display only the formatting marks, layout marks, and special content that you want to see.

Specify What You Want to See

1. Click the Office button, choose Word Options from the menu, and, in the Word Options dialog box, click the Display category in the left pane.

2. Specify whether you want to see white space between pages in Print Layout view, whether you want highlighter marks to be displayed, and whether you want to see ScreenTips (called ToolTips here).

3. Select the check boxes for the formatting marks you want to see.

4. Click the Advanced category, and, in the Show Document Content section, select or clear the check boxes for the items you want displayed.

5. Specify whether or not you want fields to be identified with shading.

6. Click OK.

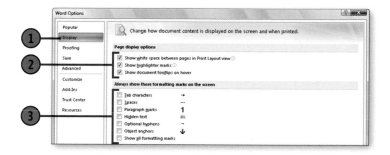

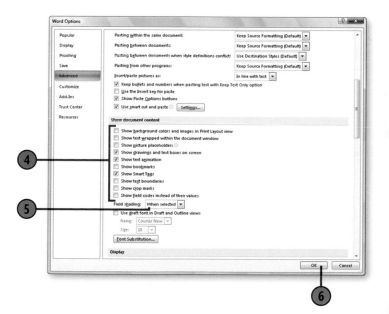

Tip

Occasionally, you might see a reference to a ToolTip in a Word window or dialog box. Don't worry—ToolTips and ScreenTips are the same thing.

Changing Your User Information

Word routinely inserts certain information into your documents, using data that you've supplied. For example, Word enters your name in the Author field; it uses your initials to identify your comments; and it can use your address to enter the return address on an envelope. However, all that automation is useless if the information you supplied to Word is incorrect or missing. Fortunately, you can easily correct or add the information.

Change Your Name and Address

1. Click the Office button, choose Word Options from the menu, and, in the Word Options dialog box, click the Popular category in the left pane, if it isn't already selected.

2. If your name is incorrect, select it, and type your correct name.

3. To change or correct your initials, select them, and type the initials you want to use.

4. Click the Advanced category.

5. In the General section, enter, correct, or replace your mailing address.

6. Click OK.

Tip

The first time you use Word, it asks you for your name and your initials but doesn't request your mailing address. This category remains blank until you've entered the information in the Word Options dialog box.

Changing the Way Word Saves Files

If you don't like the locations where Word proposes to store your documents, templates, AutoRecovery files, and other tools, you can change those locations and create the organization that works best for you. And if you're working with other people who require access to your files in a different version of Word, you can save Word 2007 files in a format that's fully compatible with earlier versions of Word.

Change the File Locations and Formats

1. Click the Office button, choose Word Options from the menu, and, in the Word Options dialog box, click the Advanced category in the left pane. In the General section, click the File Locations button to display the File Locations dialog box.

2. Click the item whose location you want to change.

3. Click Modify, and, in the Modify Location dialog box, locate and select the folder that you're designating as the new location; click OK.

4. Specify the location for any other file types, and click OK when you've finished.

5. Click the Save category.

6. Select the default format in which you want to save your documents.

7. Click OK to close the Word Options dialog box.

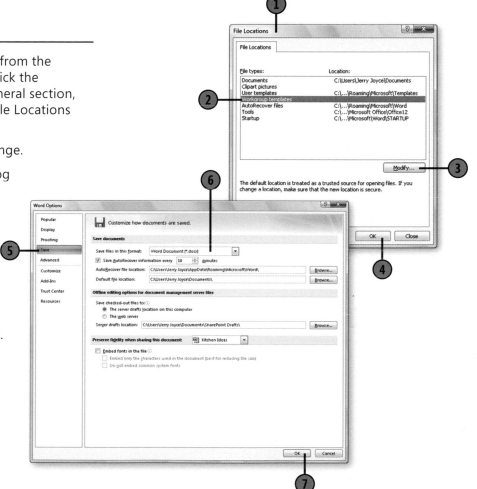

> **Tip** ✓
>
> If you consistently save your files in a format other than the Word 2007 format, you should modify the Compatibility settings on the Advanced tab of the Word Options dialog box so that your documents have the correct layout for the format in which you save them.

Customizing the Way Word Checks Spelling and Grammar

Depending on the type of document you're creating, you might need to tailor the levels of spelling and grammar checking to make them appropriate for that type of document. You can customize the types of checking Word does, and you can even designate certain text not to be checked at all.

Specify What's to Be Checked

1. Click the Office button, choose Word Options from the menu, and, in the Word Options dialog box, click the Proofing category.

2. Select this check box to instruct Word to check the spelling of each word as you type it.

3. Select this check box to instruct Word to check spelling based on the context in which a word is used (for example, to detect whether "form" should be used instead of "from").

4. Select this check box to instruct Word to check each phrase and sentence as it's completed for proper grammar.

5. Select this check box to instruct Word to check your grammar whenever it checks your spelling.

6. Specify whether you want Word to check grammar alone or grammar together with writing style. Click Settings to define the grammar rules you want Word to use to check your document.

7. Select the options you want included in the spelling check.

8. Specify if and when you want spelling and grammar errors to be hidden.

9. Click OK to use your new settings.

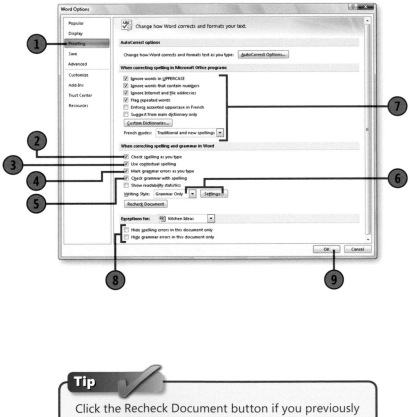

Tip

Click the Recheck Document button if you previously told Word to ignore misspellings or grammatical errors in this document but you now want any errors to be marked.

Customizing Your Spelling Dictionaries

Word uses one or more dictionaries to check your spelling. When there's a word in your document that's correct but that Word doesn't recognize—a name, an address, or an unfamiliar technical or scientific term, for example—you can tell Word to add that word to your custom dictionary. If you already have a custom dictionary that includes many of the words you want

Word to recognize as correct, you can add that dictionary to the list of dictionaries that Word is using. Also, if you discover any incorrectly spelled words in your dictionary, you should replace them with the correct spelling; otherwise, Word will consider the incorrect spelling to be correct.

Add a Dictionary

1 Click the Office button, choose Word Options from the menu, and, in the Word Options dialog box, click the Proofing category. Click the Custom Dictionaries button to display the Custom Dictionaries dialog box.

2 If you have an existing dictionary that you want to use, click Add, and, in the Add Custom Dictionary dialog box that appears, locate the dictionary file. Click Open.

3 Select the language for an added dictionary if you want it to be used only for a specific language.

4 To create a dictionary by adding entries, click New, use the Create Custom Dictionary dialog box to name the dictionary file, and click Save.

5 To add or delete words in a dictionary, select the dictionary, and click Edit Word List.

6 Do either of the following:
• Type a word you want to add, and click Add.
• Select a word you want to remove, and click Delete.

7 Click OK.

8 Verify that the dictionaries you want to use are checked and those you don't want to use aren't checked.

9 Click OK.

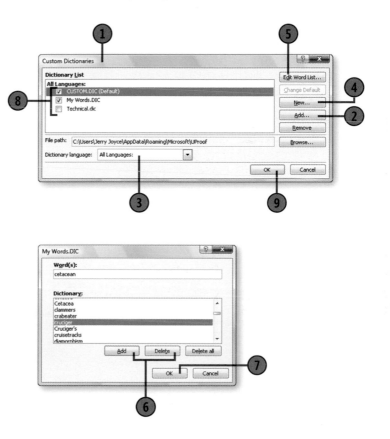

Creating Your Own Commands

If you often repeat the same series of actions as you work, you can simplify the job—and save a lot of time—by recording that series of actions to create a *macro*. For example, you can create a macro by recording the replacement of a phrase and/or a style using the Replace command. Then you can run that macro to modify other documents. Regardless of the complexity of your macro, you can run it as if it were a single Word command.

Create a Macro

1 On the View tab, click the down arrow at the bottom of the Macros button, and choose Record New Macro to display the Record Macro dialog box.

2 Type a name for the macro. (The name must begin with a letter and can't contain any spaces or symbols.)

3 Specify where you want to store the macro, type a description, and click OK.

4 Execute the series of actions you want to record as a macro, using your keyboard to select text and to move the insertion point. (Note that, other than when you click a command, most mouse actions aren't recorded.)

5 When you've completed the series of actions, click the down arrow at the bottom of the Macros button again, and choose Stop Recording.

6 Click the Macros button to display the Macros dialog box, select the macro you just recorded, and click Run to make sure the macro performs correctly.

The Recorder mouse pointer reminds you that you're recording all actions.

Tip

For the greatest control in creating and modifying macros, as well as adding items such as content controls and components of forms, use the items on the Developer tab. If the Developer tab isn't visible, click the Office button, choose Word Options, and, in the Word Options dialog box, click the Popular category, and select the check box to show the Developer tab on the Ribbon.

Transferring Styles and Macros

If you have a template that contains styles and macros and you'd like to use those elements in another template, you can copy them quickly and easily using Word's Organizer.

Transfer Items

 Open a document (or start a new document) based on the template into which you want to copy items from another template.

 On the View tab, click the Macros button, and, in the Macros dialog box that appears, click the Organizer button to display the Organizer dialog box.

 On the Styles tab, specify the template into which you're going to insert the copied items.

 Click Close File. (Note that the Close File button becomes the Open File button after you close the template.) Click the Open File button, and open the template you're going to copy from.

 Select the styles you want to copy.

 Click Copy.

 Click the Macro Project Items tab in the dialog box, and copy any macro projects you want.

 Click Close when you've finished.

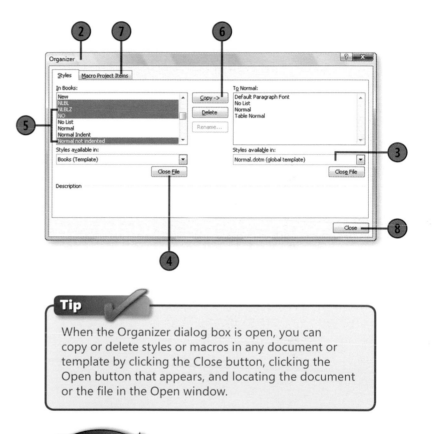

See Also

"Switching Templates" on page 111 for information about switching the template a document uses to make the styles and macros in the template available to that document.

Tip

When the Organizer dialog box is open, you can copy or delete styles or macros in any document or template by clicking the Close button, clicking the Open button that appears, and locating the document or the file in the Open window.

See Also

"Controlling Macros, Add-Ins, and ActiveX Controls" on page 230 for information about controlling access to macros.

Safeguarding a Document

At one time or another, you've probably lost some work on your computer. Whether you forgot to save a document or were the victim of a power outage, it's a frustrating and depressing experience that you vow will never happen again. You can safeguard your work and prevent most losses by doing three things. You can have Word save your changes automatically using the AutoRecovery feature; you can create a backup copy whenever you save your document; and you can keep a copy of a document on your computer, with any changes you make to it also saved to the original document stored on another computer, in case the network connection is broken or the other computer becomes unavailable.

Set Up the Safeguards

① Click the Office button, choose Word Options from the menu, and, in the Word Options dialog box, click the Save category in the left pane.

② Select this check box if it isn't already selected.

③ Set a short interval to specify how often you want the AutoRecovery information to be saved.

④ Click the Advanced category.

⑤ In the Save section, select this check box to create a backup copy of your document every time you save it.

⑥ Select this check box to create a local copy of a document that you opened from a SharePoint server or from another computer, and to simultaneously save the document to your computer and to the remote location.

⑦ Click OK.

See Also

"Changing the Way Word Saves Files" on page 217 for information about specifying or changing where your documents and AutoRecovery files are stored.

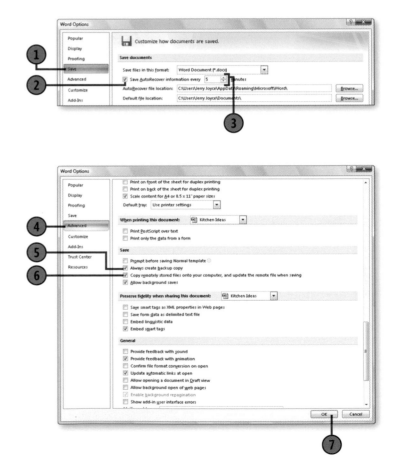

Restricting Access to a Document

Word uses a protocol called Information Rights Management (IRM) to determine who is allowed access to a document. This protocol is used either by an IRM service on a network or through the IRM Service available from Microsoft over the Internet. You identify who is granted access to a document by entering the person's e-mail address. That person must then use an appropriate IRM service to verify his or her identity, based on the e-mail address, and must download a license.

Restrict Access

1 On the Review tab—after you've completed, proofed, saved, and, if desired, marked the document as Final—click the Protect Document button, and choose Restricted Access from the menu. If you need to sign up for the IRM service, do so when prompted.

2 In the Permission dialog box, select this check box to enable restrictions.

3 Enter the e-mail names and addresses of the people you'll allow to open and read but not change the document.

4 Enter the e-mail names and addresses of the people you'll allow to open, modify, and save the document.

5 Click More Options if you want to set a date when access to the document will expire; to specify whether the document can be printed or material can be copied; or if the content can be accessed programmatically.

6 Click OK.

Tip

To remove the access restrictions, click the Protect button and choose Unrestricted Access from the menu.

Caution

The IRM service provided by Microsoft isn't guaranteed to remain available. Therefore, you should keep backup copies of the documents, with no access restrictions, in a secure location in case the service should become unavailable.

Restricting Changes to a Document

When you share a document with other people but don't want anyone to make drastic changes to it, you can specify what they can and can't do to the document.

Restrict Changes

(1) On the Home tab, after you've completed, proofed, and saved the document, click the Protect Document button, and choose Restrict Formatting And Editing from the menu.

(2) In the Restrict Formatting And Editing pane that appears, select this check box if you want to designate which styles can be used in the document.

(3) If you chose to restrict formatting, click Settings to display the Formatting Restrictions dialog box, select the styles that can be used in the document, and specify whether you want to allow AutoFormat to override your settings, or to block theme, color scheme, or style-set switching. Click OK.

(4) Select this check box if you want to restrict the type of editing that people can do to the document.

(5) Specify what type of editing you'll allow.

(6) If you'll allow only part of the document to be edited, select the part, and then select the names of those who have permission to edit that part.

(7) Click to protect the document. Save, close, and share the document.

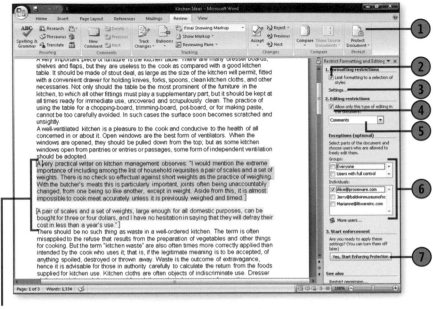

Shading shows areas where exceptions to the restrictions on editing have been applied.

> **Tip** ✓
>
> You can use these editing and formatting restrictions in conjunction with IRM access restrictions to designate who has full control of a document and to identify individual users.

> **See Also**
>
> "Restricting Access to a Document" on page 223 for information about restricting access to a document.

Signing a Document with a Certificate

If you want to prove that a document you're sending or sharing really does come from you and hasn't been changed by anyone since you finished it, you can include an invisible digital signature by attaching a digital certificate that verifies who you are. You'll need to have a digital certificate issued to you to be able to digitally sign a document. In most cases, digital certificates are issued through a third-party certificate provider or a corporate network.

Attach a Digital Signature

(1) With your document completed and saved, and with the insertion point where you want the digital signature to appear, click the Office button, point to Prepare on the menu, and choose Add A Digital Signature from the submenu to display the Sign dialog box.

(2) If you want, type a note stating the reason for signing the document.

(3) Verify that the digital signature is the one you want. If it isn't, click Change, and, in the Select Certificate dialog box, select the certificate you want and click OK.

(4) Click Sign. Close the document, and then distribute or share it.

(5) To verify that the digital signature is valid, open the document, click the Office button, point to Prepare, and choose View Signatures from the submenu to display the Signatures pane.

(6) In the Signatures pane, point to the signature name, click the down arrow that appears, and choose Signature Details to display the Signature Details dialog box to verify the signature.

(7) Click Close.

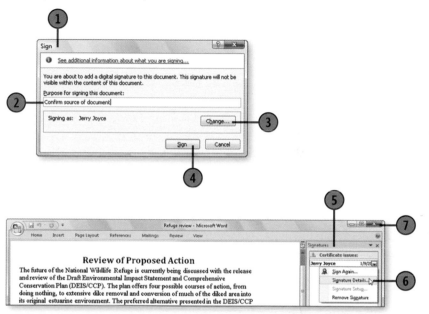

See Also

"Signing a Document with a Visible Signature" on pages 226–227 for information about obtaining a digital certificate to digitally sign a document.

Signing a Document with a Visible Signature

In the world of business and commerce, certain documents need to be signed and, often, witnessed. When a document is transmitted electronically, not only does it need to be signed, but the signature must be verifiable. Word takes care of this in two ways. It provides an easy way to set up an electronic document for a signature, by either typing the signature or using a scanned image of the signature inserted as a picture.

Additionally, Word attaches a digital certificate that has been issued to the signer from a reliable source. The digital certificate verifies the identity of the signer. With the digital certificate attached, the document is considered digitally signed. To prevent any alterations to the document after it has been signed, the digital signature is invalidated if any changes are made.

Set Up the Signature

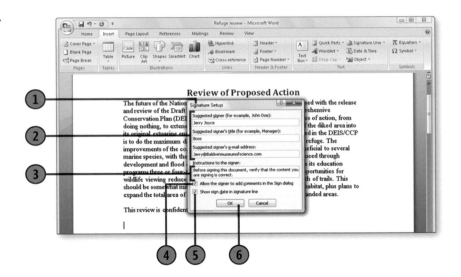

1 On the Insert tab, with your document completed and saved, and with the insertion point where you want the signature to appear, click the Signature Line button to display the Signature Setup dialog box.

2 Enter the name and, optionally, the title and e-mail address of the suggested signer.

3 Modify the instructions to the signer if you want.

4 Specify whether you want to allow the signer to add comments when signing the document.

5 Specify whether you want to include the date on which the document was signed.

6 Click OK. Save and close the document. If the document is intended for someone else's signature, send it to that person.

Tip

The typed or scanned image of a signature is used only to visually indicate who signed the document. It's the digital certificate that accompanies the document that provides the proof that the document is digitally signed.

Tip

You need a digital certificate (also called a digital ID or a digital signature) to be able to digitally sign a document. If you try to sign a document without one, you'll be prompted either to purchase one from a third party or create your own. If you create your own certificate, it will be available to validate your signature on your computer only.

Sign the Document

1. Open the document that has been prepared for your signature, and double-click the signature line.

2. In the Sign dialog box that appears, do either of the following:

   • Type your name in the box.

   • Click Select Image, and use the Select Signature Image dialog box to locate the picture file containing your signature. Click Open in the dialog box to insert the signature image.

3. If the text box that states the purpose of signing is shown, click in the box, and enter any information you want.

4. Verify that this digital signature name is the name of the digital certificate you want to use to verify your identity. If it isn't, click Change, and, in the Select Certificate dialog box, select the digital certificate you want. Click OK.

5. Click Sign, and save the document.

6. Send the digitally signed document to whoever required you to sign it. The digital certificate will accompany the document, and the recipient will be able to examine the certificate to verify that you signed it and that the document has not been altered since you signed the certificate.

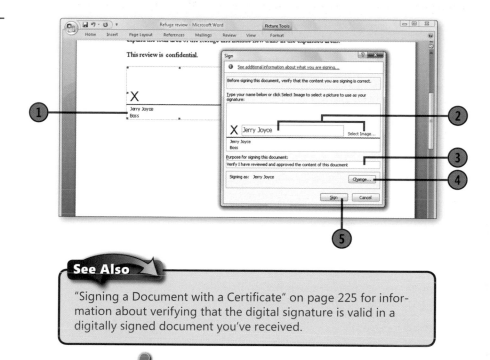

See Also

"Signing a Document with a Certificate" on page 225 for information about verifying that the digital signature is valid in a digitally signed document you've received.

Caution

A digital signature might or might not be recognized as a legal signature, depending on the type of document and your local laws.

Tip

There are various providers of digital signing certificates and other methods of digitally signing documents that might be legally recognized in many instances. To investigate these, click the down arrow at the right of the Signature Line button, and choose Add Signature Services from the menu.

Protecting a Document with a Password

If your document contains sensitive information that you don't want anyone else to see, you can encrypt the document so that no one can access its contents unless you give them the password you've created. You can further protect the document by allowing access to it but requiring a password to control who may make and save changes to the document.

Encrypt the Document

① With your document completed and saved, click the Office button, point to Prepare on the menu, and choose Encrypt Document to display the Encrypt Document dialog box.

② Enter a password.

③ Click OK, enter the password again in the Confirm Password dialog box that appears, and click OK.

④ Make any changes you want, saving the document occasionally, and then close it.

⑤ When you want to work on the document again, open it and, in the Password dialog box that appears, enter the password and click OK.

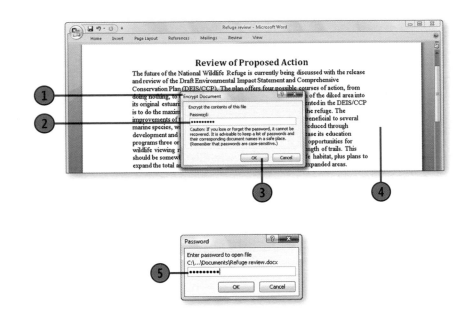

Caution

You won't be able to open an encrypted document without the password, so either keep an unencrypted copy of the document in a secure location or write down the password and store it in a secure location.

See Also

"Restricting Access to a Document" on page 223 and "Restricting Changes to a Document" on page 224 for information about other ways to control access to your documents.

Protect the Document from Modifications

1 With your document completed, click the Office button, and choose Save As from the menu to display the Save As dialog box.

2 Enter a name for the document.

3 Click Tools, and choose General Options from the drop-down menu.

4 In the General Options dialog box that appears, enter a password if you want to require a password to open the document. Enter the password again when prompted, and click OK.

5 Enter a different password if you want to require a password to save changes to the document. Enter the password again when prompted, and click OK.

6 Click OK.

7 Click Save.

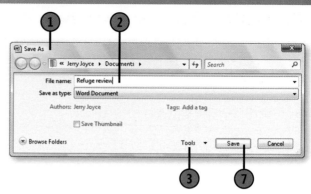

To stop requiring a password to open or modify a document, open the General Options dialog box, delete the existing password or passwords, click OK, and save the document.

Controlling Macros, Add-Ins, and ActiveX Controls

Macros are programs you use to automate actions in Word—repeating a series of commands, for example. *Add-ins* are programs or other items—more smart tags, for example—that you can add to Word to extend its capabilities. *ActiveX controls* are items that provide extra functionality—displaying special dialog boxes or toolbars, for example. Unfortunately, sometimes these items either are so poorly written that they cause operational problems or are written maliciously with the explicit intention of causing harm. To combat these risks, Word provides very strong protections against malfunctioning and malicious macros, add-ins, and ActiveX controls. However, these protections sometimes prevent good and effective tools from being used, so you might need to adjust your security settings to balance security and functionality.

Modify the Settings

1 Click the Office button, and choose Word Options from the menu. In the Word Options dialog box, click the Trust Center category in the left pane, and click the Trust Center Settings button to display the Trust Center dialog box.

2 Click the Add-Ins category, and select this check box if you want to require that all add-ins come from a trusted source. Each time an add-in from another source tries to be used, you'll be asked whether you want to use it.

3 Click the ActiveX Settings category, and select the level of security you want for ActiveX controls.

4 Select this check box if it isn't already selected.

5 Click the Macro Settings category, and select the level of security you want for macros.

6 Click OK to close the Trust Center dialog box, and click OK again to close the Word Options dialog box. Resume your work. If you find that some features you need aren't working properly, return to the Trust Center, adjust the security settings, and, when you resume your work, see whether you've fixed the problem.

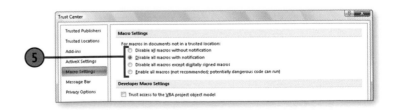

Fixing Word

Although Microsoft Word is a robust program, once in a while things can go wrong. Sometimes a problem might be severe enough to cause your computer to crash—that is, to shut down. This type of problem might be caused by a program or a support file on your hard disk being corrupted, or there might be something wrong with your computer itself. When Word, or any Office component, isn't working properly, you can run a series of diagnostic tests to find out what's wrong and, usually, learn how to fix the problem, unless Word fixes it automatically.

Run the Diagnostics

1. Close any running programs except Word, and open a blank Word document.

2. Click the Office button, choose Word Options from the menu to display the Word Options dialog box, and click the Resources category. Click the Diagnose button to display the Microsoft Office Diagnostics Wizard.

3. Click Run Diagnostics, and wait for the series of diagnostic tests to be completed.

4. Review the results, and note any item where the wizard found a problem.

5. Click Continue if you need to go to the Office Online Web site for additional help and tools.

6. If no cause was found for the problem you're having, and if the Office Online Web site didn't offer a solution, try using the tools in Windows to diagnose and solve your problem and to run full scans for viruses, spyware, and other malware.

Caution

Running the diagnostics can take a long time, so make sure that you won't need to use your computer immediately after you start the diagnostics.

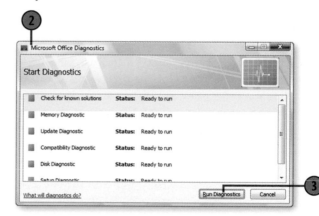

Adding or Removing Word Components

Word provides such a multitude of components that you probably haven't needed or wanted to install all of them on your computer. You can install additional components on an as-needed basis or remove components that you never use so as to save some hard-disk space.

Add or Remove Components

1 With all your Office programs closed, open the Control Panel from the Windows Start menu, click Programs, and then click Programs And Features to display the Programs And Features window. Click your Office program in the list, and click the Change button to display the Microsoft Office window. In the Change Your Installation Wizard that appears, click the Add Or Remove Features option, and click Continue.

2 Click the plus signs to expand the outline of the components until you find the item you want to add or remove.

3 Click the down arrow to display the installation choices, and specify a choice. Repeat for any other components you want to change.

4 Click Continue, and wait for the installation to be completed.

5 Start Word, and verify that the component or components have been installed or uninstalled.

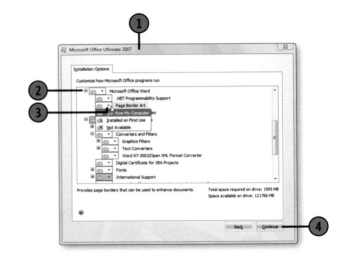

Tip

If a component is set to be installed on first use, Word automatically installs it when you need it, provided you have access to the Microsoft Office disc or the network installation files.

Tip

If you're running Windows XP, click the Add Or Remove Programs category in the Control Panel to display the Add Or Remove Programs window. With the Change Or Remove Programs tab selected, click your Office program.

Index

- (minus sign), 118, 119
+ (plus sign), 118, 119
1-dimensional equations, 147
2-dimensional equations, 147
1-page view, 16
2-page view, 16
2-sided documents, 55, 75
3-D effects
   graphics, 127
   shapes, 130
   WordArt, 134

A

accepting changes, 177
Access databases, 104
access to documents, restricting, 223
accounts, blog, 100, 101
Actions buttons, 160
actions for smart tags, 160
ActiveX controls, 230
adding
   items to toolbars, 211
   Word components, 232
add-ins, 160, 230
address book, 110
addresses
   changing information in, 216
   envelopes, 102
   mail merge fields for, 108
   printing with mail-merged data, 110
advanced options for equations, 145
advanced properties for documents, 163
alignment
   adjusting, 54

equation elements, 147
header and footer elements, 113
index page numbers, 173
keyboard shortcuts for, 19
numbers in tables, 89
shapes or pictures, 132
style definitions, 46
tab specifications, 57
table rows and columns, 89
tables in text, 92, 93
WordArt, 135
alphabetical order of tables or lists, 116
Alt key, 18
alternating headers and footers, 114–15
arrow keys, 18
arrows, 130
art. See drawing; pictures; shapes
ascending sort orders, 116, 117
assigning keyboard shortcuts, 214
attaching templates, 111
Author field, 216
Auto Check For Errors feature, 107
AutoCaption feature, 165
AutoComplete entries, 31
AutoCorrect feature
   checking spelling, 34–35
   equations and, 146
   numbering lists, 69
   smart tags and, 160
AutoMark feature, 173
automatically entered text, 31, 142.
   See also fields
AutoRecovery feature, 217, 222
AutoShapes, 130
AutoText feature, 31

B

back-to-back pages, 75
backup copies of documents, 222, 223
balloon comments, 176
bar tabs, 56
base styles, 190
bibliographic notes, 157, 168–69
bibliographies, 170
blacklining, 178
blank documents, 10
blank footers on first pages, 114
blank pages, 83
blogs, 100–101
blue squiggles, 33
bold text, 46, 51, 58
bookmarks
   deleting, 159
   indexing and, 172
   inserting, 159
   linking to, 150
   navigating with, 159
borders. See also margins
   around pages, 64
   around paragraphs, 46, 67
   around pictures, 127
   around table cells, 72, 87, 91
   artwork in, 65
bound documents, 75
boundaries in tables, 91
boxed text, 153–55
brightness of pictures, 126, 127
Browser, 9
browsing for tables or graphics, 165

Building Blocks collection
   cover-page elements and, 195
   Quick Parts feature, 30
   saving changes to, 195, 199
   tables in, 199
bullet characters, 46, 204
bulleted lists. *See also* lists
   bullets in, 46
   creating, 68–69
   formatting, 71
   modifying, 204–5
   multilevel, 206
   nested, 70
   styles in, 205
business-card labels, 103
buttons. *See* toolbars; tools

C

capital letters, 156
capitalization errors, 35
captions, 164, 165, 166
case of text, 27
categories
   clip art, 124
   pictures, 122
   Quick Parts, 30
   templates, 96
cautions. *See also* troubleshooting
   Building Blocks changes, 195, 199
   business and corporate styles, 49
   copying formatting, 61
   deleting content in table rows or
      columns, 88
   deleting paragraph marks, 97
   diagnostic tests, 231
   digital signatures, 227
   drawing tables with precision, 91
   editing Excel data, 149

editing in Outline view, 119
encrypted and passworded documents,
   228
fees for research services, 23
graphics cropping and sizing, 127
hyperlinks in documents, 99
IRM (Information Rights Management)
   service, 223
manual page breaks, 81
older and newer file formats, 15
saving Building Blocks changes, 195,
   199
spacing measurements, 53
CD labels, 103
CD or DVD program discs, 232
cells
   dividing in two, 91
   formatting in tables, 72
   margins in, 94
   markers, 87
   merging, 91
   moving to, in tables, 84
   resizing, 90
   table overview, 87
centered tabs, 56
centered text, 54
certificate providers, 225
certificates, digital, 225, 227
Change Your Installation Wizard, 232
changes. *See* editing; Track Changes
   feature
chapters in documents, 83
character fonts. *See* fonts
character formatting, 44, 61
character spacing, 46, 60
character styles, 46–47, 48, 190
characters
   AutoCorrect and, 34
   bullets, 46, 204

dingbats, 204
drop caps, 156
in equations, 145–47
ignoring in searches, 27
inserting symbols, 152
optional hyphens, 79
selecting, 38
spacing between, 46, 60, 135
specialized, in fonts, 152
typographic, 152
wildcards, 27
WordArt, 135
charges for research, 23
charts and diagrams
   creating, 138–40
   inserting, 133
   relational diagrams, 136–37
checking spelling and grammar. *See*
   grammar; spelling
citations
   bibliographies, 170
   inserting, 168–69
   legal tables of authorities, 171
clearing
   formatting, 51
   highlighting, 27
   tabs, 57
clicking hyperlinks, 151
clip art, 8, 65, 66, 124, 204
clip-art page borders, 65
Clipboard, Office, 36–37
Clipboard, Windows, 36–37
collapsing
   outlines, 118
   subdocuments, 120
collated printing, 41
colors
   page borders, 64
   paragraph borders and shading, 67

picture contents, 126
shapes, 130
SmartArt diagrams, 137
table components, 91
text, 46, 58
themes, 46, 62
window schemes, 212
WordArt text, 135
columns in tables
deleting, 88
formatting, 72
resizing, 90
sorting content, 116
table overview, 87
columns of Excel data, 149
columns on pages
column breaks, 82
flowing text in, 82
index layouts, 173
label layouts, 103
side-by-side layouts, 94
combining graphics, 131–32, 133
command tabs, 8
commands. *See* menus and commands
comments. *See* reviewer comments
comparing documents, 177–79, 181, 182
comparison calculations in mail merge,
    105
compatibility
    Compatibility mode, 14, 145
    Compatibility pack, 15
    earlier versions of Word, 14–15, 98, 187,
        217
    equations and, 145
    file formats and, 98
Compatibility Checker feature, 187
Compatibility mode, 14, 145
Compatibility pack, 15
compiling indexes, 173

components, adding or removing, 232
condensing fonts, 60
conditional expressions, 104–5, 109
consistency in formatting, 54
Contacts, mail merge and, 104, 106
content controls
    adding, 220
    citations, 169
    document properties, 162
    equations, 146
    placeholders, 97
contents, tables of. *See* tables of contents
contextual spelling errors, 33
contrast in pictures, 126, 127
converting
    citations to normal text, 169
    documents for earlier Word versions,
        98, 187, 217
    footnotes and endnotes, 157
    older documents to current Word
        version, 14–15
    tables to text, 86
    text to tables, 86
copies of documents
    creating, 12
    number to print, 41
    working on, 222
copying
    charts, 140
    Clipboards and, 36–37
    Excel data, 148
    formatting, 46, 61
    macros, 221
    styles, 46, 221
    template styles or macros, 221
    text, 36–37, 39
    translated text, 25
corporate network certificates, 225

correcting. *See* grammar; spelling;
    troubleshooting
costs of research, 23
cover pages, 30, 142, 194–95
crashes. *See also* troubleshooting
    AutoRecovery feature and, 222
    diagnosing Word problems, 231
cropping pictures, 123
cross-references
    bookmarks, 159
    as fields, 164
    hyperlinks, 150
    in indexes, 172, 173
    in text, 158
currency symbols, 152
customizing
    dictionaries, 219
    form letters, 108
    keyboard shortcuts, 214
    Quick Access toolbar, 210–11
    templates, 96–97
cutting text, 36–37

D

dashes. *See* hyphenation; special
    characters and symbols
data
    inserting from Excel, 148–49
    mail merge and, 104
    smart tags and, 160
    sorting in tables, 116
data fields. *See* fields
data sources
    charts, 139
    editing, 139
    mail merge and, 104–5, 106, 107
    record-by-record merging, 109
databases, mail merge and, 104

dates and times
   as fields, 164
   including in templates, 203
   smart tags and, 160
   sorting by, 117
decimal tabs, 56, 89
decorative bullets, 204
default folders, 11
default pasting method, 37
default styles, 49
definitions, 23
deleting
   bookmarks, 159
   cover pages, 142
   footnotes or endnotes, 157
   formatting, 51
   heading numbers, 143
   marking deletions, 176
   page numbers, 29
   paragraph marks, 97
   paragraph numbers, 68, 69
   styles from sets, 193
   tab stops, 56
   table-cell contents, 88
   table rows or columns, 88
   text, 13
   text accidentally, 13
   text in Outline view, 119
   toolbar items, 211
   watermarks, 161
   Word components, 232
   words from dictionaries, 219
delivery addresses, 102
demoting topics in outlines, 118
descending sort orders, 116, 117
descriptions in hyperlinks, 151
detecting languages, 184
Developer tab, 111, 220

diagnosing Word problems, 231.
    See also troubleshooting
diagrams. *See* charts and diagrams
dictionaries, 24, 184–85, 219
digital certificates and signatures, 225–27
dingbats, 204
direct formatting, 46, 183
direction of text, 89
displaying
   different parts of documents, 182
   documents in different views, 22
   elements in templates, 97
   fields as shaded, 203
   formatting marks, 215
   Full Screen Reading view, 16
   gridlines, 91, 132
   highlights, 215
   inconsistent formatting, 183
   items on status bar, 212
   layout marks, 215
   one or two pages at a time, 16
   optional hyphens, 79
   outlines, 118
   pages side by side, 16
   printed pages, 16, 40
   ranges of bookmarked text, 159
   review comments, 16
   Ribbon, 22, 213
   section-break markers, 77
   style names, 208
   styles, 45, 48
   subdocuments, 120
   ToolTips. *See* ScreenTips
   two documents side by side, 181
   two versions of documents, 177–79
   Word e-mail attachments, 16
distorted pictures, 123
dividing
   table cells, 91
   windows, 182

Document Inspector feature, 188
Document Map pane, 17
documents
   blank, 10
   breaking into chapters, 83
   combining changes, 180
   comparing changes, 177–79
   converting older, 14–15
   copies of, 12
   cover pages, 194–95
   creating, 10, 96–97
   creating templates from, 96
   creating with templates, 96–97
   customized toolbars in, 210–11
   digital certificates and signatures,
     225–27
   display options, 20–21
   displaying multiple parts of, 182
   displaying two side by side, 181
   Draft view, 8, 21
   encrypting, 228
   file formats, 98
   file size, 122
   Full Screen Reading view, 8, 16–17, 20
   inserting hyperlinks to, 151
   linked files, 99
   locations of, 217
   managing with master documents, 120
   online, 99
   opening, 12
   organizing and reorganizing, 118–19,
     208
   Outline view, 8, 21
   outlines, 118–19, 208
   page numbers, 29
   passwords, 228–29
   preparing final versions, 188
   preventing changes to, 224

Print Layout view, 8, 20
Print Preview, 21, 40
printing, 40–41
properties, 41, 162–63
read-only, 12, 223
reopening existing, 12
safeguarding, 222, 223, 224
saving, 11
saving for older versions of Word, 187, 217
saving as templates, 200, 202–3
selecting everything in, 38
specialized, 96–97
subdocuments, 120
tracking changes in, 176–77
unavailable on networks, 222
user information in, 216
Web Layout view, 8, 20
.docx files (Word document files), 98
.dotx files (templates), 98
double-sided documents, 75
double-spaced text, 52
double-strikethrough text, 176
double-underlined text, 176, 177
down arrows, 130
downloading
   templates, 96
   themes, 62
draft blog entries, 101
draft blog postings, 101
Draft view, 8, 21
Draw Table tool, 91
drawing
   drawing canvas, 128, 133
   inserting graphics, 133
   shapes, 125
   tables, 91
   text boxes, 154–55, 195
drawing canvas, 128, 133

drop caps, 156
DVD or CD program discs, 232

E

earlier versions of Word
   converting older documents, 14–15
   file formats, 98
   saving for, 187, 217
editing
   accepting or rejecting changes, 177
   addresses, 216
   bibliographies, 170
   citations, 169
   combining changes from multiple reviews, 180
   comparing two documents, 181
   comparing versions of documents, 177–79
   data sources, 139
   default languages, 184
   dictionary word lists, 219
   Excel data, 149
   in Full Screen Reading view, 16
   headers or footers, 113
   lists, 204–5
   mail merge recipients list, 107
   marking edits, 176–77
   in Outline view, 119
   page-number designs, 207
   page numbers, 207
   pictures, 126
   preventing changes to documents, 188, 223, 224, 229
   in Print Preview, 40
   recipient lists, 110
   SmartArt diagrams, 137
   styles, 49, 191
   templates, 200–201

text, 13, 38–39
   text-wrap appearance, 128–29
   themes, 63
   user information, 216
   WordArt, 134–35
electronic postage, 102
e-mail in Full Screen Reading view, 16
emphasizing text. *See* bold text; italic text; underlined text
encryption, 228
endnotes, 157
end-of-row markers, 87
Enter key, 18
entering text, 10
envelopes
   mail merge and, 110
   printing, 102
   return addresses, 216
E-Postage, 102
equations
   advanced options for, 145
   captions, 165
   Compatibility mode and, 14
   creating and inserting, 145–47
   linear, 147
   one-dimensional, 147
   special tables of contents for, 166, 198
   storing as Quick Parts, 30
   two-dimensional, 147
Eraser tool, 91
errors. *See* troubleshooting
Esc key, 18
even-numbered (verso or left-hand) pages, 41, 75, 115
Excel worksheets
   charts, 138–40
   inserting data from, 148–49
   mail merge and, 104

exceptions
    AutoCorrect feature, 35
    restricted documents, 224
expanding
    fonts, 60
    outlines, 118
    subdocuments, 120
expiration dates for document access, 223
exporting in file formats, 98
extensions, file, 98

F

fancy first letters, 156
Favorite Links, 12
fees for research, 23
fields
    citations as, 168
    conditional, 109
    display options, 215
    displaying as shaded, 203, 215
    document properties, 162–63
    frequently used, 30
    headers and footers, 112
    IF field, 105, 109
    inserting, 164
    legal tables of authorities, 171
    mail merge and, 104–5, 108
    page numbers as, 164
    tables of contents as, 167, 196
    TC fields, 197
    template use of, 97
    user information in, 216
    word counts, 186
figures
    captions, 165
    special tables of content for, 166, 198
file extensions, 98

file formats
    converting documents, 15
    data sources, 106
    older versions of Word and, 98, 187
    overview, 98
    saving in, 217
file-name extensions, 98
file names, 11
file size, 122
files. *See* documents
Fill-In conditional fields, 109
fills
    gradient, 135
    shapes, 130
    SmartArt, 137
    WordArt, 135
filtered HTML formats, 98
filtering data for mail merge, 105, 106
Final markings, 188
finalized documents, 188
financial symbols, 160
finding
    all instances of text, 26–27
    citations, 168
    clip art, 124
    document metadata and, 163
    graphics or tables in documents, 165
    Help topics, 42
    inconsistencies in formatting, 183
    online themes, 62
    text in documents, 26–27
first-line indents, 55
first-page running heads, 114
first-use installation, 232
fitting text on pages, 40
fixing problems. *See* troubleshooting
flowing text, 155
folders, 11. *See also* documents
following styles, 190

fonts
    adding to toolbars, 211
    changing faces or sizes, 50–51
    condensing or expanding, 60
    drop caps, 156
    formatting text with, 46–47, 58
    kerning, 60
    special characters in, 152
    themes, 62
    WordArt, 135
footers. *See* headers and footers
Footnote pane, 157
footnotes, 150, 157
form letters. *See* mail merge
Format Painter feature, 46, 61
formatting. *See also* fonts
    blog entries, 101
    charts, 139
    clearing from text, 51
    combined documents and, 180
    consistency in, 54
    copying, 46, 61
    deleting with paragraph marks, 96
    directly formatting text, 45, 46
    displaying marks for, 10
    equations, 145–47
    finding inconsistencies in, 183
    finding specific instances of, 27
    fonts, 46–47
    headers and footers, 113
    hiding or displaying formatting marks, 215
    keeping track of, 183
    keyboard shortcuts, 19
    macros, 220
    marking changes in, 176
    master documents and subdocuments, 120
    numbers in lists, 205

page numbers, 29
paragraph marks and, 96, 97
pasted text, 37
shapes, 130
sidebars and pull quotes, 153
special characters, 58
styles, 46–47, 190, 191
tables, 72, 85, 199
text in boxes, 154
text colors, 58
themes, 46–47, 62–63
underlining, 58
freezing document-property information, 162
frequently used content, 30–31
Full Screen Reading view, 8, 16–17, 20

G

galleries
adding to toolbar, 30
functionality, 4
illustrated, 8
navigating in, 18
Photo Gallery, 122
Quick Parts, 30
Quick Styles, 190
shapes, 125
styles, 48
symbols, 146
table styles, 192
generating indexes, 173
glowing pictures, 127
gradient fills, 135
grammar
checking, 218–19
correcting, 32–33
proofreading in other languages, 184–85
status icon, 9

Graph program, 138
graphics. *See also* drawing; pictures; shapes
arranging on pages, 131–32
in blog entries, 99
borders and effects, 127
brightness and contrast, 126, 127
bullets, 204
captions, 165
charts, 138–40
clip art, 65, 124
combining or grouping, 133
in cover pages, 194
cropping, 123
distorted, 123
editing, 126
equations as, 145
finding in documents, 165
formatting, 130
formatting lists with, 71, 204
frequently used, 30
grouping, 131–32
inserting, 122, 195
layering, 131–32
lines in text, 66
organizing, 122
page borders, 65
in page numbers, 207
Photo Gallery, 122
Picture Manager, 122
relational diagrams, 136–37
resizing, 123
rotating, 126, 127
shapes. *See* shapes
signatures, 226
SmartArt, 63
special effects, 63, 127
special tables of contents for, 166, 198
themes, 63

watermarks, 161
WordArt, 134–35
wrapping text around, 128–29
graphs and charts
creating, 138–40
inserting, 133
relational diagrams, 136–37
grayed features, 14
green squiggles, 33
gridlines
aligning pictures to, 132
nonprinting, 91
grouping graphics, 131–32, 133
groups of styles, 193
guidelines in tables, 87
gutters, 74, 75

H

hand cursor, 16
hanging indents, 55
headers and footers
chapters and, 83
creating and modifying, 112–15
finding text in, 26
omitting on first pages, 114
headings
cross-references to, 158
inline, 59
numbering, 143
organizing with styles, 208
outlines and, 208
tables of contents and, 196–97
Help button, 9
Help system, 42
hiding
folders, 11
formatting marks, 215

hiding, *continued*
  highlights, 215
  layout marks, 215
  Ribbon, 22, 213
  screen elements, 22
  ScreenTips, 215
  status-bar items, 212
highlighting
  all found text items, 26
  displaying, 215
  text, 177
  Track Changes notations, 176
hints for completing templates, 97
Home tab, 8
homonyms (sound-alike words), 27
horizontal lines, 66
horizontal pages, 74, 76
horizontal text, 89
HTML format, 98
hyperlinks
  automatically inserting, 150
  bookmarks and, 159
  clicking, 151
  cross-references as, 158
  inserting in text, 150–51
  online document links, 99
  tables-of-contents links, 166
  text links, 150–51
hyphenation, 78–79, 81

I

icons for hyperlinks, 99
identities, verifying, 225–27
IF field, 105, 109
ignoring
  formatting inconsistencies, 183
  misspellings, 33

punctuation or spaces, 27
  words in other languages, 184
images. *See* drawing; pictures; shapes
importing styles and macros, 221
incorrectly used words, 32
indents
  bulleted lists, 68–69
  first-line, 55
  markers, 8
  nested lists, 70
  paragraphs, 46, 55
  tables, 92
indexes, 159, 172–73
information
  researching, 23
  rights management, 223, 224
Information Rights Management (IRM),
  223, 224
initial caps, 156
initials of users, 216
inline headings, 59
Insert key, 13
Insert Ribbon, 9
Insert tab, 9
inserting
  automatic hyperlinks, 150
  bibliographies, 170
  bookmarks, 159
  captions, 165
  charts, 133, 138–40
  citations, 168–69
  clip art, 124
  comments, 176
  cross-references, 158
  document-property content controls,
   162
  drawings, 133
  drop caps, 156
  equations, 145–47

Excel data, 148–49
fields, 164
footnotes and endnotes, 157
frequently used content, 30–31
hyperlinks, 99
indexes, 172–73
mail merge fields, 108
marking inserted text, 176
pictures, 122
shapes, 195
sidebars or pull quotes, 153
smart tags, 160
SmartArt, 136
special characters and symbols, 152
tables, 84, 199
tables of contents, 167
text, 8
text in boxes, 153–55, 195
translated text, 25
watermarks, 161
insertion points, 8
inside margins, 75
inspecting documents, 188
installation
  adding or removing Word components,
   232
  add-ins, macros, and ActiveX controls,
   230
installed templates, 96
Internet resources
  blogs, 100–101
  Office Marketplace, 24
  Office Online, 96, 231
  online dictionaries, 24
  Web research, 23
IRM (Information Rights Management),
  223, 224
italic text, 46, 51, 58

J

jumps. *See* hyperlinks
justified text, 54, 78

K

kerning, 60
keyboard shortcuts, 18–19, 41, 214
KeyTips, 18
keywords for clip art, 124

L

labels. *See also* mail merge
  captions, 165
  mailing labels, 103
  smart tags and, 160
landscape page orientation, 74, 76
Language Detection feature, 184
languages
  default, 184
  proofreading in other, 184–85
  switching, 185
laws, tables of, 171
layering graphics, 131–32
laying out pages. *See* page layouts
layout marks, 215
leader characters for tabs, 56, 57
leading (line spacing), 46, 52–53
left indents, 55
left margin marker, 8
left-aligned tabs, 56
left-aligned text, 54, 78
left-hand (verso or even-numbered)
    pages, 41, 75, 115
legal blacklining, 5, 178
legal tables of authorities, 171

legally recognized signatures, 227
letter spacing, 46, 60, 135
letters
  characters. *See* characters
  mail merging. *See* mail merge
levels
  lists, 70, 206
  numbered headings, 143
  outlines, 118, 208
  tables of contents and, 197
licenses for IRM services, 223
limiting searches, 26
line breaks in text, 78–79, 80–81
line counts, 186
line spacing, 46, 52–53
line wraps, 10
linear equations, 147
lined-through text, 58, 176
lines
  clip-art page borders, 65
  dividing text, 66
  numbering, in text, 144
  page borders, 64
  paragraph borders, 67
  selecting entire, in text, 38
lining up. *See* alignment
linked files, 99
linked styles, 46, 48
linking. *See also* hyperlinks
  to Excel data, 140, 148
  to pictures, 122
  text in boxes, 155
List Library, 206
lists. *See also* mail merge
  bulleted, 46, 68–69
  creating, 68–69
  of figures, 198
  formatting, 71
  modifying, 204–5

  multilevel, 70, 206
  nested, 70
  numbered, 205
  sorting data in, 116, 117
  styles, 46, 205
  of tables, 198
Live Preview feature, 4, 45
locations of files, 217
logo watermarks, 161
looking up information, 23

M

macros
  adding to toolbars, 211
  controlling, 230
  copying from templates, 221
  creating, 220
  defined, 209
  keyboard shortcuts for, 214
  transferring, 221
  Word document formats and, 98
magazine-like columns, 82
magnifying
  pages, 194
  text, 10, 16, 22, 40
mail merge
  addressing envelopes, 110
  conditional expressions in, 109
  data sources, 107
  form letters, 104–5, 106, 108
  master documents, 104–5
  overview, 104–5
  personalizing letters, 108
  templates, 108
  values in, 105, 109
Mail Merge Wizard, 104
mailing addresses, 102, 216
mailing labels, 103. *See also* mail merge

managing blog accounts, 101
manual hyphenation, 79
manual line breaks, 81
manual page breaks, 81
margins
   changing, 77
   markers, 8
   mirroring, 75
   setting, 74
   table cells, 94
Mark As Final feature, 188
Marketplace translation services, 24
marking
   changes. *See* Track Changes feature
   citations, 171
   edits, 176–77
   index entries, 172
   section breaks, 77
marks
   cell markers, 87
   displaying formatting, 215
   end-of-row, 87
   layout, 215
   paragraph, 8, 44, 96, 97
   section breaks, 77
   space, 8
   zooming in on, 10
Markup area, 9
markups
   Markup area, 9
   printing with documents, 41
   tracking changes, 176–77
master documents
   hyperlinks, 150
   mail merge and, 104–5
   managing multiple documents, 120
mathematical equations, 145–47
measurements for spacing, 52

menus and commands
   adding items to toolbars, 211
   keyboard shortcuts for, 214
   macros, 220–21
   overview, 8–9
merging
   document changes, 180
   table cells, 87, 91
metadata, 163
Microsoft Excel. *See* Excel worksheets
Microsoft Graph, 138
Microsoft Office. *See* Office
Microsoft Office Diagnostics Wizard, 231
Microsoft Office Picture Manager, 122
Microsoft Outlook, 104, 106
Microsoft Windows XP, 5, 11, 232
Microsoft Word. *See* Word
Microsoft Works, 98
Mini toolbars, 9, 50
minimizing Ribbon, 22, 213
minus sign (-), 118, 119
mirroring margins, 75
misspellings. *See* spelling
mistakes. *See* grammar; spelling;
   troubleshooting
modes
   Compatibility, 14, 145
   Overtype, 13
modifying
   addresses, 216
   bibliographies, 170
   citations, 169
   combining changes from multiple
     reviews, 180
   comparing two documents, 181
   comparing versions of documents,
     177–79
   data sources, 139
   default languages, 184

dictionary word lists, 219
Excel data, 149
headers or footers, 113
lists, 204–5
mail merge recipients list, 107
marking edits, 176–77
page number designs, 207
page numbers, 207
pages in Full Screen Reading view, 16
pages in Outline view, 119
pages in Print Preview, 40
pictures, 126
preventing changes to documents, 188,
   223, 224, 229
recipient lists, 110
SmartArt diagrams, 137
styles, 49, 191
templates, 200–201
text, 13, 38–39
text-wrap appearance, 128–29
themes, 63
user information, 216
WordArt, 134–35
mouse actions, macros and, 220
mouse wheels, 22, 40
moving. *See also* navigating
   boxed text, 154
   graphics, 132
   items by copying, 36
   marking moved text, 176
   page numbers, 29
   paragraphs, 119
   sections, 119
   tab stops, 57
   tables, 87, 93
   text, 36–37, 39
multilevel lists, 70, 143, 206
multilingual documents, 184
multiple-file documents, 120

N

names
  documents, 11
  frequently used content, 30
  macros, 220
  read-only documents, 12
  styles, 48, 208
  templates, 201
navigating
  with bookmarks, 159
  with keyboard shortcuts, 18
  in table cells, 84
  through pages, 16–17
nested lists, 70
nested tables, 92
networks, unavailable documents and, 222
New Blog Account Wizard, 100
new blog entries, 100
new documents, 10, 96–97
newspaper-like columns, 82
nonbreaking spaces, 81
noncontiguous blocks of text, 38
noncontinuous page numbering, 29
nonprinting guidelines, 87
non-text items, replacing, 28
Normal view (Draft view), 8, 21
notes
  footnotes and endnotes, 157
  tables of, 198
numbered lists
  creating, 68–69
  formatting, 71
  modifying, 204–5
  multilevel, 206
  nested, 70
  styles, 205
numbering
  captions, 165
  footnotes and endnotes, 157
  headings, 143
  lines, 144
  pages, 29, 75, 207
  pictures or figures, 165
numbers
  aligning in tables, 89
  counting words in documents, 186
  in equations, 145–47
numeric sort order, 116

O

odd-numbered (recto or right-hand) pages, 41, 75, 83, 115
Office
  Clipboard, 36–37
  Compatibility pack, 15
  Diagnostics Wizard, 231
  menu, 8
  Marketplace, 24
  Online, 96, 231
  Picture Manager, 122
  program discs, 232
older versions of Word
  converting older documents, 14–15
  saving for, 98, 187, 217
one-dimensional equations, 147
one-page view, 16
online dictionaries, 24
online documents, 99
online Help, 42
opening
  existing documents, 12
  inserted Excel worksheets, 149
  new documents, 10
  older documents, 14
  subdocuments, 120
optional hyphens, 79, 81

Organizer feature, 221
orientation
  pages, 74, 76
  WordArt, 135
orphans in text columns, 80
Outline view, 8, 21
outlines. *See also* borders
  levels in, 118, 208
  numbered headings and, 143
  numbering, 71
  reorganizing documents with, 118–19
  selecting sections in, 119
  styles and, 208
  tables of contents and, 167, 196–97
  viewing, 8, 21
Outlook, mail merge and, 104, 106
outside margins, 75
overall looks. *See* themes
Overtype mode, 13
overwriting older files, 15

P

page breaks, 81
page counts, 186
page headers or footers. *See* headers and footers
page layouts. *See also* page numbers
  bound documents, 75
  chapters, 83
  columns of text, 82
  double-sided, 75
  elements in, 73
  hyphenation adjustments, 78–79
  margins, 77
  side-by-side, 94
  standard-sized, 74
  tables. *See* tables
  widows and orphans, 80

page numbers
 adding, 29
 in cross-references, 158
 customizing, 207
 on double-sided pages, 75
 as fields, 164
 graphics in, 207
 in indexes, 172, 173
 omitting on first pages, 114
 onscreen indicators, 9
 in tables of contents, 196
page orientation, 74, 76
pages. *See also* page numbers
 arranging graphics on, 131–32
 borders around, 64
 clip-art page borders, 65
 counting, 186
 covers, 142
 displaying as printed, 16, 40
 displaying one or two at a time, 16
 frequently used, 30
 magnifying, 40
 orientation, 74, 76
 page breaks, 81
 paper size, 41
 printing, 41
 ranges of, in indexing, 172
 turning, 16–17, 40
 white spaces between, 215
paper, 41, 74
"paperless office," 16, 40
paragraph marks, 9, 44, 96, 97
paragraph styles
 applying, 45
 creating, 190
 defined, 44
 formatting text with, 46–47
 symbols for, 48

paragraphs
 alignment, 54
 copying formatting, 61
 indenting, 55
 inline headings, 59
 lines around, 67
 moving, 119
 numbering, 68–69
 selecting, 38
 shading, 67
 sorting, 117
 spacing, 52–53
 starting new, 10
 in tables, 87
 widows and orphans, 80
passwords, 228–29
pasting
 charts, 140
 Excel data, 148
 text, 36–37, 39
 translated text, 25
paths to files, 217
patterns on shapes, 130
personalizing form letters, 108
phone numbers, 160
Photo Gallery, 122
photos. *See* pictures
phrases
 storing frequently used content, 30
 translating, 24
picas and points, 52
picture bullets, 204
Picture Manager, 122
pictures. *See also* shapes
 arranging on pages, 131–32
 in blog entries, 99
 borders and effects, 127
 brightness and contrast, 126, 127
 bullets, 204

 captions, 165
 charts, 138–40
 clip art, 65, 124
 combining or grouping, 133
 in cover pages, 194
 cropping, 123
 distorted, 123
 editing, 126
 equations as, 145
 finding in documents, 165
 formatting, 130
 formatting lists with, 71, 204
 frequently used, 30
 grouping, 131–32
 inserting, 122, 195
 layering, 131–32
 lines in text, 66
 organizing, 122
 page borders, 65
 in page numbers, 207
 Photo Gallery, 122
 Picture Manager, 122
 relational diagrams, 136–37
 resizing, 123
 rotating, 126, 127
 shapes. *See* shapes
 signatures, 226
 SmartArt, 63
 special effects, 63, 127
 special tables of contents for, 166, 198
 themes, 63
 watermarks, 161
 WordArt, 134–35
 wrapping text around, 128–29
placeholder text
 in citations, 168
 in headers, 112
 paragraph marks with styles, 203
 in templates, 97, 201

plain Text format, 98
plus sign (+), 118, 119
point measurements, 52
portrait page orientation, 74, 76
postage, 102
postal codes, 104–5
posts in blogs, 101
precedents, tables of, 171
precision
    point measurements, 52
    table measurements, 90, 91
prefixes, searching for, 27
preventing editing. *See* protecting
        documents
previewing
    fonts, 50
    headers and footers, 112
    Live Preview feature, 45
    mail-merged envelopes, 110
    mail-merged results, 107, 109
    printed documents, 21, 40
    styles, 48
Print Layout view, 8, 20
Print Preview feature, 21, 40
printing
    document properties, 41
    documents, 40–41
    envelopes, 102, 110
    Help topics, 42
    keyboard shortcuts, 19
    mailing labels, 103
    mail-merged documents, 103, 110
    markups, 41
    previewing documents, 21, 40
    shortcut-key assignments, 41
    styles, 41
problems. *See* troubleshooting
professional equations, 147
program discs, 232

Programs And Features window, 232
promoting topics in outlines, 118
prompting for mail merge information,
        109
proofreading
    equations, 146
    finalized documents, 188
    languages, 184–85
    Proofing Errors feature, 33
    spelling check options, 218
Proofing Errors feature, 33
properties of documents, 41, 162–63
protecting documents
    bad macros, add-ins, or ActiveX
        controls, 230
    digital certificates and signatures,
        225–27
    passwords, 228–29
    preventing editing, 188, 224
    restricting access to documents, 223
    safeguarding documents, 222
    saving and backing up automatically,
        222
publishing blogs, 100
pull quotes, 153
punctuation. *See also* special characters
        and symbols
    ignoring in searches, 27
    inserting, 152

Q

Quick Access toolbar, 4, 8, 22, 210–11
Quick Parts feature, 30–31
Quick Print feature, 41
quick shortcuts, 18–19
Quick Styles feature
    applying, 45, 48
    creating styles based on, 190

inline headings, 59
sets of styles, 49, 193
themes and, 44
Quick Tables feature, 85, 199
quotes, pull, 153
quotes, tables of, 198

R

ragging text, 78–79, 81
ranges of pages
    indexing, 172
    printing, 41
reading documents, 16–17
Reading Highlight option, 26
read-only documents, 12, 223, 226
rearranging toolbar items, 211
reassigning keyboard shortcuts, 214
rechecking spelling and grammar, 33, 218
recipients
    editing list of, 107, 110
    envelopes for letters, 110
    specifying in mail merge, 106
recording macros, 220
records, merging for form letters, 109
recovering lost documents, 222
recto (right-hand or odd-numbered)
        pages, 41, 75, 83, 115
red squiggles, 32
references
    bibliographies, 170
    captions, 165
    citations, 168–69
    cross-references, 158
    footnotes or endnotes, 157
    legal tables of authorities, 171
    See or *See also* in indexes, 173
    tables of contents, 167

reflections of pictures, 127
registering blogs, 100
rejecting changes, 177
relational diagrams, 136–37
remote locations, unavailable documents
   and, 222
removing. *See also* deleting
   access restrictions, 223
   formatting from text, 51
   items from toolbars, 211
   page numbers, 29
   password protection, 229
   styles from sets, 193
   Word components, 232
renumbering endnotes and footnotes, 157
repetitive content, inserting, 30
replacing
   content in templates, 97
   misspelled text, 34
   non-text items, 28
   text, 13, 28
Research pane, 23
researching information, 23
resetting. *See* restoring
reshaping text wrap, 128–29
resizing
   pasted Excel data, 149
   pictures, 123
   shapes, 125
   SmartArt diagrams, 137
   tables, 87, 90
   text, 50–51
   toolbars, 210
   view of text, 16
resolution, screen, 6
restarting list numbering, 69
restoring
   deleted text, 13
   original fonts, 51

original Quick Styles, 49
original themes, 62
   pictures to original appearance, 127
   text-wrap appearance, 128–29
restricting. *See also* protecting documents
   access to documents, 223, 228–29
   edits in documents, 224
retrieving frequently used content, 30
return addresses, 102, 216
Review tab, 23
reviewer comments
   in balloons, 176
   combining into one document, 180
   displaying, 16
   illustrated, 9
   inserting with Track Changes feature,
      176
   in Reviewing pane, 176, 179
reviewing documents
   combining all comments into one
      document, 180
   comparing sections of one document,
      182
   comparing two documents, 181
   comparing versions of documents,
      177–79
   default languages, 184
   finding inconsistent formatting, 183
   preparing finalized documents, 188
   Reviewing Pane, 176, 179
   Track Changes feature, 176–77
Reviewing Pane, 176, 179
Ribbon
   adding items to toolbars, 210
   displaying, 22, 213
   functionality, 4, 6
   hiding, 22, 213
   illustrated, 9
   minimizing, 22, 213

Rich Text format, 98
right indents, 55
right-aligned paragraphs, 54
right-aligned tabs, 56
right-aligned text, 54
right-hand (recto or odd-numbered)
   pages, 41, 75, 83, 115
rotating
   pictures, 126, 127
   shapes, 125
   SmartArt, 137
   WordArt, 135
rows in Excel data, 149
rows in tables
   deleting, 88
   formatting, 72
   illustrated, 87
   resizing, 90
   sorting content, 116
rows of labels, 103
.rtf format, 98
rulers, 8, 55, 56, 57
rules
   mail merge and, 105
   tables of, 171
run-in headings, 59
running heads. *See* headers and footers
running macros, 220

S

safeguarding documents
   bad macros, add-ins or ActiveX controls,
      230
   digital certificates and signatures,
      225–27
   macros, 230
   methods, 222
   passwording documents, 228–29

preventing changes to documents, 118, 224

restricting access to documents, 223

saving and backing up automatically, 222

Save As dialog box, 11

Save dialog box, 11

saving designs

  boxed text, 154

  Building Blocks, 195, 199

  Quick Style sets, 193

  tables, 199

  themes, 63

saving documents

  automatically, 222

  based on templates, 97

  to default folders, 11

  in different formats, 98, 217

  for older Word versions, 15, 187, 217

  overview, 11

  as read-only, 12

  recovering lost documents, 222

  as templates, 200, 202–3

saving equations, 147

saving keyboard shortcuts, 19

scaling

  objects. *See* resizing

  print jobs, 41

schemes, 212

screen elements, 8–9, 22

screen resolution, 6

ScreenTips

  adding for hyperlinks, 151

  describing hyperlinks, 150

  displaying, 215

  illustrated, 8

  keyboard shortcuts in, 19

  table descriptions, 199

  translation-related, 24

scroll bars, 9

scrolling

  splitting windows, 182

  two documents side by side, 179, 181

searching

  for all instances of text, 26–27

  for citations, 168

  for clip art, 124

  document metadata and, 163

  for graphics or tables in documents, 165

  for Help topics, 42

  for inconsistencies in formatting, 183

  for online themes, 62

  for text in documents, 26–27

section breaks, 77, 83

sections

  chapters, 83

  margin settings and, 77

  moving, 119

  page numbers and, 29

  section breaks, 77, 83

  section-break markers, 77

  switching page orientation, 76

security

  bad macros, add-ins or ActiveX controls, 230

  digital certificates and signatures, 225–27

  macros, 230

  passwording documents, 228–29

  preventing changes to documents, 118, 224

  restricting access to documents, 223

  saving and backing up automatically, 222

See and *See also* references in indexes, 173

see-through shapes, 130

selecting

  keyboard shortcuts for, 19

  linked text, 155

objects with text wrap, 129

sections in outlines, 119

tables, 199

text, 13, 38–39

setting up pages. *See* page layouts

shading

  field display options, 203

  paragraphs, 67

  tables, 87

  types of formatting, 46

shadows

  on pictures, 127

  on shapes, 130

  types of formatting, 46

shapes. *See also* pictures

  adding, 125

  arranging on pages, 131–32

  AutoShapes feature, 130

  borders or outlines, 130

  bullets, 204

  clip-art page borders, 65

  combining or grouping, 133

  cover pages, 194

  formatting, 130

  gallery of, 125

  grouping, 131–32

  inserting, 195

  layering, 131–32

  lines in text, 66

  in lists, 71, 204

  in page numbers, 207

  patterns on, 130

  resizing, 125

  SmartArt, 63

  tables of, 198

  text inside, 130

  theme special effects, 63

shapes, *continued*
    WordArt, 135
    wrapping text around, 128–29
sharing files with older versions of Word, 14, 98, 187, 217
sheets of labels, 103
shortcuts, 18–19, 41, 214
showing. *See* displaying
Shrink One Page feature, 40
shrinking pages, 40
sidebars, 153
side-by-side layouts, 94
side-by-side viewing, 16, 181
signatures, digital, 225–27
single-lined equations, 147
size. *See* file size; paper; resizing
smart tags, 160
SmartArt diagrams, 5, 14, 63, 136–37
soft edges on pictures, 127
sorting
    lists, 117
    mail merge data, 104
    mail merge fields, 106
    table data, 116
sound clips, hyperlinks to, 99
sound-alike words (homonyms), 27
source documents, 179
Source Manager feature, 168–69, 170
"space before" or "space after" spacing, 52–53
spaces
    ignoring in searches, 27
    nonbreaking, 81
    space marks, 9
spacing
    around tables, 93
    between characters, 60
    hyphenation adjustments and, 78–79
    between lines or paragraphs, 52–53

between pages, 215
styles and formatting options, 46
special characters and symbols
    AutoCorrect and, 34
    bulleted lists, 46, 204
    currency symbols, 152
    dingbats, 204
    equations, 145–47
    footnotes or endnotes, 157
    ignoring in searches, 27
    inserting, 152
    optional hyphens, 79
    smart tags and, 160
    style types, 48
    Symbols gallery, 146
special effects
    3-D graphics, 127
    3-D shapes, 130
    SmartArt, 137
    themes, 63
    WordArt, 134
spelling
    AutoCorrect feature, 34–35
    correcting, 32–33, 34–35
    customizing options, 218–19
    proofreading in other languages, 184–85
    skipping words in other languages, 184
    status icon, 9
splitting windows, 182
spreadsheets, 148–49. *See also* worksheets
squiggles, 32, 33
starting Word, 10
statistics, 186
status bar, 18, 212
Step By Step Mail Merge Wizard, 107
stock symbols, 160
storing frequently used content, 30
strikethrough text, 58, 176

structuring equations, 146
styles
    adding to toolbars, 211
    applying, 44, 45, 48
    basing on existing definitions, 190
    character, 46–47, 48, 190
    citations, 169
    copying from templates, 221
    creating, 190
    displaying, 48, 208
    editing, 49, 191
    examining in documents, 183
    fonts in, 50
    formatting text with, 44, 46–47
    inline headings, 59
    keyboard shortcuts, 19, 214
    lists, 41, 205, 206
    in master documents and subdocuments, 120
    names, 208
    numbered headings, 143
    organizing documents with, 208
    page numbers, 207
    paragraph. *See* paragraph styles
    printing lists of, 41
    Quick Styles. *See* Quick Styles feature
    sets of, 49, 193
    SmartArt diagrams, 137
    symbols for, 48
    tables, 46, 85, 192, 199
    tables of contents and, 167, 196, 197, 198
    in templates, 96, 111
    themes and, 44
    updating after switching templates, 111
    WordArt, 135
subdocuments, 120
subheadings, 208
sublevels in lists, 70

subscript text, 46
suffixes, 27
suggested spellings, 32
superscript text, 46
suppressing
  heading numbers, 143
  line numbers, 144
switching
  between header and footer content,
    113
  Quick Styles sets, 49
  templates, 111
  views, 22
symbols
  AutoCorrect and, 34
  bulleted lists, 46, 204
  dingbats, 204
  equations, 145–47
  in equations, 145–47
  footnotes or endnotes, 157
  ignoring in searches, 27
  inserting, 152
  optional hyphens, 79
  smart tags and, 160
  style types, 48
  Symbols gallery, 146
Symbols gallery, 146
Synchronous Scrolling feature, 181

T

tab spacing, 46
tab stops, 8
table styles, 46, 85, 192, 199
Table Styles gallery, 192
tables
  adding rows or columns, 88
  aligning items in, 89
  aligning with text, 92

captions, 165
converting to or from text, 86
creating, 84
customizing, 90–91
deleting rows or columns, 88
elements of, 87
finding in documents, 165
formatting, 72
frequently used, 30
gridlines, 91
illustrated, 9
inserting Excel data as, 148
mail merge and, 104
moving, 93
nested, 92
predesigned, 85
resizing, 87
saving designs, 199
selecting, 199
side-by-side layouts, 94
sorting data in, 116
special tables of contents for, 150, 166,
  198
styles, 46, 85, 192, 199
using instead of tabs, 56
tables of authorities, 171
tables of contents
  creating, 167, 196–97
  entries in text boxes and, 172
  as fields, 164
  hyperlinks, 150
  special, 150, 166, 171, 198
  wrapped text around items and, 166
tables of equations, 150, 166
tables of figures, 150, 166, 198
tables of tables, 150, 166, 198
tabs
  bar, 56
  center, 56

decimal, 56, 89
leaders, 57
left, 56
right, 56
in headers and footers, 113
in indexes, 173
in table cells, 84
in text, 56–57
tags, smart, 160
tall pages, 74, 76
TC fields, 197
telephone numbers, 160
templates
  attaching, 111
  automatically inserted text in, 97
  copying styles and macros from, 221
  creating from existing documents, 96
  designing, 202–3
  displaying elements in, 97
  .dotx files, 98
  downloading, 96
  equations, 146
  locations of, 217
  mail merge and, 104, 108
  modifying, 200–201
  overview, 95
  saving documents as, 200
  starting new documents with, 96–97
  switching, 111
  tables, 85
  watermarks, 161
  Word Macro-Enabled, 98
temporarily displaying Ribbon, 22, 213
tests, diagnostic, 231
text
  in boxes, 153–55, 195
  centered, 54
  converting to or from tables, 86
  copying, 36–37, 39

text, *continued*
  direction, 89
  editing, 13
  entering, 10
  finding in documents, 26–27
  flowing in boxes, 155
  fonts, 50–51
  formatting, 44–45
  highlighting, 177, 215
  hyphenation adjustments and, 78–79
  inserting Excel data as, 148
  inside shapes, 130
  justified, 54, 78
  left-aligned, 54, 78
  lines in, 66
  linking in boxes, 155
  moving, 36–37, 39
  orphans in, 80
  pasting, 39
  ragging, 78–79, 81
  replacing, 28
  resizing, 16, 50–51
  right-aligned, 554
  selecting, 13, 38–39
  SmartArt, 136–37
  sorting, 117
  spacing, 46, 52–53, 60, 78–79
  in table cells, 88
  text wrap. *See* wrapping text
  translating, 24–25
  watermarks, 161
  WordArt, 134–35
text boxes, 153–55, 195
text file formats, 98
text wrap. *See* wrapping text
themes
  applying, 46–47
  cover pages, 142, 194
  downloading, 62

  fonts in, 50
  Quick Styles, 44
  setting and changing, 62–63
third-party digital certificates, 226, 227
three-dimensional effects
  graphics, 127
  shapes, 130
  WordArt, 134
thumbnails, 17
times and dates
  as fields, 164
  including in templates, 203
  smart tags and, 160
  sorting by, 117
title pages, 194–95
TOCs. *See* tables of contents
toolbars
  customizing, 210–11
  shrinking, 22
tools
  adding to toolbars, 210
  ScreenTips, 215
ToolTips. *See* ScreenTips
topics, reorganizing, 118–19
Track Changes feature, 5, 176–77, 180
tracking
  changes to documents, 176–77, 180
  changes to formatting, 183
transferring styles and macros to new
    documents, 221
translating text, 24–25
Translation ScreenTips, 24
transparency of shapes, 130
trimming pictures, 123
troubleshooting. *See also* cautions
  ActiveX controls, 230
  add-ins, 230
  applying styles, 45
  copying formatting, 61

  detecting languages, 185
  diagnosing Word problems, 231
  displaying inconsistent formatting, 183
  distorted pictures, 123
  macros, 230
  mail merge, 104–5
  preparing finalized documents, 188
  selecting text in boxes, 154
Trust Center feature, 230
"Try This!" exercises
  autocorrecting equations, 146
  AutoText, 31
  bookmarks, 159
  checking spelling and grammar, 33
  citation placeholders, 168
  cross-references, 158
  decimal numbers in tables, 89
  drop-cap styles, 156
  examining styles, 183
  finding graphics or tables in documents,
    165
  indexing, 173
  inserting Excel data, 149
  measuring tables, 90
  nested tables, 92
  outline levels, 118
  page borders, 64
  previewing fonts, 50
  Quick Styles, 48
  Ribbon display options, 213
  smart tags, 160
  SmartArt diagrams, 137
  table rows and columns, 88
  text wrap, 129
  word counts, 186
  WordArt, 134
turning numbering on or off
  line numbering, 144
  numbered headings, 143

turning pages, 16–17, 40
two-dimensional equations, 147
two-pages at a time view, 16
two-sided documents, 55, 75
typefaces
    adding to toolbars, 211
    changing fonts or sizes, 50–51
    condensing or expanding, 60
    drop caps, 156
    formatting text with, 46–47, 58
    kerning, 60
    special characters in, 152
    themes, 62
    WordArt, 135
typing
    entering text, 10
    replacing text, 13
    style names, 48
typographic characters, 152

U

underlined text. *See also* smart tags
    adding emphasis, 58
    applying with styles or formatting, 46
    clearing, 51
    double-underlined text, 176, 177
    marked-up text, 176
    in outlines, 118
undoing
    actions, 13, 19
    ignore actions, 33
    search and replace, 28
    text replacements, 28
ungrouping graphics elements, 194
unnumbered paragraphs, 69
up arrows, 130

updating
    bibliographies, 170
    data from Excel, 148, 149
    dates and times automatically, 203
    indexes, 172, 173
    older documents, 14–15
    styles, 111, 191
    tables of contents, 167
user information, 102, 216

V

values in mail merge, 105, 109
variable headers and footers, 114–15
verifying
    digital signatures, 225
    identities, 225–27
versions of documents
    combining changes into one, 180
    comparing, 177–79
versions of Word, compatibility, 14–15,
        98, 187, 217
verso (left-hand or even-numbered)
        pages, 41, 75, 115
vertical pages, 74, 76
vertical text, 87, 89
videos, hyperlinks to, 99
viewing. *See* displaying
views
    Document Map, 17
    Draft, 8, 21
    Full Screen Reading, 8, 20
    Outline, 8, 21
    Print Layout, 8, 20
    Print Preview, 21
    Thumbnails, 17
    Web Layout, 8, 20
viruses, 98, 230

W

warnings. *See* cautions;
        troubleshooting
watermarks, 161
Web Layout view, 8, 20
Web logs (blogs), 100–101
Web pages. *See also* Web sites
    inserting hyperlinks to, 150–51
    saving documents as, 98
Web sites. *See also* Web pages
    blogs, 100–101
    Office Marketplace, 24
    Office Online, 96, 231
    online dictionaries, 24
    Web research, 23
wheels, mouse, 22, 40
white spaces
    ignoring, 27
    space marks, 9
whole words, searching for, 27
wide pages, 74, 76
widows in text columns, 80
wildcard characters, 27. *See also* special
        characters and symbols
windows
    customizing display, 212–13
    schemes, 212
    screen elements, 8–9
    screen resolution and, 6
    splitting into two portions, 182
Windows Clipboard, 36
Windows Photo Gallery, 122
Windows XP, 5, 11, 232
wizards
    Change Your Installation Wizard, 232
    Mail Merge Wizard, 104
    Microsoft Office Diagnostics Wizard,
        231

wizards, *continued*
  New Blog Account Wizard, 100
  Step By Step Mail Merge Wizard, 107
Word
  adding or removing components,
    232
  converting older documents, 14–15
  diagnosing problems, 231
  earlier versions of, 14, 98, 187, 217
  Help system, 42
  interface, 8–9
  keyboard shortcuts, 18–19
  multiple techniques for working in,
    38–39
  program discs, 232
  saving documents for older versions,
    187, 217
  starting, 10
  viewing options in, 20–21

word counts, 9, 186
Word Macro-Enabled documents, 98
Word Macro-Enabled templates, 98
WordArt graphics, 134–35
words
  adding or deleting in dictionaries, 219
  definitions, 23
  drop-cap styles, 156
  hyphenating, 78–79
  incorrectly used, 32
  searching for all forms of, 27
  selecting, 38
  storing frequently used content, 30
  translating, 24
  word counts, 9, 186
Works Cited lists, 170
Works word processor, 98
worksheets
  charts, 138–40

inserting data from, 148–49
  mail merge and, 104
wrapping text
  around graphics, 128–29
  around tables, 92, 93
  around WordArt, 135
  table positioning and, 92
  tables of contents and, 166
writing style, 218

X

XML (eXtensible Markup Language), 98

Z

ZIP codes, 104–5
Zoom Controls, 8, 10, 22, 40, 194

About the Authors

Jerry Joyce is a marine biologist who has conducted research from the Arctic to the Antarctic and has published extensively on marine-mammal and fisheries issues. He developed computer programs in association with these studies to simplify real-time data entry, validation, and analysis that substantially enhanced the quality of the research. He has also had a long-standing relationship with Microsoft: Prior to co-authoring 15 books about Microsoft Windows, Word, and Office, he was the technical editor for numerous books published by Microsoft Press, and he wrote manuals, help files, and specifications for various Microsoft products. Jerry is Seattle Audubon volunteer and represents Seattle Audubon on the Washington State Oil Spill Advisory Council and the Washington State Ballast Water Working Group.

Marianne Moon has worked in the publishing world for many years as proofreader, editor, and writer—sometimes all three simultaneously. She has been editing and proofreading Microsoft Press books since 1984 and has written and edited documentation for Microsoft products such as Microsoft Works, Flight Simulator, Space Simulator, Golf, Publisher, the Microsoft Mouse, and Greetings Workshop. In another life, she was chief cook and bottlewasher for her own catering service and wrote weekly cooking articles for several newspapers. When she's not chained to her computer, she likes gardening, cooking, traveling, writing, and knitting sweaters for tiny dogs. There's a children's book in her head that she hopes will find its way out one of these days.

Marianne and **Jerry** own and operate **Moon Joyce Resources,** a small consulting company. They've been friends for 25 years, have worked together for 21 years, and have been married for 15 years. They are co-authors of the following books:

Microsoft Word 97 At a Glance

Microsoft Windows 95 At a Glance

Microsoft Windows NT Workstation 4.0 At a Glance

Microsoft Windows 98 At a Glance

Microsoft Word 2000 At a Glance

Microsoft Windows 2000 Professional At a Glance

Microsoft Windows Millennium Edition At a Glance

Troubleshooting Microsoft Windows 2000 Professional

Microsoft Word Version 2002 Plain & Simple

Microsoft Office System Plain & Simple— 2003 Edition

Microsoft Windows XP Plain & Simple

Microsoft Windows XP Plain & Simple—2nd Edition

Microsoft Windows Vista 2007 Plain & Simple

The 2007 Microsoft Office System Plain & Simple

If you have questions or comments about any of their books, please visit *www.moonjoyce.com*.

What do you think of this book?

We want to hear from you!

Do you have a few minutes to participate in a brief online survey?

Microsoft is interested in hearing your feedback so we can continually improve our books and learning resources for you.

To participate in our survey, please visit:

www.microsoft.com/learning/booksurvey/

...and enter this book's ISBN-10 number (appears above barcode on back cover*). As a thank-you to survey participants in the United States and Canada, each month we'll randomly select five respondents to win one of five $100 gift certificates from a leading online merchant. At the conclusion of the survey, you can enter the drawing by providing your e-mail address, which will be used for prize notification only.

Thanks in advance for your input. Your opinion counts!

*Where to find the ISBN-10 on back cover

ISBN-13: 000-0-0000-00000-0
ISBN-10: 0-0000-00000-0

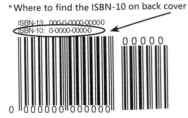

00000

0 000000 000000

Example only. Each book has unique ISBN.